PATIENT A AND OTHER PLAYS

PATIENT A AND OTHER PLAYS

FIVE PLAYS BY LEE BLESSING

Two Rooms

Down the Road

Fortinbras

Lake Street Extension

Patient A

HEINEMANN
Portsmouth, NH

Heinemann
A division of Reed Elsevier Inc.
361 Hanover Street
Portsmouth, NH 03801–3912

Offices and agents throughout the world

CIP is on file with the Library of Congress.
ISBN: 0-435-08662-6

Editor: Lisa A. Barnett
Production: Vicki Kasabian
Series design and cover: Jenny Jensen Greenleaf
Photograph of author: Susan Johann

Printed in the United States of America on acid-free paper
99 98 97 96 95 DA 1 2 3 4 5

CONTENTS

❖

INTRODUCTION

❖

In the summer of 1987, while I was working with Des McAnuff on the La Jolla Playhouse production of *A Walk in the Woods* (he'd premiered it at the Yale Repertory Theater and would subsequently direct it on Broadway), Des asked me if I'd accept a commission to write a new play for the next La Jolla season. I'd never been commissioned to write a full-length play before, and my first question was, "A play about what?"

"Anything you like," Des said, "I'll direct it."

That conversation began a period of commissioned full-length plays that has extended to the present. This collection includes the first five. Des and the La Jolla Playhouse commissioned three and the Ensemble Theatre of Cincinnati another. The last was a private commission. For each of the projects, I had at least a year's lead time. While that seemed like a lot, it wasn't.

For example, while the subject of the first play, *Two Rooms,* occurred to me almost immediately, its essential device—that of two divided realities taking place at once, impossibly, in the same room—didn't come for a few months, after various other strategies had been examined and rejected. More time went by planning and structuring the work and suddenly—at roughly the point where I usually begin writing a play—I realized there were only a few weeks before the Playhouse's February auditions in New York and Los Angeles were due to begin.

Thus, *Two Rooms* had to be cast when the play was only half written; there was almost nothing beyond the first act. We were fortunate enough to cast the marvelous Amanda Plummer for the lead, as well as one of the finest pure actors I've ever known, Jo Henderson. *Two Rooms* was the last play Jo ever performed, and the play will always be dedicated to her luminous memory.

The last half of *Two Rooms* was written from February to June 1988—the month it opened. Thus the usual process of a new play's being workshopped, read in public, etc., was abandoned. There simply wasn't time.

The production was excellent—extraordinarily well acted, directed, and designed (with a particularly effective set by Marjorie Kellogg and lighting by Peter Kaczorowski)—and featured nine TV monitors, among other things.

Although response to the play was positive, for me the script was not completely finished. I took it "back into the shop," primarily to simplify and focus its central issues. A second production of a significantly rewritten version took place almost a year later in Minneapolis, under the direction of Jeanne Blake. This time I was more satisfied with it as a dramatic document—and it's this second version that's published here.

The process for *Down the Road,* a year later, was nerve-rackingly similar. I didn't choose the play's subject until November, had only half of it done for La Jolla's February auditions, and had barely finished a draft by the start of rehearsals in May. In the middle of the six or seven weeks of rehearsal I rewrote eighty of the play's one hundred pages and the extraordinary cast had to discard the version they'd already memorized and learn an entirely new version before opening night.

The first audience of any sort for *Down the Road* held opening-night critics, but miraculously things once again went well. The production garnered some deservedly excellent reviews. Still, once again I was left with a script I felt needed to go farther. I reworked it over the next several months and received a second production from that wellspring of intelligent and clear-eyed support for living, working, breathing playwrights, the Humana New Play Festival of the Actors Theatre of Louisville. Jeanne Blake directed, and once again it's that version of the play found here.

I did commissions three out of four straight years for Des McAnuff at the La Jolla Playhouse (in 1990 I worked with Lloyd Richards, who directed the world premiere of my play *Cobb* at the Yale Repertory Theater). The final project was the only one in which Des asked for anything even mildly specific.

La Jolla was opening a rather amazing new second stage (the Mandell Weiss Forum—a facility most theatres in the country would dream of for a mainstage), and Des asked if I could create something "biggish, preferably on a classic subject, and with numerous roles for graduate-student actors." None of this was required, he stressed, but if I just happened to have an idea . . .

Coincidentally, I had been considering a variation or two on *Hamlet.* The project was soon titled *Fortinbras,* and while it had to compete with a TV-film I was writing, I felt things were going pretty well—until February arrived, and I once more had written only a bit more than the first act from which to audition actors. Luckily, all fifteen roles had at least *some* lines by that point in the play, so it was feasible.

Fortinbras, a dark farce predicated on the reign of Prince Fortinbras in Denmark after Hamlet and his family have self-destructed, allowed Des to show off the myriad technical possibilities of his new theatre, continued a series of brilliantly designed productions (including the irresistibly lush costumes by Susan Hilferty), and had a keenly clever original score by Michael Roth—much of which he improvised personally every night.

Three-fourths of the way across the country, a smaller theatre, the Ensemble Theatre of Cincinnati, led by another energetic artistic director, David White III, had been talking to me about doing an open-ended commission for a new play. David was ready to commit a slot in his next season for a new play from me, sight unseen. That kind of faith in my ability to deliver a producible script on time made it easy for me to accept the commission. Financial support for the production came from a private gift made by Lois and Richard Rosenthal, a Cincinnati couple whose dedication to new and challenging American drama is genuinely impressive.

Neither the Rosenthals nor ETC expressed the slightest alarm when I told them my new play, *Lake Street Extension,* was about molestation, child prostitution, incest, *and* relations between the United States and El Salvador in the Reagan years. No one demanded to see the script early. There were no secret agendas, no tests for political correctness, no last-minute qualms about content. I worked on the world premiere with director Jeanne Blake in a relaxed and extremely supportive environment—and the production proved very successful.

The final play in this collection, *Patient A,* is the most unusual commission I've undertaken. Jeanne and I had presented *Two Rooms* at the Theatre Club of the Palm Beaches, in Florida. Through Lou Tyrrell, its artistic director, we met the lawyer for Kimberly Bergalis, a woman who claimed to have been infected with HIV by her dentist. No mention of her case came up at the time, but a few months later Lou called and asked if I'd consider a commission to write a play about her experience.

The first question I asked was, "What kind of play do Kim and her family want?" When the answer came back, "Whatever play you write," I knew I could accept the commission. Jeanne and I went to visit Kim and her family in April of 1992. We saw them all again in October, two months before she died.

It took two years to research, write, and produce the play. In that time, neither the lawyer nor Kim's family asked to see the script. The family never experienced a word of it until they sat in the audience on opening night. The fact that my politics were not the same as the family's—nor the same as those of their strongest critics—left me with no idea whether *anyone* would respond favorably to the play.

My hope all along had been somehow to raise the material above the narrow and acrimonious debate over the public policy issues surrounding her case and create a portrait of a society struggling to do what's most humane in the face of an inhumane tragedy.

The Signature Theatre Company, under the leadership of Jim Houghton, had committed its 1992–93 New York season to producing four of my works, and the first three happened to be revivals of *Fortinbras, Lake Street Extension,* and *Two Rooms.* The final slot would be reserved for the world premiere of *Patient A.* With Jeanne directing, the play opened downtown in April 1993. Much to my relief, it was met with praise from people on both sides of the issue.

One of my greatest challenges as a playwright is my unwillingness to write the same play over and over. At times I feel interviewers scrutinizing me (as though searching for the spot marked "Attach Type-of-Playwright Label Here") and I don't know what to tell them. I've written broad farces, political commentaries, family dramas, sports plays, work plays, plays about crime, personal biographies, marriage plays—even a Western.

The five plays collected here reflect this diversity. *Two Rooms* is about America's experience with its hostages in Beirut; *Down the Road* explores the phenomenon of serial murder and our relationship to it as consumers; *Fortinbras* is a loving liberty taken with Shakespeare's masterpiece—containing at the same time a dark, political undertone; *Lake Street Extension* is a willful linking together of two forms of incest—one familial and one internationally political; finally, *Patient A* examines not only the Bergalis case but my own feelings in the first decade of AIDS.

I always hope that a reader or audience member, at the point of experiencing a new work of mine, won't be able simply to"dial in" a set of expectations before the lights go down: such and such a genre, tone, context, set of characters—all with relatively minor variations. While that may be good for the business side of playwriting, it can be a starvation diet for an artist. I want the world of each new play to open as many doors as possible, for the audience and for myself. I love exploring different kinds of human experience and different kinds of theatre. For me it keeps the process alive.

I owe a tremendous debt of gratitude to those who helped in the creation of these plays—particularly since they were commissions. Des McAnuff, Robert Blacker, and the La Jolla Playhouse; Jon Jory and the Actors Theatre of Louisville; David White III, the Ensemble Theatre of Cincinnati, and the Rosenthals; Louis Tyrrell and the Theatre Club of the Palm Beaches; Jim Houghton and the Signature Theatre Company, as well as Kimberly Bergalis, her family, and their lawyer, Robert Montgomery—all played important roles in bringing these plays into being, and all have my deepest thanks.

Beyond that, and beyond everything else, I want to thank Jeanne Blake, whose willingness to listen, respond, appraise, and edit my early drafts—as well as her insightful direction of my final drafts—has made her the person most responsible for these plays being in the versions you see here.

TWO ROOMS

❖

To Jeanne, and to the memory of Jo

Two Rooms received its world premiere at the La Jolla Playhouse (Des McAnuff, Artistic Director; Alan Levey, Managing Director), La Jolla, California, on June 21, 1988. It was directed by Des McAnuff; the set was designed by Marjorie Bradley Kellogg; the costumes were designed by Susan Hilferty; the lighting was designed by Peter A. Kaczorowski; the music was by Michael S. Roth; the sound was by Serge Ossorguine; video production was by Dennis McNabb; and slide photography was by Harry Hendrickson. The cast was as follows:

LAINIE WELLS. . . . . Amanda Plummer

WALKER HARRIS . . . . Brent Jennings

ELLEN VAN OSS . . . . Jo Henderson

MICHAEL WELLS. . . . . Jon DeVries

A revised version of *Two Rooms* was produced at the Cricket Theater (William Partlan, Artistic Director) in Minneapolis, Minnesota, in October 1989. It was directed by Jeanne Blake; the set design was by Rick Polenek; the lighting design was by Tina Charney; the costume design was by Anne Ruben; and technical direction was by John David Paul. The cast was as follows:

MICHAEL WELLS . . . . Terry Edward Moore

LAINIE WELLS . . . . Camille D'Ambrose

WALKER HARRIS . . . . Steven Hendrickson

ELLEN VAN OSS . . . . Shirley Venard

CHARACTERS

MICHAEL WELLS, 30s, educator
LAINIE WELLS, 30s, educator, married to Michael
WALKER HARRIS, 30s, reporter
ELLEN VAN OSS, 40s, representative of the State Department

TIME

The recent past, the present

PLACE

A room

ACT ONE

Scene One

Lights rise to reveal a dull-colored emptiness. A narrow mat lies on the floor. The sense of an entry upstage, but no more than that. Michael lies on the mat. He has an unkempt beard, wears a t-shirt and pajamas. He also wears handcuffs. He is blindfolded.

MICHAEL. Mathison had a gun. Under his jacket. A little automatic pistol or something — I'd never seen it before. Silver. I remember it gleamed in the sunlight when he pulled it out. It was just as they were forcing us both into the car — just as he put one hand on the roof of the car. He was right in front of me, there was nowhere I could go. And suddenly this shining little fantasy pistol appeared. Can you imagine? I taught for two years with the guy and never knew he carried it. As though that was supposed to save us. As though that pitiful gun — that absurd, miniscule tribute to one man's utter lack of realism . . . I mean, he had to know what the world can do — if it just *feels* like it — to a man. To any man. And to carry a gun? The size of a cigarette case? In Beirut? *(He starts to laugh, stops because it hurts.)* He didn't even know what to do once he pulled it out. I think he really believed all those kidnappers would take one look at this mighty weapon of the West, drop their AK-47's and flee. "Run! It's a trap! He's got a tiny gun!" *(Starts to laugh again, stops.)* God, Lainie, I love

5

you. I wish this was a real letter. *(A beat.)* What Mathison forgot was these people have been taking hostages for thousands of years. They know how to do it. He yelled, "I'm armed!" I remember, and that same instant one of them shot it out of his hand, along with some of his fingers, and they slammed us into the car, did the old Kalashnikov-to-the-forehead routine, wrapped Mathison's hand up with his own shirt, blindfolded us and drove us . . . wherever this is. No one spoke. The only sound was Mathison weeping. I wasn't paying that much attention. I was busy counting my own fingers. And toes. *(A beat.)* Ok, this is a digression, but I'm suddenly thinking of your toes. Really. I'm remembering them on the beach at the ocean. First few dates — somewhere in there. You had a bathing suit on — which could have been the first time I saw you in one — and we were lying on towels and you dug your toes down in the wet sand. You dug them around very slowly, and suddenly I felt overwhelmed by this powerful image of . . . a sea turtle, coming ashore, digging in the sand and laying millions, or hundreds — you'd know — of eggs. And it's stupid, but it made me feel connected in a way I'd never felt before, to amphibians. I mean, there they are — forever faced with the choice: go on land and risk their life to lay eggs, or stay in the sea where it's warm and safe and eventually die out. And it occurred to me in that moment that marriage is exactly the same proposition. And I looked at your toes in the sand once more, and . . . married you anyway. *(A beat.)* I wear a blindfold. I can take it off, but if I do they beat me. Or if they come in and it looks re-tied, they beat me. Sometimes it doesn't look like I've taken it off, but since I'm an American they're sure I must have, and they beat me anyway. Their voices are so young. I'm sure it's a delusion, but sometimes I think I've had one or two of them in my class. *(A beat.)* Now I'm in theirs. *(The lights fade quickly to black. When they rise again, Lainie is alone in the room. She stands staring at the empty mat. The room is much brighter — light from an unseen window surrounds her. When she speaks, she addresses the mat at first, then moves around the room. She does not address the audience.)*

LAINIE.   I'm talking to myself. All last night, taking the furniture out of this room, I was talking to myself. It's not the worst habit. Besides, for the last year, what else have I been doing? *(She regards the mat critically, slides it toward one corner of the room, silently appraises its new position.)* Talking to everyone in power — which is, of course, the definition of talking to yourself. I don't know about it here. It'd probably be in a corner, but this one? Which one? *(Sliding it to another corner of the room.)* It's hard to know which was worse: talking to Moslems or talking to Christians. Talking to Lebanese or talking to Syrians. Going across the Green Line to beg, or to Damascus — or Washington. *(Suddenly nods her head decisively.)* Washington. Definitely Washington. The Arabs wouldn't help me, but at least they'd respect the pain. In Washington, I *was* the pain. *(Of the position of the mat.)* This is absolutely wrong. *(She moves it to another corner, stares at it.)* The head of the University said they'd do everything humanly possible to get you back. So did the head of Amal. So did the Lebanese President. So did the Syrian Foreign Minister, our embassy in Beirut, our embassy in Damascus, the Undersecretary of State, the President, and everyone running for President. This doesn't work at all. *(She moves the mat to the center of the room again.)* This is just going to have to stand for all the corners of the room. Why not? It's . . . not an exact science. *(She stares at the mat.)* You'll be here. *(She moves towards the source of light from outside, mimes pulling down a shade and lights dim. She goes to the mat, sits on one side of it, then lies on it, allowing space as though another person were lying on it with her. Tentatively, she reaches out as though stroking the cheek of her 'companion.')* From now on, I'm only talking to you. *(Lights fade to black. When they rise again, Lainie sits on the floor a few feet from the mat, staring at it. Walker stands staring at her.)*

WALKER. How long has this room been like this? *(A beat.)* Do you redecorate often? *(A beat.)* Rest of the house looks real nice. Very normal. *(A beat.)* This room, though. This room you seem to have done something to. *(A beat.)* Lainie? Can I call you Lainie? *(A beat.)* I want to thank you for letting me come. I know a lot of other reporters would like to be here. I'm glad you chose to talk to me. *(A beat.)* Lainie? *(A beat.)*

So — what is it you'd say you've done to this room?

LAINIE.   I cleansed it.

WALKER.   Cleansed it? *(Attempting to break the mood.)* Is that a new thing? In decor? Cleansing? *(A beat.)* Lainie? *(A beat.)* It's hard to ask the right questions if you won't —

LAINIE.   I scrubbed and painted all the walls. I took all his things out.

WALKER.   Was this his room? 1 mean — is it?

LAINIE.   His office. His things were here.

WALKER.   Where are they now?

LAINIE.   In the basement.

WALKER.   What if he comes back? Soon, I mean.

LAINIE.   I painted everything. Walls, ceiling.

WALKER.   A lot of consistency. What's the mat for?

LAINIE.   I look at it.

WALKER.   Why? *(A beat.)* Do you mind if I open the shade? *(A beat.)* Lainie? *(Without attempting to open the shade.)* So — does the government keep in contact with you?

LAINIE.   She's coming today.

WALKER.   She?

LAINIE.   The government. Her name is Ellen. She's been attached to me. My case. *(A beat.)*

WALKER.   Ellen. What time is she coming?

LAINIE.   I liked your voice.

WALKER.   What?

LAINIE.   Your voice on the phone. I liked it.

WALKER.   Why?

LAINIE.   It took its time. *(She stares steadily at the mat.)*

WALKER.   When is Ellen coming? *(A beat.)* Did you want me to meet her? Is that why I'm here? *(A beat.)* The government hasn't always told the truth on this issue. You do know that. *(A beat.)* I could write about this right now. With what I've got. Just having been here. I could write about this room. What you're saying, what you're not saying. But I won't — if you'll just look at me. *(Again, no response.)* What is it you're staring at?

LAINIE.   His hands. *(Lights fade to black. Quickly they fade up again. Ellen now stands where Walker did. Lainie remains in the same position.)*

ELLEN. We think they've moved him. Not far. A different section of town, perhaps. Or even just across the street. We're reasonably certain it's no further than that. It's good strategy for them to move him from time to time. It enhances their power. *(A beat.)* Still, they may have moved him all the way to the Bekaa Valley. That is possible. *(A beat.)* They may not have moved him at all. They may only be pretending to move him. As you know, our intelligence in Beirut isn't the best. Even pretending to move him could enhance their power. *(She sighs.)* Frankly, almost everything enhances their power. It would be hard for Michael's captors to make a mistake, at the moment. Lainie, are you listening to me? *(Walker enters with a small ottoman.)*

WALKER. Here you go.

ELLEN. Thank you.

WALKER. *(Setting it down for her.)* I'm getting your tea. Lainie?

LAINIE. Nothing. *(Walker exits U.)*

ELLEN. Why is he here?

LAINIE. Shouldn't he be here?

ELLEN. He's from a newspaper. What have we been talking about for the last year, Lainie?

LAINIE. It's better to be quiet.

ELLEN. We have no way of knowing what public statements by hostage relatives may do. No way at all. It could make it even harder for us to secure a safe return. I'm disappointed that you called him.

LAINIE. He called me.

ELLEN. I'm disappointed he's here. It's absurd for you to talk to newspapers. Besides, one doesn't talk to newspapers in any case. One lights their fuse. Please, get rid of him.

LAINIE. I can't do that.

ELLEN. *(Starting to go.)* Then I'll go.

LAINIE. No.

ELLEN. I won't be able to be free with information.

LAINIE. When is there ever any information?

ELLEN. *(Sighs, sits.)* When are you going to do something about this room? *(A beat.)* Where were we?

9

LAINIE.   You said they were moving him. Or maybe they weren't.

ELLEN.   The most important thing to remember is that we're not speaking of a country of terrorists here.   We're barely speaking of a country at all. We're speaking of factions. Some friendly to Iran, some to Syria, some to Israel, some to us. They're all fighting for power.   For all we know your husband —

LAINIE.   Michael.

ELLEN.   Michael may be liberated by a faction that favors us. Something like that could happen at any time.

LAINIE.   What are the chances?

ELLEN.   The important thing is to maintain cautious optimism. Advised hope, I call it. We're hopeful, but we're advised. We're not unintelligent. We recognize the reality of the situation, then we inject hope. Into that reality. Because without hope there can be no foreign policy. *(Walker reenters with a small tray-table. On it is a tea set. He sets it all down next to Ellen and pours.)*

WALKER.   I let it steep in the kitchen.

ELLEN.   Thank you. *(A beat.)* I'm so odd. Everyone in Washington pumps down coffee all day as fast as they can. And then there's me — with my little cup of tea. I feel like a foreigner. *(She studies the tea a moment.)* The main thing — the crucial thing — is knowing that hope is a real and present possibility. Men have disappeared in Beirut, men have reappeared.

WALKER.   So when's Michael Wells going to reappear?

ELLEN.   Well — that is what I mean by hope. *(A beat.)*

WALKER.   Sorry?

ELLEN.   I mean, for example, there are pictures. We have pictures of Michael. Taken just a month ago. Pictures of him alive.

WALKER.   He had the shit beat out of him. He was barely recognizable.

ELLEN.   The point is, he's alive.

WALKER.   He was alive then.

ELLEN.   And hope keeps him alive, right up to the present

moment. That's why we use hope. Hope enhances our power.

LAINIE.   When will my husband be released?

ELLEN.   We can't say.

WALKER.   What do you mean, you can't say?

ELLEN.   I really should go. I didn't come here for a news conference. *(Ellen moves to leave.)*

LAINIE.   Ellen. *(Ellen stops.)*

WALKER.   It's our Middle-East policy that's keeping your husband hostage. Nothing else.

ELLEN.   That's ridiculous.

WALKER.   In terms of priorities, Michael comes below oil, below U.S.-Soviet relations —

ELLEN.   He's totally uninformed —

WALKER. Below U.S.-Israeli relations, U.S.-Syrian relations —

ELLEN.   Lainie —

WALKER.   U.S.-*Iranian* relations —

ELLEN.   *(To Lainie.)* You'd be well-advised to reflect on *your* relations with the press.

WALKER.   Can I quote you? *(To Lainie.)* Have you ever wondered why other governments can get their hostages out and we can't?

ELLEN.   They pay ransom.

WALKER.   And it works!

ELLEN. This government is using every ethical means to bring your husband back to you.

WALKER.   This government wouldn't care if your husband died.

ELLEN.   Mr. Harris!

WALKER.   Because then he's not a problem anymore.

ELLEN.   Either he goes — right now — or I do.

WALKER.   *(To Ellen.)* How does she get you to come out here, anyway? It's a thirty-minute drive.

ELLEN.   Lainie?

LAINIE.   I won't talk to her on the phone.

WALKER.   Really?

LAINIE.   I hang up the minute I hear her voice.

WALKER.   How come?

ELLEN.   Lainie.

LAINIE.   I don't want to be alone when I hear about Michael.
I want to hear it from her face to face.
ELLEN.   I come out here because I wish to!
LAINIE.   I told them I'd fast. I'd chain myself to a building.
ELLEN.   We have never taken her seriously.
WALKER.   You're here.
ELLEN.   The Department feels that since Lainie does live close
by, and is only asking for one personal visit per week —
LAINIE.   I want two next week.
ELLEN.   One or two visits per week, it's a small price to pay
for keeping her —
WALKER.   Quiet?
ELLEN.   From embarrassing herself. You're a newsman, Mr.
Harris. Certainly you understand the degree to which media
can adversely affect a sensitive situation.
WALKER.   Sure. That's why I investigate every goddamn story
I can. *(A beat.)*
ELLEN.   We encounter all sorts of emotional responses in
these situations. This we are prepared for. My job is to help
victims learn which responses are appropriate, and which are
not. The response of running to the papers, in the vain belief
that they are somehow the repository of virtue and kindness,
is woefully inappropriate. I urge you to ask yourself what's in
it for them. *(Starting out, then stopping.)* The government is
doing all it can along every avenue. There are however acts of
God, for example, over which no government has power.
LAINIE.   You think this is an act of God?
ELLEN.   No. But it is . . . as remote. *(Starting out again.)* I'll
be back next Wednesday.
LAINIE.   Monday.
ELLEN.   *(A glimpse of irritation crossing her face.)* Monday. *(Ellen
exits U.)*
WALKER.   *(Once she is gone.)* You wonder why the government
can't do anything. Right there — that attitude. That's the
reason.
LAINIE.   Walker, goodbye.
WALKER.   Goodbye? What do you mean?
LAINIE.   Goodbye.

WALKER. We've just gotten started.

LAINIE. Goodbye. *(A beat.)*

WALKER. When can I come back? *(No response.)* You know, I've got better things to do than chase down stories of unco-operative people. *(A beat. He starts to go, stops.)* Do you want me to leave? I'll do what you want me to do. *(A beat.)* Lainie? What is it you want me to do?

LAINIE. Bring back my husband. *(He stares at her, then leaves. Lights quickly fade to black. When they rise again, Michael is alone onstage, as he was at the beginning.)*

MICHAEL. I have new guards now. It's been more than a year, hasn't it? They don't tell me exactly. I've discovered some things here. For example, your hands can become friends if they're in handcuffs long enough. *(A beat.)* I once saw a hand just lying in the street. You remember that day I came home, after walking past a car-bombing? I didn't tell you at the time, but I saw it. Just a hand, lying there, unclaimed. It wasn't even horrible so much as . . . terrifyingly lonely. *(A beat.)* I ask myself all the time, "Why did we stay here? Why did we stay here? Why?" *(A beat.)* I look back now and can't believe we stayed. Can't believe we actually sat there at the University and said, "One last term. Then we'll leave." One last term. I wonder if we would've left even then. I wonder if somehow, some part of us even liked the danger. Or was in awe of what we were witnessing. I mean, why does anyone stay? This city's in the hands of boys. Teenagers roam the streets carrying AK-47's and somebody *stays*? I don't know if there's ever been a city that has for this long been such a horror. That's taken itself apart brick by brick, life by life. And so many of us stayed. We walked down the street, through the rubble, past the checkpoints, past the bombings — we had days full of ordinary moments. Amid — what? — devils from Hell. Boys who might shoot you the next moment. Cars that might drive up, park and explode. *(With a growing tension that finally breaks through.)* And none of us seemed ready to say, "Leave it. Let us out of here! Please, *God* anything but this! *Stop it!!*" *(A beat. He recovers himself.)* And none of us was ever quite ready to leave. *(He moves towards a wall. Lainie enters and sits next to the mat, reaching out as though stroking Michael's hair. Michael is oblivious to her.)*

LAINIE. Michael? This bothers me. Here on this side, just below your mouth. It's a line here. A little tuck, almost. A wrinkle. It's not on the other side. I don't mind you growing older, but you should do it all over your face, evenly. Don't you think? *(A beat.)* This, though. Here at your temple. I like this. The way the hairs glide along the side, over your ear, into the tangle in back. Just these hairs on the side, running straight back, like they're in a hurry. *(With a slight laugh.)* But all this ear-hair. This has got to go. *(Quieter.)* A beard. I can't imagine it. *(A beat.)* I suppose you don't get enough sleep. Or maybe you do. Maybe all you do is sleep. I hope so. I wish you could sleep from first to last. That you'd never open your eyes again, till I was in front of you. Your eyes are so . . . Why do women love eyes so much? They say it's men that are visual. *(A beat.)* Michael? *(Lights fade to black.)*

Scene Two

A slide appears on the U. wall. It's a picture of a heavily-damaged building in Beirut. We see Lainie and Walker silhouetted on the floor, looking up at it.

LAINIE.   This is a hotel in Beirut near where we lived. It was destroyed in some shelling a couple of months before . . . before he was taken. *(We hear the sound of a slide projector. The picture changes: the site of a car-bomb explosion.)* A car bombing. Michael used to take pictures as he walked along. He wasn't looking for these kinds of things. You just couldn't avoid them. People at the University told him it was dangerous. It made people notice him. Even more, I mean. And he did stop a few weeks before . . . *(Another slide: a Lebanese youth, perhaps 15, with an automatic weapon.)* This guy commanded a whole block. He liked Michael. He wanted to pose. *(Another slide: the coast. A few indistinct figures at the shore.)* Michael heard that people had started fishing with grenades. They'd just toss a grenade in the water, and . . . fish that way. *(Another slide: a Lebanese woman, weeping bitterly.)* Michael said he could've taken this picture a hundred times. I'm not sure what it was about her. He didn't know her. He saw something different as he passed. Maybe the sun's shining on her in a different way. Maybe it's something

14

about the way she's standing, or — whatever it is, all the values just seem to . . . hold you. *(Suddenly the projector shuts off. The image disappears. Blackness.)*

WALKER. What's wrong?

LAINIE. I want to stop now.

WALKER. We just started.

LAINIE. I'm sorry.

WALKER. I'll get the lights.

LAINIE. Don't.

WALKER. You want to sit in the dark?

LAINIE. Do you think they still blindfold him?

WALKER. They might. Who can know?

LAINIE. Do they chain him?

WALKER. They might. *(Walker flicks on the lights. He stands at the U. wall. Lainie still sits on the floor.)* Those are good pictures. He's a good photographer.

LAINIE. He's a good teacher, too. I'm sorry. These pictures were harder than I thought. I shouldn't have agreed to show them to you.

WALKER. It's a shame. They'd go awfully well with an interview. If you'd ever give me an interview.

LAINIE. I can't decide.

WALKER. It's been two months. *(A beat.)*

LAINIE. Why haven't you written anything up to now? You have more than enough without me talking.

WALKER. I guess I'd like to have your permission. *(With a self-deprecating laugh.)* My editors think I'm crazy, of course. But that's why. *(A beat.)* I won't write anything if you don't want me to. That's a promise.

LAINIE. What's a promise?

WALKER. You were teaching, weren't you? After you got back here? *(Lainie nods.)* But recently you took a leave of absence?

LAINIE. You've been asking about me?

WALKER. Why'd you leave?

LAINIE. It's hard to teach natural sciences when . . . *(She trails off.)*

WALKER. When what?

LAINIE. When nothing's natural. *(A beat.)*

WALKER. So. Do you sit in here all day?

15

LAINIE.   No. I'm working on a project. It's something I couldn't do in Beirut.

WALKER.   What is it?

LAINIE.   I watch birds. I go down to the marsh a couple miles away, and. . . . Warblers, mostly. I'm working on them.

WALKER.   Does it relax you?

LAINIE.   It teaches me.

WALKER.   And the rest of the time you're in here? Not much of a life. *(A beat.)*

LAINIE.   Michael's here. I can't explain it, but for me he is. In this room. The moment I come in, I feel . . . the warmth of his body. The rest of the house — everywhere else — is cold.

WALKER.   You need to talk to people. Away from here. At work, or —

LAINIE.   I work in a marsh.

WALKER.   You should talk to friends. How about the other hostage families?

LAINIE.   It's like looking in a mirror.

WALKER.   Then talk to the public. That really hasn't been tried enough. We could start with an interview. In depth, about —

LAINIE.   My pain?

WALKER.   Among other things. We could run it in the paper. Two, three installments. Maybe more.

LAINIE.   We could run my pain in installments?

WALKER.   It's better than hiding in a marsh. *(A beat.)*

LAINIE.   Ellen says that won't help anyone but the kidnappers.

WALKER.   *No* one knows what will help. That's the first thing. No one knows. All we know is what we've done, and what hasn't worked. Keeping silent hasn't worked.

LAINIE.   Why do you care about this? You don't have anyone over there.

WALKER.   I care about people who are going through what you're going through.

LAINIE.   But why? Why our pain? There's so much to pick from. The world is full of terrible . . . outcomes. Why did you choose this? Is it because you can win an award?

WALKER.   An award? What are you talking about?

LAINIE.   Intense suffering. A long series. Lots of installments. A

16

Pulitzer prize.

WALKER. Is that what you think I'm here for? I've been waiting for months! You think that's how I 'd go after a Pulitzer prize? You think I'd wait for you to ask me here? I'd be on your doorstep every day. I'd be out in the marsh with you.

LAINIE. I'm sorry.

WALKER. I've stared into too many faces — yours included — of people who've been told, "Your husband's gone. He may be dead. There's nothing you can do." *(A beat.)* The reason I'm here is because more than anyone this has happened to — any family, I mean — you understand what's really going on.

LAINIE. What's really going on?

WALKER. What's really going on is that they'll let him die. They've already made the value judgment on him and the others. To this administration, it's more effective to use his captivity — and even his death — to push a bunch of policy points, than it is to use every means to get him back.

LAINIE. You really think that?

WALKER. I know it. So do you. The day he's reported dead, do you think they'll be taking any responsibility? They'll be all over TV, pointing the finger at every terrorist in the Middle East and saying, "These are barbarians. Don't try to understand them, just let us do what we must do." And we'll let them.

LAINIE. What do you think I should do?

WALKER. I've said. Speak out. Do interviews. Go on TV if you have to. *(She considers this.)*

LAINIE. No.

WALKER. Why not?

LAINIE. *(Shakes her head.)* It's too public for me. It's too . . . public.

WALKER. Well. Fear of speaking. Right up there with — what? Fear of falling, fear of loud noises —

LAINIE. That's not fair.

WALKER. Oh, I'm not being fair? Sorry. You're right. Loud noises can be pretty rough. *(He suddenly claps his hand loudly behind her ear. She pulls away from it, holding her ear in pain.)*

LAINIE. *Stop* that!

WALKER. That's probably going to be the last thing Michael ever hears. Only it won't be two hands clapping, it'll be a gun.

LAINIE. Get out of here!

WALKER. Care about your husband.

LAINIE. I do!

WALKER. Do something!

LAINIE. I *am!*

WALKER. Do more!

LAINIE. *No!! (A beat.)* You know what will get him back? Nothing we can understand. Whatever took Michael, whatever will bring him back is a power so incomprehensible we'll never understand it. And all the running around screaming about injustice won't change a thing. All we can do—all *anyone* can do —is take pictures of mourning widows. Write stories about mourning widows. Become fascinated with widows of men who aren't even dead yet. But nothing — *nothing* — will make a difference.

WALKER. Lainie, I'm only —

LAINIE. Get out! If I want to see a scavenger, I'll go to the marsh. *(A beat. Walker hesitates, then exist. Lights fade to black. When they rise again, Michael sits alone on the mat. He is blindfolded.)*

MICHAEL. *(A beat.)* War isn't a tear in the fabric of things, it is the fabric. If earth is our mother, our father is war. The chief priority we have on earth is to vie with each other for a place to stand. Does any of this make sense, Lainie? I'm trying to explain why this has happened to us. Americans fight all the time — lots of wars. But always far away. We haven't had to fight for the soil we stand on in a century. We've forgotten that level of sacrifice. These people haven't. Everyone in this country — Christian, Sunni Moslem, Shi'ite, Palestinian, Israeli — everyone is fighting for the ground. The ground itself. They stand here or nowhere. So it's easy for them to give up their lives. Small sacrifice. It's easy for them to kill, too. Small sacrifice. You know how being here, being swallowed up by it, makes me feel? Like I'm finally part of the real world. For the first time. Lainie, something in me never felt . . . affected . . . until this happened. You know what it makes me think of? Shiloh. Vicksburg. The Wilderness. What those places must have been like: suffocating, endless, bleeding disaster. Stacking of bodies ten deep for a few feet of *our ground.* Don't you see? We're not different from these people, we've just forgotten. We think this urge doesn't exist anymore. We abstract everything, we objectify. We talk about

18

global politics, how all this affects the balance of power. Do you know what a twenty-year-old Shi'ite thinks of the balance of power? *(Lights fade to black.)*

Scene Three

Lights fade up to reveal Ellen sitting in a chair. Lainie sits on the floor facing her.

ELLEN.   I got a call today.

LAINIE.   About Michael?

ELLEN.   Not exactly. About Walker. He's been visiting you now and then, hasn't he?

LAINIE.   What's wrong with that?

ELLEN.   Nothing. He was here about a week ago. You looked at slides, I believe.

LAINIE.   How do you know that? Did he tell you?

ELLEN.   Walker? Oh, no. *(Laughs slightly.)* No, no, no. Sometimes we watch your house.

LAINIE.   You do?

ELLEN.   Of course. You're on the list.

LAINIE.   What list?

ELLEN.   The Watch Your House list. You've made threats. You're a potential embarrassment. In the realm of international politics, that can be serious. Terrorists can use what you do. What Walker does, too. Americans are often naive in their efforts to affect things like the media, public opinion. They can end up helping this country's enemies far more than themselves. In a situation like this, where so little can be done, the temptation must be irresistible to do something irrational, counterproductive. That's the only way I can understand what Walker's done.

LAINIE.   What's he done?

ELLEN.   Oh, that's right. You don't know yet. That call I got? It was from one of his editors. Walker's written a story. About you. It'll be out tomorrow. Not an interview. He doesn't quote you directly. But he details the kidnapping, and all your various meetings with people during the early months, and . . . I'm afraid

19

. . . also this room.

LAINIE.   He'd never do that without telling me.

ELLEN.   That's what I thought. That's why I'm here, in fact. To find out if he really has done this behind your back. *(A beat.)* Is that the case?

LAINIE.   Can we get them not to print the story?

ELLEN.   No. But I'd like to make a suggestion or two, if I could.

LAINIE.   What?

ELLEN.   If you were to make a public statement disavowing the article, that might help. Perhaps having a different reporter, from a newspaper we could recommend, come in and see this room in a more normal state —

LAINIE.   No.

ELLEN.   Whatever you like. Perhaps only a photographer. Just a picture of you sitting in this room with furniture, the window open . . . *(Lainie is silent.)* Well. Let's see what damage is done before we look for solutions. *(A beat. Ellen rises.)* I probably should be getting back to the office. *(She moves to leave. Lainie is motionless.)* Lainie? Are you all right?

LAINIE.   Are you pretending to care?

ELLEN.   I care very much. I think you know that.

LAINIE.   If you did, you'd do something.

ELLEN.   I told you, there's nothing we can do about Walker —

LAINIE.   Not about Walker; about Michael.

ELLEN.   We do things all the time. Every day. We just can't tell you about them.

LAINIE.   Nothing happens.

ELLEN.   Sometimes something happens. People do get released.

LAINIE.   Not because of anything you do.

ELLEN.   You can't know that.

LAINIE.   I can't know much, given how little you tell me.

ELLEN.   A government must have secrets.

LAINIE.   Why?

ELLEN.   I'm not conducting a course for children. *(A beat.)* We need silence. From you, from all the hostage families. And a willingness to let us do our job. It isn't easy for you, we know that. But talking with people like Walker doesn't help anyone, and as we've learned today, it's its own punishment. The one thing you can do — the only thing that will be of any use — is to hope.

LAINIE. Hope?

ELLEN. Hope.

LAINIE. Hope doesn't come from you, does it?

ELLEN. What do you mean?

LAINIE. It comes from God, doesn't it? Or Allah? Jehovah? Fate? A higher power — isn't that right? Certainly not the government. The government doesn't dole out hope. It's not an entitlement program.

ELLEN. I don't see how this —

LAINIE. I study hope all the time. You know where? The marsh. I watch the warblers there, nesting. I know their whole life cycle. Little, friendly I-won't-bore-you-with-the-Latin-name warblers. Thousands of them. Going about their business. Not too many predators, plenty of insects to eat. They wouldn't need hope at all if it weren't for one thing.

ELLEN. Which is?

LAINIE. The cuckoo. A much larger bird. Fewer of them, but . . . larger.

ELLEN. I'm not sure I see the connection.

LAINIE. You're right. Cuckoos don't eat warblers. They also eat insects. But cuckoos don't build nests. Instead, they wait till the warblers are away from theirs. Then they lay their eggs in the middle of all the warbler eggs. Neat, eh? Camouflage.

ELLEN. Sounds . . . effective.

LAINIE. Oh, it works every time. The warblers return, and because they have — literally — bird brains, they don't seem to notice the great big egg among the little ones. They sit on them all. And what do you think happens? I mean, what's evolution for? The cuckoo hatches first. And there he is — nearly as big as his step-parents, demanding an immense volume of food, and waiting for the warbler eggs to hatch one by one. And when they do, do you know what happens then?

ELLEN. Inform me.

LAINIE. They crawl around — blind, as the cuckoo chick is blind — in the nest, waiting for their parents to return with food. But as they do, one by one, they encounter a miracle of natural selection: the back of the baby cuckoo.

21

ELLEN.   The back?

LAINIE.   Its back, unlike other birds' backs, is indented. There's a hollow. And you know what it's shaped like? What it's just big enough for? A baby warbler. And yet another miracle of nature: the baby cuckoo has an instinct. To do what? Push against anything that touches its back. Push and push until that thing is not there anymore. And with great effectiveness, one by one, this blind, newborn, totally innocent bird murders each of the blind, newborn, totally innocent warblers, by pushing them out of the nest where they'll starve or be eaten by rats and snakes.

ELLEN.   Thank you for sharing such a wonderful story.

LAINIE.   I'm not done. Warbler Mom and Dad come home. What do they find? One baby — which is as big as a Buick, and doesn't chirp like them. What do they think? Who will ever know? What do they do? Feed the only baby they have. Until one day it flies off, fully-fledged, a different species. And God or Allah or Nature or Fate — which we've already agreed is the author of hope — looks on with something more than indifference. With approval. *(A beat.)* The indentation in the cuckoo's back — that is the face of God. That is the chance of hope in the world.

ELLEN.   Not every nest is visited by a cuckoo.

LAINIE.   Mine was. Now offer me hope. *(Lainie turns, exits quickly U. Ellen sighs, starts to follow after her. Before she can reach the door, Michael enters, in handcuffs. He is blindfolded. Ellen is unsurprised to see him.)*

MICHAEL.   They take me to the bathroom once a day. If I'm lucky I can shower once a month. Pardon my appearance.

ELLEN.   That's perfectly all right.

MICHAEL.   I imagine you dream about all your hostages.

ELLEN.   Just you.

MICHAEL.   Really?

ELLEN.   Well, I'm assigned to you. The State Department is very big. Other hostages are dreamt about by others.

MICHAEL.   *(Nods.)* Ah.

ELLEN.   Don't misunderstand. The dreams don't bother me.

MICHAEL.   They don't?

ELLEN.   What do you . . . think about all day?

MICHAEL.   I think about a man as a stored object. As a broom in a broom closet. I think about brine shrimp in the Kalahari.

ELLEN. Brine shrimp?

MICHAEL. Tiny shrimp that live in the desert, in Africa. Lainie told me about them. They can live for years in suspended animation in the mud of a dry lakebed. When rain comes — if it comes — they wake up, and swim around, and procreate as fast as they can and get eaten by everything around them. Then after a week or two the lake dries up again, and the lucky ones hit the mud for another . . . decade. Ninety-nine percent of their life is spent waiting for their life. You get out of the United States, you see a lot of that. Whole cultures waiting to be alive.

ELLEN. You're sympathetic to your captors' cause. The Stockholm Effect. A common syndrome — it's documented.

MICHAEL. It's convenient. You're sure your dreams don't bother you?

ELLEN. No more than the student's dream of being late to the exam bothers the student. There's some real anxiety at first, but ultimately —

MICHAEL. Indifference?

ELLEN. I realize it's not real.

MICHAEL. I am real.

ELLEN. Of course. But I'm not required to treat you that way. (*She exits quickly U. Lights fade to black.*)

Scene Four

Lights rise to reveal Lainie and Walker. The chair is gone.

WALKER. I want to be able to give you my side of things. (*A beat.*) I want to show you that what I did —

LAINIE. You promised me. (*A beat.*)

WALKER. That what I did —

LAINIE. You promised me.

WALKER. Lainie —

LAINIE. This room. You put this room in a newspaper.

WALKER. It's in a newspaper every day. It's Michael's room. It's

23

the room they're all in. Hell, everyone's in it. We can't get out.

LAINIE. People call me. They've been calling all week. They want to know if this room really exists. They want to know if they can come over.

WALKER. I'm sorry.

LAINIE. You're sorry?! My life hasn't been that different, you know. I've had friends take advantage of me before. I've had them hurt me, betray me. I know what it's like. But I never thought someone would come into my life now — as it is now — and do this.

WALKER. Lainie —

LAINIE. *Why*!?

WALKER. 'Cause you were smothering, that's why. You were sitting in here and pumping the air out, and for all Washington cared you could do it forever. Your husband, the men in Lebanon, the people in this country need you. They need you to say "I hurt" — in public. They need you to say, "I don't believe my government," and "We have to try new ways." They need to hear you say it over and over.

LAINIE. *That's for me to decide! That's my choice! You took my choice!* *(A silence.)* You think that just because you've been in this room, you understand it? It's the one place I can go and find Michael. Where I can feel — however imperfectly — what he's experiencing. No barrier between us. No one coming between. No one. I don't have to hear about him from a government spokesperson, or a reporter or concerned friends — I have him here. He's mine.

WALKER. *(Quietly.)* It's an illusion.

LAINIE. *What isn't?* How do you want me to experience Michael? On the news? In the faces of all the sick human beings I've had to beg for his freedom? Holding hands with how many other helpless relatives? You're a great one to talk about illusions — that's your whole business. If I can have Michael — no matter how I do it — I'm going to have him. Do you understand?

WALKER. Lainie —

LAINIE. *Do you understand?!* *(A beat. Walker nods, turns to leave.)* People are calling me. Reporters — other reporters — want to do articles about me and this room. What are we going to do about that?

WALKER. I don't know. I'm sorry. *(A beat. He starts out again.)*

24

LAINIE. I'm going to give you an exclusive interview.

WALKER. Why?

LAINIE. Because now that you've written what you've written, talking to someone is inevitable. Unless I just want to be thought of as . . . odd, I'll have to speak out. A lot of reporters would work, I suppose. But with you there's a special advantage. I know how far I can trust you. *(Walker exits. Lights fade quickly to black and quickly rise again. Lainie is with Michael, who is blindfolded.)*

MICHAEL. Some days I go around a room at home. Any room. Doesn't matter, they're all wonderlands compared to where I'm kept. Today it's my office. I try to remember everything about every piece of furniture. Where I bought it, what it was like that day, the smells in the air. It's really very sobering, how much the mind recalls when it's forced to. I remember my chair, my filing cabinet — and not just my filing cabinet, but the exact order of files: household, course-plans, medical, automobile, retirement — all of it. As if I took a picture. I remember the *smell* of my desk. And each day. I think I remember each day in my office — all of them. Cold days, wet days, days of incredible light. *(A beat.)* Did I tell you I was making a new country? On the wall. I feel the tiny bumps. They're mountains, of course. And the cracks are rivers. I work on it all day, sometimes. Every mountain has a name. There's Mount Freedom — of course. There's Mount Hope and Mount Sense of Humor. And Mount Forgiveness. There's Mount Forgiveness. Most days though, I fill up with the people we know. You, mostly. *(Lainie carefully removes Michael's blindfold. He smiles at her.)* You know that child we thought about having? We had him. He's um . . . almost six months now. I'm aging him faster than normal so we can talk together sooner. His name is Andrew. Because I like it. He has your hair and eyes, and . . . I can't tell about his nose yet. We may have a daughter later, I'm not ruling it out. *(A beat. They stare at each other.)* Who can predict the future? *(Lights fade quickly to black.)*

END OF ACT ONE

ACT TWO

Scene One

A tight spot comes up on Ellen, sitting on a chair in the room. She smiles.

ELLEN. What does it mean to be an American? Well, here it means — for most of us — "to be comfortable." Elsewhere in the world it means to be punished. To be punished justly, some would say, for the crime of having been born here and not there. *(We suddenly see a slide of a young Shi'ite terrorist on the same wall Lainie's slides appeared in Act One.)* This is one of those who does the punishing. He may be college-educated. He may well be a graduate of the American University in Beirut. He may be a shepherd, with no education whatsoever. He may speak English, or only Arabic. He may be devout — he may not. He may be utterly committed to his cause, or only doing this because it provides work and food and some measure of security. Perhaps he likes the excitement. Perhaps, like most young men, he just likes the guns. He may be relatively humane; he may be monstrous. *(Another slide — another young Shi'ite terrorist.)* Here's another one. *(Another slide — another young Shi'ite terrorist.)* And another. *(Another slide — another young Shi'ite terrorist, then several more in quick succession. She speaks as they flash past.)* And another, and another, and — thousands in this country. And this of course is only one country. Think of it — enormous numbers of people all over the world hating Americans. Hating other Westerners too, of course, but particularly Americans. Willing to kill even the most innocent of us. To make an example of our men, women, children, infants, of the aged, the infirm — of *any* American. To imprison us without trial. For years. Why? *(Another slide — a very young Shi'ite terrorist, complete with rocket-launcher.)* They watch our television, you know. See our films, wear our clothes, drive our cars, listen to our music. They use our technology — what they can afford of it. They learn in our universities. What do they learn? That by sheerest accident, they have been born in a part of the world which has no power. That to be an uneducated person in a small country, speaking a bypassed language, worshipping an old-fashioned god is worse than death. That to be such a person without a *revolution* — or promise of a revolution — is to be shut in a room, blindfolded, with a chain around your ankle for life. *(More slides — pictures of slain hostages William Buckley, Peter Kilburn and William Higgins.)* These men are dead. They were American hostages taken in Lebanon, and later apparently murdered. They were not killed for who they were so much as for who they might have been: that is, any of us. They were our representatives in death. Their lives were erased by those whose lives otherwise might never have been written. *(Another slide — Shi'ite militiamen celebrating in a Beirut street.)* Men whose only reality is to reject and destroy what they can of the Western world — which floats before them as an unreachable illusion, both detested and desired. Infinitely powerful, infinitely weak. In a real sense, the Crusades are here again. We in the State Department understand that. It's our job to be ready to sacrifice the few for the many when necessary, and we do. It's our job to look down the road, to ascertain what is and isn't likely to happen, and form our judgments accordingly. For example. *(More slides: Americans who have been kidnapped in Lebanon since 1984.)* These men, all kidnap victims, are of course undergoing dehumanizing conditions in their false imprisonment. No one denies this. They are being held by men who would as soon kill them as anything else. Yet, since 1984 out of the total of more than sixty foreigners taken, only a few have died. Over thirty have been released. We in State have to believe that the kidnappers are no more interested in dead hostages than we are. We have to believe that time is therefore on our side, not theirs. That ultimately the situation will be resolved — after a presidential election here, or a shift in the military or political situation there or whatever. A break will come. *(The slides stop on a picture of Peter Kilburn.)* But if I'm wrong, if these men in fact all suffer torture and die as a direct result of this country's policy in the Middle East, I must be ready to accept that too. American citizens have to realize that when we take a risk, the U.S. government can't always save us. That the time comes when we — on an individual basis — will simply have to pay. *(The slide goes out. Total blackness. When lights rise again, Lainie and Michael sit on the mat in the same position as at the end of Act One.)*

LAINIE.   Do they move you very often?

MICHAEL.   Now and then.

LAINIE.   Are the rooms ever different?

MICHAEL.   It's always the same room. Whatever it looks like.

LAINIE.   Why do they move you?

MICHAEL.   They're nervous. I'm a prize, remember? The Army could steal me away, another faction could steal me. Sort of like sea gulls fighting over an orange rind on the beach.

LAINIE.   What do you do all day?

MICHAEL.   Write letters to you. What do you do?

LAINIE.   Well, I . . . I do a lot of things. I do my work.

MICHAEL.   And how's that?

LAINIE.   Oh, you know . . . never-ending.

MICHAEL.   *(With a smile.)* That's the trouble with nature. What else do you do?

LAINIE.   Nothing.

MICHAEL.   Still?

LAINIE.   I'm still getting used to it.

MICHAEL.   It's been a —

LAINIE.   I know how long it's been — it's been longer than my life, all right?

MICHAEL.   I know.

LAINIE.   I wish they kidnapped women.

MICHAEL.   They do. Sometimes.

LAINIE.   They let them go. *(A beat.)*

MICHAEL.   Does anything make you happy?

LAINIE.   Sometimes Walker does.

MICHAEL.   What's he like?

LAINIE.   He's like you. He likes to be where he's told he shouldn't be. *(A beat.)* I gave him an interview.

MICHAEL.   You did?

LAINIE.   I talked about you. I talked about how little anyone's doing. All the standard things. I feel like such a fool when it's all over and nothing's happened. We all of us seem that way to me sometimes — all the ones who speak out. Going around the country, grabbing the whole nation by the elbow, saying, "Please? Can't you do something?" *(A beat.)* Do you ever hear gunfire where you are? Or shelling?

MICHAEL.   Yes.

LAINIE.   Close?

MICHAEL.   Close enough. I fantasize sometimes that the place gets hit. A hole opens up, and I run out of it. Like someone escaping from a crashed plane. About the same odds, I suppose. I like the room this way. Thanks.

LAINIE.   Ellen always want me to open the window.

MICHAEL.   Maybe you should.

LAINIE.   You think so?

MICHAEL.   You know what I'd give for a window?

LAINIE.   Yes. *(He rises, moves towards the window. He makes a gesture as though opening a curtain. Light pours into the room. He looks out, smiles. Lainie rises and joins him at the window. After a moment Michael exits U., leaving Lainie staring out. Lights fade to black. When they rise again, Ellen and Lainie stand across the room from each other. The light in the room window is apparently still open, since the light remains brighter.)*

ELLEN.   Well. This is certainly an improvement.

LAINIE.   Thank you.

ELLEN.   When did you start opening the window?

LAINIE.   A couple of weeks ago. Right after you were here last.

ELLEN.   Really. It's much more pleasant. Maybe I should stay away longer next time.

LAINIE.   If you do, don't come back.

ELLEN.   Don't be cross. You know I've had to be in the office every minute lately. That's the whole point of a crisis, isn't it? Keep the bureaucrats in their place.

LAINIE.   How's the crisis coming?

ELLEN.   You should know. You're doing enough to intensify it.

LAINIE.   That's not what I'm doing.

ELLEN.   It isn't? Let me remind you of your phone call to me yesterday.

LAINIE.   You don't have to —

ELLEN.   *(From memory — perfectly, of course.)* Walker says I should go on TV. I think he may be right. Maybe this is a real opportunity to put pressure on people.

LAINIE.   I didn't mean you.

ELLEN.   Of course you meant me. You meant the State Department.

LAINIE. All right, so I did mean you. So what?

ELLEN. Lainie, this crisis has been manageable so far. But there's no telling what can happen. We have a lot of Americans trapped with some exceedingly dangerous terrorists in a very cramped charter terminal in Crete. If you and other hostage relatives start jumping onto TV screens now, God knows what effect it will have.

LAINIE. Maybe a good effect.

ELLEN. I doubt it. Lainie, there are twenty-three American lives in that building. We can't break in, they have the building rigged to explode. We have to bargain. Fast. It's important that no other issue gets involved.

LAINIE. You mean Michael.

ELLEN. We're speaking of innocent lives here.

LAINIE. What's Michael? Guilty?

ELLEN. *(With a frustrated sigh.)* There's a dead serviceman lying twenty feet from the door of that terminal. At the moment they won't even let us take his body away.

LAINIE. I know.

ELLEN. He just thought he was on vacation. He wasn't even in uniform. But he was unfortunate enough to have a military I.D., and —

LAINIE. *I know. (A beat.)* Can't we just wait them out? Can't we — ?

ELLEN. This group likes to die for what they believe in. They're not like a bunch of bank robbers. As far as they're concerned, when they die, they win. *(A beat.)* Now, they *have* made demands. They want some fellow terrorists released. Those demands are being studied by various . . . governments, and just between you and me, we may be able to come to an agreement. Or somebody may. It's rather complicated, you can imagine. But believe me, when terrorists take a group as large as this, everyone understands it's a short-term project.

LAINIE. Project? Is that how you see it? What's Michael — a long-term project?

ELLEN. Sadly, in a sense, yes.

LAINIE. Because he wasn't lucky enough to be abducted in an airport? With a bunch of other people?

ELLEN. Lainie, there are physical realities.

LAINIE. What about moral realities?

ELLEN. Please — don't mix apples and oranges. If you go public, if you make demands, you'll only delay matters and increase the danger for everyone involved. And frankly, no matter what you do, we won't ask for Michael's release.

LAINIE. You won't?

ELLEN. It's not his time.

LAINIE. His *time?*

ELLEN. It's nice with the window open. You should leave it this way, I think. *(Rising to leave.)* Well. I don't have much free time. I'm afraid I'll only be able to talk on the phone, at least until this present emergency's over. It's hard for me to be away right now. Lainie? *(Lainie hasn't moved.)* Soon it will be over and everything will be back to normal. *(A beat.)* I *am* sorry it can't be now. *(Ellen exits. Lights fade to black, then quickly rise again on Walker entering with a photograph in his hand.)*

WALKER. *(Calling out loudly.)* Lainie! This is great! This is fantastic! Thank you!

LAINIE. *(Entering.)* It's just a picture.

WALKER. Are you kidding? Michael and Jim Mathison together at the University of Beirut? You never told me you had this.

LAINIE. I didn't see any reason to —

WALKER. Look at it. They've got their arms around each other, they look warm, human, vulnerable — it's perfect.

LAINIE. Walker —

WALKER. We've got to bring this along. They'll want to use it on the show, I know it.

LAINIE. You think so?

WALKER. They'd kill for it. It's got everything you'd want: simple, affecting — this'll communicate.

LAINIE. I don't want to bring it.

WALKER. You don't?

LAINIE. I look at that picture. I don't want it flashed all over the country.

WALKER. Why not? That's exactly what you want to do. It's the perfect one. It affects you. It'll affect other people. *(She takes it from him.)*

LAINIE. I'll find another one.

WALKER.   No.

LAINIE.   No?

WALKER.   Either you're going to do this or you're not. You have a chance to make a statement here. But it's only going to be heard if you make it as strong as possible. "Quietest Hostage Wife Speaks Out" is a headline. "Quietest Hostage Wife Sort Of Speaks Out" isn't.

LAINIE.   But this is a picture.

WALKER.   Doesn't matter. It's all imagery. The pictures we choose, the copy we write, the interviews you give — it's all a matter of giving the proper image. That's how people think. Images — not ideas. Images.

LAINIE.   *(Of the picture.)* If I give this up, I give it up. I won't be able to look at it. *(A beat. She gives it to him.)*

WALKER.   Good. Thanks. They'll pick this up everywhere, believe me. They'll run it all over — all the networks. This is the perfect time. Couldn't be more perfect. I was afraid this would all be over by now, I really was.

LAINIE.   Have they let anyone go? Women, children?

WALKER.   Nobody. Not a one.

LAINIE.   What if they decide to . . . to — ?

WALKER.   Kill more of them? It's possible. But it's not all that likely. They've already made their point with the soldier. We know they're serious.

LAINIE.   They could get nervous. Someone could make a mistake.

WALKER.   No one's going to make a mistake. These things are rituals. Everyone knows the role they're playing. Our role is to get Michael into the deal. We can, too. We're going to help him — starting with this . . . *(Indicates the picture.)* and one very intense interview. Come on — let's get you down to the studio. *(He moves to leave, turns, sees that she's not moving.)* Come on.

LAINIE.   What happens after the interview?

WALKER.   Another interview. Maybe a lot of them.

LAINIE.   And after that?

WALKER.   Everybody. Everybody who asks. 7 o'clock, 11 o'clock, late-night news shows. You name it.

LAINIE.   And after that?

WALKER.   I don't know. Threatening phone calls from the State

Department — or the White House, if we're lucky.

LAINIE. And from the families of the new hostages. They're going to hate me — you know that, don't you? If I try to complicate this negotiation by insisting that Michael —

WALKER. Bullshit.

LAINIE. It's not bullshit. They will.

WALKER. Do you care?

LAINIE. Of course I care. I know what they're going through —

WALKER. How long have they been going through it? *(A beat.)* You've been in line. It's your turn, too — not just theirs. *(Michael enters, handcuffed but not blindfolded. Walker is oblivious to him, but Lainie sees him. Michael smiles at her, goes and lies down on the mat, closing his eyes.)*

LAINIE. All right.

WALKER. *(Taking her by the hand, exiting.)* Come on. Believe me, you'll get used to it. *(They exit. Michael suddenly bolts straight up, screaming.)*

MICHAEL. *LAINIE!! LAINIE!!* (A beat. He looks around fearfully, as though expecting someone to enter. When no one does, he relaxes slightly.) They moved me again. That's why I dreamed. They have a box that they put me in when they move me. It's the shape of a coffin. And it's soundproof. The first time they tried it, they put the box in the back of a van with a bad exhaust system. I was unconscious when they took me out. I know this is an illusion, but sometimes — usually right in the middle of the night — it occurs to me that I don't know, I don't absolutely *know*, whether I'm alive or dead. *(A beat.)* They brought Mathison here — you know that? No, of course you don't. I never actually saw him. They moved him into a room just down the hall. I could hear him go by once a day when they took him to the bathroom. He said something in the hall the first time he passed by. They shouted at him to shut up, but I could tell his voice. I was afraid they'd take him away again if I said anything back. I'd been warned about that sort of thing before. So for a week I'd just listen to him shuffle past, once a day. Then one day, I heard them moving him — for good, I thought — so I shouted to him. "Mathison!" Once, real loud. It got very silent in the hall. Then the sound of them shoving him out, and then my door opened. Two guards came into my room and beat me. They never would admit

33

he'd been there. But I knew. I heard him. He heard me. *(Lights fade out on Michael.)*

Scene Two

Lights up on the empty room. Walker enters carries a glass of champagne. He calls out.

WALKER. Hey, Lainie! Come in here! What are you doing?

LAINIE. *(Off.)* I'm getting some coffee.

WALKER. Coffee?

LAINIE. *(Off.)* We need to sober up.

WALKER. Why!? We did it! We got the message out! We put those bastards on the spot. They're going to have to ask for everybody — I know it!

LAINIE. *(Entering with a cup of coffee.)* I can't remember the last time I had alcohol.

WALKER. *(Holding his glass towards her.)* Have some more. I'm sure it's a very good month.

LAINIE. No, thanks. This'll be fine. *(Gradually a silence surrounds them. They look at each other, can't help a smile and a slight laugh.)*

WALKER. You were fantastic. Fantastic. Everybody in America felt for you. And that picture. Was I right or what? The cameramen were tearing up.

LAINIE. They were not.

WALKER. They were. I saw tears. Sixty-year-old union guys. Men who've seen every disgusting, pitiful atrocity that ever happened. I bet they haven't cried since the doctor hit 'em. But they cried tonight. For Michael. For you.

LAINIE. No one has to cry for me.

WALKER. They *do*. That's the point. That's the power. You have whatever it takes. You have authority. People feel what you say. You can't help it. They look at you, and they trust what you say.

LAINIE. What if what I say isn't for the best?

WALKER. They'll believe it anyway. Right now — not a week ago, not a week from now — but *now*, this instant, people believe what you say. They're moved by it. They may even act on it. How do you

34

think things happen in the world? They happen because every once in awhile enormous numbers of people become ready to hear something. And if you've got what they're ready to hear, then you're a very powerful person.

LAINIE. Walker —

WALKER. Use it. You have to use it. You have to push at the ones who are pushing you.

LAINIE. No one's pushing me.

WALKER. Nothing in this world happens because it ought to. You have to push people into it. Right now, you have a quality that lets you push. You have a thing to say, and the means to say it. If you're lucky, when you look back on it, it'll have been moral. If not, too bad — you made your best guess.

LAINIE. When did you first decide I had this . . . quality?

WALKER. First time we talked.

LAINIE. And that's why you've kept at this? With me?

WALKER. Lainie —

LAINIE. I mean it. Is that all this has been? You've just been waiting for me to . . . blossom into some kind of spokesperson for you?

WALKER. Not for me, for yourself. For Michael. How do you think you're going to get him back? ESP? You going to pray he'll show up? He won't. You'll get him back when you make this government uncomfortable enough to make some other government uncomfortable enough to lean on somebody — that's it. *(She stares at her coffee.)*

LAINIE. You'll write a lot of articles now, won't you? No matter how it comes out.

WALKER. Yes, I will. That's my job. That's how I push. *(A beat.)* So look — in my business, when you make the government uncomfortable you drink champagne, not coffee. What do you say? *(He offers her his glass. She doesn't take it.)*

LAINIE. Go home.

WALKER. Go home?

LAINIE. I don't feel like celebrating.

WALKER. Why not?

LAINIE. Because for all I know, I haven't done anything more than risk the lives of innocent people tonight. That's no reason to celebrate.

WALKER.   That's not what you were saying earlier.

LAINIE.   Earlier I didn't think I was with someone who — *(She stops herself.)*

WALKER.   Someone who what? Who what, Lainie?

LAINIE.   Who makes friends just so he can . . . push.

WALKER.   I have to be able to do my job.

LAINIE.   That's what Ellen says. It's probably what the Shi'ites say.

WALKER.   What's wrong with that? It's a world of work, Lainie.

LAINIE.   It's a world of crime. We call it work so we can keep doing it. *(A beat.)*

WALKER.   I'm sorry you feel this way. I think I've been pretty damn patient, all things considered. I've waited a year for a story that —

LAINIE.   *Michael's* waiting. Not you. Not me. Michael.

WALKER.   *I know! That's why I'm writing about the stupid fuck!! (A long beat.)* Lainie? *(A beat. He takes a hesitant step towards her, pulls back.)* I'll call you in the morning. *(He exits quickly U. with the champagne, his glass and her cup. Lainie sits on the mat thoughtfully for a moment, then lies back on it, and closes her eyes. Lights change, isolating her on the mat.)*

LAINIE.   Michael? The first time I saw you, time turned a corner. I'd always thought of it as gray, impassive. But it wasn't. When I married you, I felt as though time were our child. That somehow we could . . . *(She stops, sits up.)* We could shape it to our lives. *(Lights fade. In the darkness we hear Walker's voice. When lights rise, Lainie is sitting in a corner on the floor.)*

WALKER.   *(Off.)* Lainie? It's me, Walker. Can I come in? *(Off.)* Lainie? *(Off.)* Your car's in the garage; I know you're here. *(Off.)* Lainie? *(After a moment, Walker enters. He looks at Lainie with concern but not surprise.)* It's not a defeat. It's a step closer. *(No response. He moves to her.)* They released Mathison. Plus everybody from the charter terminal. That's a step. They recognized a linkage. They bargained. We can take credit for that. You're as responsible as anyone that Jim Mathison's free now.

LAINIE.   Why him?

WALKER.   No one knows. *(A beat.)* You haven't been answering your phone.

LAINIE.   Reporters call. *(Of the mat.)* I can't see him anymore. All

36

morning I haven't been able to feel him. I can't remember what
he looks like.

WALKER.   He'll come back. I know he will. *(She moves to the mat
on all fours, places a hand at its center.)*

LAINIE.   He may as well have disappeared into the earth. Right
here. On this spot. I would feel more hope.

WALKER.   Lainie, he's ... For God's sake, we got Mathison back.

LAINIE.   Did you see the President? On the news? "We have them
back now, after eight harrowing days of captivity."

WALKER.   *Plus Mathison.*

LAINIE.   Is that what they tell mothers of dead soldiers? "Your
boy's dead, but don't worry — the one right next to him was just
fine."

WALKER.   I'm just saying that Mathison —

LAINIE.   *I didn't do this for Mathison! HE'S NOT MINE! (A beat. She
collapses on the mat, crying. Walker hesitates, moves to the door, stops,
moves to her. He strokes her shoulder and arm awkwardly, tenderly. She is
on her side, facing away from him. He stares up and away while she cries.
As her crying abates, his stroking moves to her hair. After a moment, she
moves closer to him, so that her head rests on his lap. She slowly grows silent
as he continues to stroke her hair. Lights fade to black. Lights back up on
Michael sitting alone on the mat.)*

MICHAEL.   Sometimes I wake up with the most intense desire to
know what day it is. Sunday? Thursday? I feel like I'm going to die
the next minute if I don't find out. Other times I'll wake up and
suddenly realize that months have gone by — must have gone by —
since I last had a conscious thought about time. It makes me feel
like the astronaut who travels forty years at the speed of light and
then returns, no older. "What's happened to everyone?" he must
think. "Time must be for them, not me." I never thought of time
as a coat you could take off and put on again. Too cold to live
without it — so we all keep it on. We hug it to ourselves, because
if we can't ... *(A beat.)* Time is change. That's all it is. When there's
no change. When there's no change ... Yesterday one of my guards
told me I'd been here three years. *(A beat.)* I didn't know what he
meant. *(Lights fade to black.)*

Scene Three

Lights rise on Ellen, sitting on the ottoman. The window is open.

LAINIE.   *(Off.)* Oh — Darjeeling or English Breakfast? I can't remember.

ELLEN.   English Breakfast. Always.

LAINIE.   *(Entering with the tray-table and tea.)* Good. That's what I made. Imagine me forgetting. *(She sets down the tray-table and pours tea for them both.)* How've you been?

ELLEN.   Fine. Just got back from a vacation, actually.

LAINIE.   Really? Where'd you go?

ELLEN.   St. Thomas.

LAINIE.   You went there last year, didn't you?

ELLEN.   It's where I go every year. I even go to the same hotel there every year. It's the one my husband and I used to stay in when we were married. We both still go there. Only he goes a month before I do now.

LAINIE.   That's an interesting arrangement.

ELLEN.   It's not an arrangement at all. It's a circumstance. *(A beat.)* How are you holding up?

LAINIE.   About the same. It's been a long time.

ELLEN.   We're aware of that —

LAINIE.   Since I've seen you, I mean.

ELLEN.   Yes, well —

LAINIE.   I've just gone back to work.

ELLEN.   Really?

LAINIE.   Last month. I'm teaching again. Everyone there is being very considerate. No "What's it like?" questions.

ELLEN.   Good.

LAINIE.   Strange to be around so many people all day. I'd gotten out of the habit. *(A beat.)* Have you heard anything new about Michael?

ELLEN.   Not specifically —

LAINIE.   I thought when you called —

ELLEN.   No, it wasn't that we'd heard anything new about Michael, precisely.

LAINIE. What was it then?

ELLEN. Nothing, actually. Nothing official.

LAINIE. Is there something you want to say to me?

ELLEN. Of course. I'm here, aren't I?

LAINIE. Then why don't you say it?

ELLEN. It's just a little tricky, to be frank. It's — well, I'd like to feel I'm not here in my official capacity this time. That is, if you could feel that way.

LAINIE. Why?

ELLEN. Could you feel that way? *(A beat.)*

LAINIE. All right.

ELLEN. Good. I wanted to tell you about something that happened last night. It, um — well, it certainly took me by surprise.

LAINIE. What happened?

ELLEN. We intercepted someone. A terrorist. Not a Shi'ite, not even Lebanese. But an Arab, and . . . we killed him.

LAINIE. You what?

ELLEN. He fought back. He resisted. It made no sense — he was completely surrounded, but . . . he resisted.

LAINIE. Where?

ELLEN. In a small Italian coastal town. It should be on the news within an hour or so. We've managed to hold it back a bit, but —

LAINIE. What are you saying?

ELLEN. I think you know what I'm saying.

LAINIE. Michael's in more danger now?

ELLEN. They all are. *(A beat.)* It was bad enough for Michael that we intercepted this man. But to kill him. I'm afraid it's a very dangerous situation.

LAINIE. Not for you.

ELLEN. Lainie —

LAINIE. Whose idea was this?

ELLEN. I couldn't tell you if I knew.

LAINIE. What was the point? What did you think you had to gain?

ELLEN. This man was implicated in the deaths of scores of American citizens. He was behind at least three bombings.

LAINIE. So somebody at State said, "Kill him."

ELLEN. They *did not.* They decided to capture him. If possible.

LAINIE. And it wasn't. So now Michael's going to —

ELLEN.   Nothing will happen to Michael, for all we know. The risks were carefully analyzed, and —

LAINIE.   The President's image — that's what was analyzed. Did he need to look forceful this week?

ELLEN.   We can't assume that any of the hostages will be harmed simply because one terrorist leader was intercepted.

LAINIE.   Killed! Use English! *(A beat.)*

ELLEN.   Killed. It was the judgment of the Department that Michael and the others would not be overly . . . endangered.

LAINIE.   Was that your judgment? *(A beat.)* You never answer questions like that, do you?

ELLEN.   No.

LAINIE.   Is it because you know if you started you'd never be able to stop? *(A beat.)*

ELLEN.   Early in the war between Iran and Iraq, there was an offensive. Iranian soldiers — Shi'ites, like the people holding Michael — needed a way to break through Iraqi minefields. They chose and all-out frontal assault, classic World War I stuff. But with one difference. To clear the mine fields, the Iranian army — which has some significant technical limitations — used boys. The boys didn't go out and dig up the mines. They ran over them. The mines blew up, killing the boys, and the soldiers followed after, across the newly-cleared fields. These boys were fourteen, fifteen — up to twenty. Some were as young as ten. They had . . . volunteered for the duty. They wanted to be martyrs. And their families too, many of them, freely gave their sons to this honor. The boys wore white headbands, ran into the fields shouting "Shaheed", which means martyr. Some of them wrapped themselves in blankets first, so that when they were killed the explosions wouldn't blow them apart quite so much, and their bodies could be . . . gathered more easily, and returned home to inspire other boys to take the same path. Their parents do not grieve. They are proud, and satisfied their sons are in heaven — to them a place as tangible as this, without pain. *(A beat.)* There are times when it becomes impossible to negotiate. When the very act of negotiating legitimizes a philosophy that's . . . not human anymore. Those places where such a philosophy reigns have to be isolated. Those people who try to extend such a philosophy must be stopped. At any cost.

LAINIE.   Any cost?

ELLEN.   Any cost. *(Lights fade to black. They come up quickly again on Lainie and Walker. Lainie is very agitated.)*

WALKER.   I don't think it means anything.

LAINIE.   What do you mean, it doesn't mean anything? They said they were going to kill him!

WALKER.   It's a radio report. They've been wrong dozens of times. They're almost never right.

LAINIE.   What if they're right this time?

WALKER.   It's a tactic. That's all it is. We hit them, they threaten the hostages. Nothing happens. It's just a pressure game.

LAINIE.   This isn't a threat. They said they were going to kill him.

WALKER.   That announcement didn't even come from his captors. It came from an entirely different faction. They wouldn't even know where he is, let alone how he is.

LAINIE.   Oh, God — I can't stand this. I can't. Not knowing — this is . . . oh, *GOD*!!

WALKER.   Lainie — *(She moves away from him, pacing the room with increasing agitation.)*

LAINIE.   There is a circle of hell for these people. There is a circle of hell so deep —

WALKER.   Lainie, calm down —

LAINIE.   *NO*!!

WALKER.   You know, there might even be an advantage in this.

LAINIE.   Advantage!!

WALKER.   Listen to me! A false story's been broadcast. Michael's kidnappers may have to show pictures of him alive now.   There could be a video tape, or —

LAINIE.   And if there's nothing?

WALKER.   That doesn't mean anything either. They can play this a lot of different ways.   The point is, they've kept him for three years. And now they're just going to kill him? When they've got nothing to gain? It's not rational.

LAINIE.   What's rational about killing? *(A beat.)* I want to go on TV. I want to talk to somebody. To everybody. I want to —

WALKER.   You shouldn't do that.

LAINIE.   Why not?!

WALKER.   Nothing's known yet. We have to wait and find out the status of things.

LAINIE. *Status*!?

WALKER. We killed one of their people. I don't think Michael's captors want to hear from any American right now — even you.

LAINIE. I didn't kill anyone.

WALKER. *We* did. The country did. We have to wait for some time to pass.

LAINIE. How am I supposed to sleep? Till we hear. How am I supposed to live? Not knowing.

WALKER. I don't know. But that's the situation we're in. They can say he's alive, they can say he's dead —

LAINIE. They can say *anything*! They can do *anything* . . . to him. *(A beat.)* We should obliterate the city.

WALKER. Lainie —

LAINIE. Why not!!? Don't you want to!? Lebanon, the Middle East — let's *get rid of it*! *(Walker grabs Lainie and hugs her to him tight.)* I want to kill them.

WALKER. It's all right.

LAINIE. I want to kill them.

WALKER. I know. It's all right.

LAINIE. I want to kill a million people. *(He continues to hold her. Reluctantly, her arms finally go around him. They freeze in this position. Michael enters — handcuffs, no blindfold. He circles them as he speaks, but doesn't look at them. He finishes his speech staring out the window.)*

MICHAEL. One night someone came to move me. It was no one I knew — none of my guards. I was blindfolded, but I could tell by his voice. He spoke English better than any of them. He said I had to be moved at once — that the Syrian Army might have learned where I was. He was nervous, but there was a softness in his voice, too. I think he was young. *(A beat.)* Some clothes were thrown on me and I was hustled into the back seat of a car by three men. All the voices were new — not one of them was familiar. It was actually a cool night. The feeling of being outside was incredible. I listened for anything — any sound, any voice — over the noise of the car. Not because I was planning to escape. Just for the sheer, sensual pleasure of it. A sound, at random. A voice. Anything that was completely disconnected from my being a hostage. That just . . . existed in the world. And I thought for some reason about all the things that always exist in the world simultaneously — with or without us. Innumerable parts of a system designed to not even recognize itself as a system. Dogs barking in the streets, wind in the shop awnings, people talking on corners, flowers letting go their fragrance, people riding bicycles, pigeons mourning nobody we know, people driving in cars, people buying oranges, distant explosions, people carrying guns, people dying of poison gas, oceans rocking on their stems, people making love for the first time in their lives, people designing clothes-hangers, people designing the end of the world, people in movie theaters, people singing in languages we don't understand, insects filling the world — *filling* the world — people in restaurants ordering the best meal of their lives, people using the phone, petting their cats, holding each other in each other's arms. *(A beat.)* All of it, at once. *(A beat.)* They drove me to a quiet neighborhood and shoved me into a building. I was taken down, still blindfolded, to a small, cramped room that smelled like . . . clay, and I was shot to death. *(Michael exits, but not U. He passes through the 'wall' of the room. Lights fade to black.)*

Scene Four

Lights rise. The room is empty. Walker enters carrying the chair. He sets it down. Ellen appears at the door.

ELLEN. Do we have to be in here?

WALKER. That's what she wants. *(A beat.)*

ELLEN. There are three reporters outside. They seemed to know I was coming. Did you tell them?

WALKER. Not me. I like exclusives. Maybe they're just here because it's an important story. Then again, maybe they like watching the State Department deal with the consequences. *(A beat.)* So, when's the phone call from the President?

ELLEN. He's sending a letter.

WALKER. A letter? No post-game phone call? No national hookup?

ELLEN. Not this time.

WALKER. Have you done a lot of this kind of work? Bearer of ill-tidings?

43

ELLEN. Some. When I worked in the Defense Department.

WALKER. Now there's a job.

ELLEN. It's nothing one looks forward to.

WALKER. What did you say to them?

ELLEN. What can you say? I told them their men were heroes. I said, "Your husband, son, brother, father was a hero. He died of bad luck." Not bad planning at the top, not tactical mistakes of his commanders. Bad luck.

WALKER. And they believed you?

ELLEN. Oh, yes. *(A beat. He looks out the window.)*

WALKER. Is that what you're going to tell Lainie? That Michael died of bad luck?

ELLEN. No, Lainie gets the truth.

WALKER. Which is?

ELLEN. Off the record?

WALKER. Nothing's off the record. *(Ellen shrugs, sits silently. Walker sighs and looks out the window.)* All right, all right — off the record. *(As Ellen speaks, Lainie enters silently U. Neither of them sees her.)*

ELLEN. We miscalculated. We valued Michael's life below a chance to make an international point. We increased the danger for all the hostages. We chose to.

LAINIE. Thank you. *(They turn with surprise.)*

ELLEN. Lainie, I . . . I wasn't —

LAINIE. Going to say it like that? I'm glad you did. *(A beat.)* Is that all your business?

ELLEN. The President is sending you a letter.

LAINIE. I'll burn it.

ELLEN. Your husband's remains will arrive tomorrow morning at Andrews Air Force base. If you have no objections, there will be a short ceremony —

LAINIE. I object.

ELLEN. The body will be transported at government expense to a funeral home of your choice.

LAINIE. I get a choice?

ELLEN. Simply inform us where. *(A beat.)* Allow me to take this opportunity to convey the deep sympathy of the Secretary of State.

LAINIE. Go to hell.

ELLEN. And the President.

LAINIE.   Why are you saying this?!

ELLEN.   It's my job to say this.

LAINIE.   You don't have a job. You have a license to manipulate. *(A beat.)* I want to be like you. Tell me how to be like you.

ELLEN.   What do you mean?

LAINIE.   I want to think like you. I want to be able to put people away, in my head. I want to forget them there. I want to lock them in whatever room you have for that.

WALKER.   Lainie —

LAINIE.   Teach me! *(A beat.)* You won't, will you? That's your most closely-guarded secret. That's where all the real weapons are.

WALKER.   *(To Ellen.)* You should go.

LAINIE.   No. Not till I say. Ellen, I think you and government did your best. I think everyone did his best. Michael did his best, Walker did his best, you did, the Shi'ites — even the ones that killed Michael. Probably everyone has done his best. That's what frightens me. That's why I don't know if I'll ever be able to walk out of this room anymore. Into what? A world filled with people doing their best?

ELLEN.   I wish I could take your pain away.

LAINIE.   I wish you could remember it. *(Ellen exits U. A beat.)*

WALKER.   Do you need me to be here?

LAINIE.   Not right now. Not for awhile.

WALKER.   I'd like to be.

LAINIE.   No.

WALKER.   Why not? *(A beat.)* I don't think you should be alone.

LAINIE.   I'm not. *(A beat.)*

WALKER.   What about tomorrow? I'll drive you to the Air Force base.

LAINIE.   Thank you. You should go now.

WALKER.   Are you sure? *(She nods, stares at the mat. He looks around the room.)* I'll call you later. All right? Lainie? *(A beat.)* Lainie? *(She moves to the mat, kneels down beside it, stares at it. Walker studies her for a moment, then starts out U.)*

LAINIE.   *(Pointing at the chair.)* Could you take that out? Too much furniture. *(Walker picks it up, stares at her, then leaves. She is again focussed on the mat. Her hand strokes through the air, as though caressing Michael's face. At this point Michael enters U., silently. He moves to the mat and reclines on it, so that her hand now strokes his hair.)* I think my favorite is the African hornbill.

MICHAEL. Of all birds. Why?

LAINIE. After they mate, the male walls the female up, in the hollow of a tree. He literally imprisons her. And all through the weeks of incubating the eggs, he flies off and finds food, and brings it back and feeds her — through a little hole in the wall he's built. After the eggs are hatched, he breaks down the wall again, and the whole family is united for the first time. You see? It hasn't been a prison at all. It's been . . . a fortress.

MICHAEL. Their devotion, you mean?

LAINIE. Their devotion. *(He smiles, closes his eyes. She continues to stroke his hair. Lights fade to black.)*

THE END

DOWN THE ROAD

❖

For Jeanne Blake

Down the Road was first produced at La Jolla Playhouse (Des McAnuff, Artistic Director; Alan Levey, Managing Director) in La Jolla, California, on August 8, 1989. It was directed by Des McAnuff; the scene design was by Neil Patel; the costume design was by Susan Hilferty; the lighting design was by Peter Maradudin; the sound design was by John Kilgore; and the original music was by Michael Roth. The cast was as follows:

DAN HENNIMAN . . . . Jonathan Hogan

IRIS HENNIMAN . . . . Susan Berman

WILLIAM REACH . . . . James Morrison

Down the Road was presented at the Actors Theatre of Louisville (Jon Jory, Producing Director) at the Fifteenth Annual Humana Festival of New American Plays, in Louisville, Kentucky, on March 6, 1991. It was directed by Jeanne Blake; the scene design was by Paul Owen; the costume design was by Hollis Jenkins-Evans; the lighting design was by Mary Louise Geiger; the sound design was by Darron West; and the production stage manager was Debra Acquavella. The cast was as follows:

DAN HENNIMAN . . . . Mark Shannon

IRIS HENNIMAN . . . . Bernadette Sullivan

WILLIAM REACH . . . . Markus Flanagan

CHARACTERS

IRIS HENNIMAN, early 30s, free-lance writer
DAN HENNIMAN, 30s, free-lance writer, married to Iris
WILLIAM REACH, late 20s, a serial killer

TIME

The present

PLACE

A maximum security prison. A motel.

Scene 1

The set consists of two areas: a motel room with only a double bed and two chairs, and the interview room of a maximum-security prison. In it should be only a table and three chairs. All the chairs should be simple. Other realistic set elements are discouraged. While a tv is heard in the motel at times, and its glow is visible, there should be no tv.

Lights up on Dan and Iris in the motel. Day. Iris stands looking out the window. Dan stands across the room, looking at her.

IRIS. You all unpacked?

DAN. Totally and completely. *(She continues to stare out.)* So, feel like taking a walk, or — ?

IRIS. What's sitting out there? Is that a water heater?

DAN. Where?

IRIS. Leaning against that house across the street.

DAN. Uh, yes — that is a water heater.

IRIS. It's just sitting there on the front porch.

DAN. They're probably going to throw it away — it's all rusty.

IRIS. It's rusty because they're *not* throwing it away. I bet it's been sitting there for years.

DAN. *(Putting his arms around her from behind.)* Do you consider this a big issue?

IRIS. *(Moving away from him easily.)* It just caught my eye, that's all. So — you think you're ready?

DAN. As I'll ever be.

IRIS. You can't let him get to you. That's the main thing.

DAN. I know.

IRIS. We don't want him to clam up. We'd lose the book.

DAN. I *know*. You're not the only one who's interviewed criminals.

IRIS. What criminals have you ever interviewed?

DAN. Those Wall Street guys.

IRIS. Working with you on a crime book. I must be crazy.

DAN. Hey, I'll be great.

IRIS. You will be great, as long as you let me guide you.

DAN. I wish he'd let us interview him together.

IRIS. Maybe he thinks he can shock us more one at a time. But it's better this way. We can set up two psychologies with him — see more sides.

DAN. How come I have to go first?

IRIS. So he'll respect you. If I go first, he'll treat you like the second string.

DAN. Ah.

IRIS. Don't know why I'm trying to sound like such an expert. I've interviewed lots of murderers, but never a serial killer. *(A beat.)* Are you worried about what he'll tell you?

DAN. Of course.

IRIS. Whatever he says, you can't react. If you do —

DAN. I know. He might clam up.

IRIS. Or start playing games. *(Dan turns, looks at her, smiles.)*

DAN. Tell you the only games *I'm* interested in.

IRIS. Dan —

DAN. *(Reaching for her.)* It's the motel. I can never control myself in a motel.

IRIS. Well, learn. We'll be here for months.

DAN. *(All the more inflamed.)* Months!

IRIS. We haven't even walked outside yet. *(He kisses her, moves her to the bed.)* Dan, this isn't professional. *(Lights fade to black.)*

Scene 2

Between scenes we hear the voices of Dan and Reach over speakers. Lights rise on Iris in the motel. Evening. She sits on the bed with a small tape recorder, listening. At the same time, the conversation we've been hearing shifts and now emanates from the tape recorder.

DAN. April second. 11:30 am. First interview with William Reach.

REACH. You're organized.

DAN. You understand that you can in no way profit by the publication of the book we're writing about you?

REACH. I understand.

DAN. You have no objection?

REACH. No objection. *(Lights crossfade, shifting from the motel room to the prison interview room. We see Reach and Dan sitting across the table from each other. Reach — who's in handcuffs — wears drab, institutional clothing. On the table is a briefcase and tape recorder. It's the same conversation we've been listening to on the tape, and now their voices take over from the tape.)*

DAN. Bill, we're here to facilitate your book. This is your account, your ... actions. Other books have been written about you, but this is the first to come directly from you. We want to help make this an important and useful document. *(A beat.)* So. Is there anything you want to know about me?

REACH. What's your name again?

DAN. Dan. Dan Henniman.

REACH. Ever write about someone like me, Dan?

DAN. No. But my wife —

REACH. The publisher — Mr. Scanlon — said you write for *Business Week*?

DAN. I used to. Now Iris and I —

REACH. I don't mean to criticize. It's just that I want to get the story told. The best way.

DAN. Certainly.

REACH. That's why I'm finally talking.

DAN. It's not the appeal?

REACH. Sorry?

DAN. You just appealed your sentence of life without parole, right? And your appeal was denied?

REACH. Yes, I'm afraid it was.

DAN. So, isn't that the reason you're speaking out now? Since in a sense you have nothing to lose. *(Reach stares at him.)* Sorry, I'm putting words in your mouth.

REACH. That's all right.

DAN. You tell me your reasons if you want to — fair enough? *(Reach nods.)* So. How many people have you killed?

REACH. At least nineteen.

DAN. You don't know the exact number?

REACH. I know it was at least nineteen.

DAN. Are you saying there are others you haven't admitted to? *(Reach is silent.)* Are there others? *(Reach is silent.)* We'll say nineteen then.

REACH. I hope you're not nervous talking to me.

DAN. Not really.

REACH. You're completely safe. Your wife will be, too. Guard's right outside, looking through that little window. He could be in here in a second.

DAN. Have you ever been violent? In prison, I mean.

REACH. No.

DAN. Why not?

REACH. It's not so bad here. *(Lights shift to the motel.)*

Scene 3

Iris stands looking out the window. Evening. She holds a tape recorder and speaks into it.

IRIS. Took my first walk yesterday. Gas station, gas station, mini-mart, KFC, quick-stop, gas station, Taco Bell, a worse motel than this one and the Interstate. Dan's out walking right now. The prison's ten miles from here. Twenty miles from anywhere else. *(A beat.)* Dan, you sound fine on these tapes. I think he feels very positive about you. *(A beat.)* I'm feeling pretty positive about you myself tonight. Yesterday was nice. *(Something outside catches her eye again.)* I can*not* stop looking at that water heater. At night there's a yellowish light from the gas station that makes the water heater look almost extraterrestrial. Why do they keep it? Whoever lives there must think of it as — what? Adornment? Why am I looking at it? I'm *not*. *(She looks away. Slowly she looks back out the window. Lights shift to the interview room.)*

Scene 4

Dan and Reach are as before.

DAN. Let's start with Cindy Lauterber. She was the first person you ever ... she was the first, right?

REACH. Of the nineteen? Yes. *(A beat.)*

DAN. She was a stranger.

REACH. Yes.

DAN. How did you ... um, how did you — ?

REACH. Meet her? In a mall. Middle of the day. I called in sick to work.

DAN. *(Consulting his notes.)* To the ... the vending machine company?

REACH. Yeah, I called in sick and —

DAN. You had a route and filled machines, right?

REACH. You know that.

DAN. Yes, sorry. You called in sick?

REACH. I couldn't face it that day, so I went to the mall. Saw this woman — God, how old? She was —

DAN. Eighteen.

REACH. Picked her up.

DAN. How?

REACH. She was pretty. I told her I was a magazine photographer. Asked her to come out to my car so I could take a

55

couple pictures — show my editor.

DAN. And she went?

REACH. They always went.

DAN. She wasn't suspicious?

REACH. Not really.

DAN. Why not?

REACH. I was charming.

DAN. Had you ever done this before?

REACH. Picked up girls with that line? Sure.

DAN. Had you killed them? Or had you stopped at raping them?

REACH. Dan, I'm really uncomfortable talking about any more victims than nineteen. I hope that's not a problem.

DAN. Cindy and you got to your car. Your camera was in the car? You unlocked the car?

REACH. Right.

DAN. You took your camera out?

REACH. No. It was in the back, on the floor. I pretended it was caught under the seat. You know, the strap. I asked her to slide the seat up. She had to sit in the seat to do that.

DAN. And when she sat in the seat, what did you do?

REACH. Pulled a knife. Grabbed her. Pulled her door shut. Took about two seconds.

DAN. She was yours, then? What did you feel when you took control of somebody like that?

REACH. What did I feel? Relief.

DAN. You had succeeded.

REACH. It was by far the best part of it. Always.

DAN. It wasn't killing them?

REACH. Killing was necessary, but it wasn't ... *(Reach trails off.)*

DAN. Same for the sex? Necessary, but not ... the best?

REACH. You think you know a lot about this.

DAN. No, I only —

REACH. Maybe I should interview you.

DAN. I don't mean —

REACH. Since you're such an expert.

DAN. I'm sorry, all right? *(A beat.)* I really do apologize. What about the mutilation? Was that secondary too? To the control

56

of another human being?

REACH. You mean was control the engine that pulled the train? Yes, it was.

DAN. How would you characterize it? The control. Was it control over women? Society? Life and death? Your mother?

REACH. Does it matter?

DAN. That's not much of an answer.

REACH. It's not much of a question.

DAN. You don't think it's important? Why you did this? *(A beat. Dan sighs.)* All right, we'll write down control over everything. Fair enough?

REACH. I can go with that. *(Lights shift to the motel.)*

Scene 5

Iris is as before, speaking into the tape.

IRIS. I spent the afternoon talking to a prison guard's wife. She says if you're in a prison, you must deserve to be there. Innocent or guilty she says, if you're there, the Good Lord meant you to be. I asked her if she thought that was true for the guards as well. "Especially the guards," she said. "Including your husband?" I asked. "Especially my husband." *(She turns it off as Dan enters from the bathroom.)*

DAN. So, you listened to the tape?

IRIS. Most of it. He sounds like a lot of fun.

DAN. He is. Straining at the seams to convince me he's human. What's scary is, he almost can. The whole time I was trying to make him comfortable — apologizing to a serial killer.

IRIS. He's a source, like anyone else. You're putting him at ease.

DAN. Who's going to put me at ease?

IRIS. I'm actually looking forward to going in tomorrow.

DAN. Yeah, now that I've gone first. Made all the mistakes, cleared the way for the pro.

IRIS. *(Smiling.)* Yeah, thanks. You didn't make any mistakes, though. Not any big ones. He likes you.

DAN. *(Sitting.)* Not sure how to take that.

IRIS. Why are you sitting down? I thought you wanted to go to a movie.

DAN. Oh — right. Forgot.

IRIS. We'll need all the escapism we can get.

DAN. *(Starting to rise tiredly.)* True.

IRIS. You're really not up for this, are you? I know what you need. Lie down on the bed.

DAN. What about the movie?

IRIS. I'll make one. Get on the bed and close your eyes. *(He lies on the bed, face up.)* Roll over. *(He does so. She kneels on the bed, rubs his back.)*

DAN. Ohh, yes ...

IRIS. You feel like you've been beaten with a rope. Are your eyes closed?

DAN. Yes. *(They aren't.)*

IRIS. Good. Tonight's movie is a travelogue.

DAN. A what?

IRIS. Quiet, these used to be quite popular. The title is, *A Map Of What She'll Look Like.*

DAN. That's a travelogue?

IRIS. *(Rubbing him hard.)* Shhh! *(Dan groans deeply.) A Map Of What She'll Look Like,* directed by Iris Henniman. With help from Dan Henniman. We start with her hands. They're tremendously strong. They hold us with the first need. Almost as if it's the earth itself that holds us, not her. We lift her up, and her body works in the air as though she's walking to heaven. Her eyes ... are heaven — the only time we'll see it in our lives.

DAN. That's good.

IRIS. Don't interrupt. She bears us, just as we've borne her. She gives us the world she's come from, and all we can give in return is this one. We owe her everything. We'll never be able to pay. Staring into her face, we realize she looks exactly the way we always dreamed our souls looked. More than innocent. More than pure. Completely untouched. *(As her hands range up to the back of his neck and then through his hair.)* Her hair will be exactly like ... mine, I think. But her skin will be yours. The same feel, the same life rising through it — like nothing I've ever felt before. Something I'd never known I'd lost until the moment I found it. *(She starts to kiss the back of his neck. He rolls over, stares up at her.)* We still can, you know. Tonight.

DAN. We can?

IRIS. You still want to go for a girl, don't you? *(He smiles, nods.)* Then let's get started. *(They kiss again, with an easy passion.)*

DAN. Should we be thinking of names while we — ?

IRIS. Shut up. *(They kiss. Lights fade to black.)*

Scene 6

Lights fade up again on the motel. Morning. We hear Dan's and Iris's voices from the bathroom.

DAN. Madeleine.

IRIS. No.

DAN. Hillary.

IRIS. I'm sick of Hillary. Everyone has a Hillary. Hordes of little Hillarys running around.

DAN. Mike.

IRIS. Mike's a boy's name.

DAN. I knew a woman named Mike.

IRIS. *(Entering.)* And a very lucky woman she was, too.

DAN. *(Entering.)* Iris.

IRIS. One's plenty. I had a great time last night.

DAN. Me, too. What if it didn't take?

IRIS. You're right. We'd better do it again immediately.

DAN. Time out! If last night didn't get you pregnant, nothing's going to.

IRIS. We have to do it a lot at certain times —

DAN. I understand; we'll get a girl. *(Handing her the briefcase.)*

You going to be all right with him?

IRIS. You're still in one piece. *(She kisses him, moves to go.)*

DAN. Don't let him get to you.

IRIS. I think I'm pregnant. 'Bye. *(Dan smiles. She exits. Lights shift to interview room.)*

Scene 7

Reach sits with Iris, reading her something he's written.

REACH. "Hi, lover. Bet you wondered why I've been so late writing back. Must be 'cause I'm writing all my other girls. Ha. Just kidding. How are things in Mobile? I think of you all the time, the way you are in that picture you sent. You know the one I mean. It's my connection with you. Connections are so important. You like the one I sent of me? I was in college then, but I still look the same. Same great looks. Ha. I think we were meant to meet and hold hands together, no matter how far away we might be. Holding hands in a world of uncertain destinies. All my love ..." What do you think?

IRIS. Who is she?

REACH. Just a fan. You like my style?

IRIS. It's ... conversational. Can we have a copy?

REACH. *(Handing letter and photo to her.)* Go ahead; use it. *(Iris puts them into her briefcase.)* You know, I've read all your books. Scanlon sent them to me. You're very good.

IRIS. Thanks.

REACH. You never have a picture on the jacket. *(A beat.)* You're younger than I thought. Prettier.

IRIS. *(Turning on the tape recorder.)* So are you. Tell me, Bill — when you had sex with Cindy Lauterber, was she alive or dead? *(A beat.)* We're not quite sure from yesterday's tape, that's all. *(A beat.)* We really do depend on you for accuracy. *(A beat.)* Do you have trouble talking about the sexual part of it? *(A beat.)* Why do you think you have trouble talking about that?

REACH. I don't like why questions.

IRIS. Why not?

REACH. Ask me a how question.

IRIS. How come you don't like why questions? (*He looks off disgustedly.*) How did you kill Cindy?

REACH. With a knife.

IRIS. And you did this right away, or — ?

REACH. I drove her to the lake first.

IRIS. Sugar Lake?

REACH. That's right.

IRIS. How many bodies did you leave in the hills near Sugar Lake?

REACH. Nine. No — ten.

IRIS. Once you and Cindy got there, did you kill her in the car, or — ?

REACH. I made her get out. She yelled. No one was around.

IRIS. Did she try to run?

REACH. I had hold of her. Are you afraid of me?

IRIS. Desperately. What happened next?

REACH. She tried talking. I told her to shut up.

IRIS. Were you afraid you'd get to know her? (*A beat.*) When did you stab her?

REACH. Right then.

IRIS. How many times?

REACH. Seven, eight — I don't know. She fought. I was nervous. I cut myself. Finally she went unconscious. She made a sound, and ... my arm was bleeding.

IRIS. Is that when you raped her?

REACH. Is it rape if they're dead?

IRIS. So she was dead?

REACH. When I finished, I threw her down the hill.

IRIS. Didn't bury her?

REACH. No, the ... animals. You know. Then I bandaged myself, drove home.

IRIS. How did you feel? As you drove.

REACH. Scared. Perfect.

IRIS. Perfect?

REACH. Like God. (*Lights shift to the motel.*)

Scene 8

Day. Dan sits in a chair talking into a tape recorder.

DAN.   Walked to McDonald's this morning. Car dealer, gas station, Dairy Queen, gas station, tire store, muffler shop, gas station, McDonald's. Incredible landscape. They should get honest and call these strips theme parks: "Oblivion World." Step right up and disappear. *(He turns off the tape, turns it on again.)* Actually, I've walked to McDonald's almost every day for the last two weeks. Pretty easy to get into a rut here. *(A beat.)* Um, Iris? Speaking of ruts, I notice you've been including lots of notes about water heaters. I know it's one of those well-observed details we're always looking for, but you have ... golly, six or seven entries here, and maybe that's enough? *(He turns off the tape, turns it on again.)* I finished rereading the background material on Reach. Every book, newspaper article, magazine spread, talk-show tape, etc., etc. Even reread the t-shirt. Never felt so paranoid in my life. I'm sure this feeling will fade, at some point. *(Staring out the window.)* That water heater's just red with rust. *(Lights fade quickly to black.)*

Scene 9

Lights rise on interview room. Reach and Iris are as before.

IRIS.   Cindy's body —
REACH.   Who?
IRIS.   Cindy. *(Suddenly catching herself.)* Oh — I'm sorry. I got them confused. Paula. Paula's body.
REACH.   Cindy was a couple weeks ago. We're on number five. You need a break?
IRIS.   No, no. Just sometimes they ... run together. *Paula's* body — in fact, all ten of the bodies you left at Sugar Lake — weren't found for years. The remains were fragmentary.

REACH. So?

IRIS. I'm just trying to examine your patterns. Through the first several.... We know you used a knife on some of them. But not always?

REACH. I hit some of them with a rock. Strangled — you know. Sometimes it was kind of messy. I got angry with myself.

IRIS. For killing them ... so badly?

REACH. I got smoother as I went on.

IRIS. Did you ever torture a victim?

REACH. No, I liked being quick.

IRIS. Why?

REACH. I don't know why. That's your job.

IRIS. This is your book, Bill. I can't speculate about your motives. So. Why did you like to be quick?

REACH. Most people don't torture what they hunt. *(A beat.)*

IRIS. Fair enough. What was it like choosing someone?

REACH. Moving targets. I'd stand around — mall, carnival, bar. I don't know what I was looking for. The way someone looked. Or if she acted tentative. If I smiled and she smiled back. Even just her clothes.

IRIS. Skimpy clothes? Expensive?

REACH. Just nice. Nice, clean look. Done up, not careless. I'd see a girl like that and want her.

IRIS. Why didn't you just have her?

REACH. What?

IRIS. You were single, good-looking. You probably could've gone to bed with a lot of these women.

REACH. Sure, but what's the point? That wouldn't've been different from what anybody else does. *(A beat.)*

IRIS. Let's take a different angle. Paula Milstrom —

REACH. Number five.

IRIS. Right, I'm with it now. You met Paula in a bar and took her home. You were living alone at that time. You had sex with her? *(He nods.)* In a more or less normal — ?

REACH. Yeah.

IRIS. And afterwards, when she was asleep — ?

REACH. I stabbed her.

IRIS. Why? *(He's silent.)* You kept her in the apartment, right? After you'd killed her. For how long? Six days, is that right? Before you brought her body to Sugar Lake?
REACH. Yeah.
IRIS. You just kept her there. Why?
REACH. I liked her. *(Lights fade quickly to black.)*

Scene 10

Instantly we hear a woman's scream: long, terrified — very disturbing. A beat. The woman screams again. Another very short beat, then a hesitant smattering of applause that quickly builds to a crescendo and then dies down. During the applause lights fade up in the motel room to reveal Dan watching tv. It's night. We hear the voice of a Talk-Show Host.

HOST. Well, well, *well*. So what's this picture called again? *Bambi Meets Godzilla?*
MALE GUEST. *(With a laugh.)* You could call it that.
HOST. No, you play a killer.
MALE GUEST. A serial killer.
HOST. Right. There's more of that these days, isn't there?
MALE GUEST. Lots more.
HOST. Gruesome thought. Who does your guy kill?
MALE GUEST. Very beautiful women. Cover girls only: *Vogue, Elle, Cosmopolitan —*
HOST. *Sports Illustrated. (Mild audience laughter.)* That's what we think of with *Sports Illustrated* nowadays, isn't it?
MALE GUEST. Depends on what you call sports.
HOST. I know what *I* call sports. *(Big audience laugh. Dan rises and moves toward the glow. He gestures and the tv turns off.)*
DAN. We got a call from Scanlon. Iris?
IRIS. *(Calling from the bathroom.)* What?
DAN. Scanlon called.
IRIS. *(Entering from the bathroom.)* What did he want?

DAN. Wanted to know how it was going. Told him it was going fine, we're marching through the first several of the famous nineteen murders —

IRIS. If there were only nineteen.

DAN. And that Reach was cooperative, informative and graphic when pressed.

IRIS. What did Scanlon say?

DAN. He wanted to know how graphic.

IRIS. Publishers.

DAN. What's he want us to do? Hype the gore?

IRIS. It hypes itself. *(Moving to the bed, sitting.)* I've interviewed men who murdered their friends, their wives, eight people in a City Hall. No one like him.

DAN. Scanlon also wanted to know how the other side of it was going. The note file. Our impressions.

IRIS. What did you say?

DAN. Said it was going great. Hopeless town, empty lives, wilderness that's practically Biblical.

IRIS. Good. *(She starts for the bathroom again.)*

DAN. Didn't say a word about this. *(Dan turns on the tape recorder. We hear Iris's voice.)*

IRIS. *(On tape.)* There's a woman sitting next to the water heater. Middle-aged, shapeless house-dress. She's wearing sunglasses, staring east. I believe she serves the water heater in some way. Perhaps she's the high priestess, I'm not sure.

DAN. *(Turning it off.)* What am I listening to?

IRIS. Nothing. I was just kidding around. *(Dan fast-forwards the tape, turns it on again. Iris on tape.)* Able-bodied men walk in and out of the house. These are obviously her slaves. She or the water heater itself exerts a highly-sophisticated form of mind-control —

DAN. *(Turning it off.)* Whole paragraphs of "kidding around"?

IRIS. It's an impression. We agreed to record our impressions.

DAN. Our impressions, not our fixations.

IRIS. If you have a problem with this, say so. Don't pull a grand inquisitor routine with the tape.

DAN. I thought things were going fine.

IRIS. They are.

DAN. Is this something you always do when you're interviewing? Does it break the tension, or —

IRIS. I happened to see a water heater, get fascinated, record a lot of silliness — ok?! It was a lapse.

DAN. What kind of lapse?

IRIS. *Dan —*

DAN. I'm trying to learn, that's all. Why a water heater?

IRIS. What else is there!? There's an Interstate and a water heater — that's it! Oh, and at the prison we get to spend half our time with the sickest man on the planet. What do you want me to fixate on?

DAN. I still don't see why you have to make a novella out of a water heater.

IRIS. *Is this just a style-point, or what!? (A beat. She sits in a chair. As she does so, lights come up faintly on the interview room. Reach is sitting there.)* With most murderers it's, "I hated this, I hated that, I hated everything." With Reach, it's just ... a wall. "Why did you kill her?".

REACH. I don't know.

IRIS. "How did you kill her?".

REACH. Stabbed her ten times. Strangled her with a nylon rope, nearly severed her head from her body.

IRIS. "What did you do then?".

REACH. Raped her.

IRIS. "Then what?".

REACH. Cut her head off, took it home, set it on a table, stared at it.

IRIS. "Then what?".

REACH. Had sex with it.

IRIS. "And how did you feel?".

REACH. What?

IRIS. "When you did that, how did you feel?". *(Reach hesitates, shrugs.)* He could have been stripping a chair. *(Lights fade out on the interview room.)* I thought nothing could bother me — that I could listen to the most horrible things. *(Lights crossfade to the interview room. As they do so, Dan simply crosses from the motel room to the interview room with his briefcase. Reach is still sitting there.)*

Scene 11

Reach is reading Dan a letter Reach has received.

REACH. "... no one who looks like you, and talks like you, could do what they say you have done. It's not possible, and even if it was, God would forgive it. You are obviously a man of worth and not trash like some. You have a rare quality of charm not even the man on *Sixty Minutes* can refuse. I hope you don't think I'm forward to send my picture ..." *(Reach pulls a snapshot out of his pocket and hands it to Dan.)* "... but since I know what you look like, I thought it could make us equal in a small way. All my prayers and love ..." And then she signs her name.

DAN. Can I see that?

REACH. *(Giving Dan the letter.)* Enjoy yourself. I've got plenty of 'em. *(Dan stares from letter to picture.)* She's cute.

DAN. What? Oh.... Let's get to work. *(Dan puts the letter and photo in the briefcase.)*

REACH. What about the title?

DAN. What?

REACH. Of the book. Scanlon keeps giving me the runaround. Won't give a firm yes to any of the titles I've suggested.

DAN. You're talking titles with him?

REACH. I like *First Blood,* but he said it was a movie.

DAN. It was.

REACH. He didn't like *Blood Trail,* either. Sounded like a Western.

DAN. Well —

REACH. He thought *Blood Fury,* but I don't know.

DAN. Maybe Iris and I should give Scanlon a call and suggest some of our own.

REACH. If you think it'll help.

DAN. *(Turning on the tape.)* April 30th. 11:30 am. Bill, today I'd like you to talk about the death of Melanie Bryce.

REACH. Great.

DAN. She was your, um ... *(Looking at his notes.)* Your ninth victim, right?

REACH. About that, yeah.

DAN. This one involved a trip of some days, isn't that right?

REACH. Six days.

DAN. You were in another state.

REACH. I took a few days off.

DAN. Did the vending company know where you were?

REACH. No.

DAN. You didn't tell them you were leaving.

REACH. The machines would be there when I got back.

DAN. You didn't tell your fiancee, either?

REACH. She was never my fiancee. We never set a date.

DAN. I thought she was.

REACH. I gave her a ring, that's all. I'd practically left her by then anyway.

DAN. I thought she left you.

REACH. I thought we were talking about Melanie Bryce.

DAN. Did you often leave for days at a time?

REACH. Yeah.

DAN. And your ... um, Donna never got worried or suspicious?

REACH. She got puzzled. I told her not to be. Told her I needed time to be alone. Men need that, don't they?

DAN. You met Melanie Bryce — she was sixteen? — in, um —

REACH. Edwardsville.

DAN. Three hundred miles from your home. You picked her and a friend up near their high school.

REACH. It was raining. Real downpour. They stuck their thumbs out.

DAN. Her friend was Gina Miller.

REACH. Guess so. I dropped her off at her house.

DAN. Why?

REACH. Why what?

DAN. Why didn't you kill them both? Later you killed two at a time. Weren't you sure you could handle it, or — ?

REACH. I could handle it.

68

DAN. But you dropped Gina off. *(A beat.)*
REACH. She wasn't right. She looked — I don't know — she looked unimportant. Messy.
DAN. Ugly?
REACH. No. She was pretty enough.
DAN. Just badly dressed.
REACH. She wasn't right.
DAN. So. You were alone with Melanie. What happened?
REACH. I pulled a gun right away. Made her bend down out of sight. Had her put her hands behind her back. Taped her hands, taped her mouth.
DAN. As you drove?
REACH. While we were stopped at a light. Then I took her down the road.
DAN. Where?
REACH. Sugar Lake.
DAN. But before that?
REACH. An empty farmhouse I knew about.
DAN. *(Looking at notes.)* This was the farm owned by —
REACH. Don't know.
DAN. John Berthelsen, about thirty miles from your home.
REACH. Right.
DAN. So you drove Melanie two hundred seventy miles while she was alive and conscious? What did you talk about?
REACH. Her mouth was taped.
DAN. Sorry.
REACH. Don't you listen?
DAN. Did you talk to her?
REACH. Asked if she was comfortable.
DAN. You got her in the farmhouse, you ... broke in? You ... did she struggle?
REACH. No. She was pretty tired, cramped from how she was sitting.
DAN. You entered the farmhouse. You took her where? The bedroom?
REACH. The kitchen.
DAN. Why?
REACH. There was a sink. *(A beat.)*

69

DAN. Did you kill her right away?

REACH. No, I tied her in a chair.

DAN. Did you have sex? At that point?

REACH. At that point. At that point. That's all you guys want to hear about, isn't it? Yeah, orally.

DAN. You mean you — ?

REACH. She blew me. I made her do that.

DAN. Did you have an orgasm?

REACH. What's wrong with you?

DAN. Nothing —

REACH. Are you getting excited?

DAN. No, Bill, I'm not getting excited. I'm asking you questions for the book.

REACH. Well, if you're not getting excited, who is?

DAN. Hopefully, no one.

REACH. Uh-huh. And this is a scholarly publication we're working on, isn't it?

DAN. Are you ashamed you had an orgasm, or ashamed you didn't?

REACH. I came in her mouth and killed her. Bim-bam. Next question.

DAN. How did you — ?

REACH. Slit her throat with my fishing knife.

DAN. That's a lot of blood. Weren't you afraid — ?

REACH. I know how not to leave clues.

DAN. You cut her head off. Did you do that then?

REACH. Yes. Put it in a plastic bag, threw it in the trunk of my car.

DAN. The body?

REACH. Garbage bag. Threw it in the trunk. Washed up the kitchen, got in my car and — zip.

DAN. To Sugar Lake. The dumping ground. You tossed the body, and ... took the head home?

REACH. Not directly. I had to stop and see my therapist. The guy the court assigned me.

DAN. After your rape conviction?

REACH. It wasn't rape. I bargained that down to third-degree. Never served any time for that. So I had my last session with

70

the therapist that day.

DAN. And you drove there, with Melanie Bryce's head in your car's trunk, and had your last session with him?

REACH. That's right.

DAN. What did he say to you, that last day?

REACH. He said he thought I'd made real progress. *(Lights fade to black.)*

Scene 12

Lights rise on the motel. Day. Iris sits with some papers in her lap. We hear the sound of a radio news report.

ANNOUNCER. The bodies of the two girls were found at the bottom of an abandoned well, in a wooded area. Their uncle led authorities to the site as part of an agreement which will allow him to be charged with two counts of second-degree murder only —

IRIS. Christ.

ANNOUNCER. A spokesman for the county attorney's office expressed regret that this was the only way to discover the victims' remains. The children's parents —

IRIS. *(Rising, moving towards the tv.)* Christ.

ANNOUNCER. ... when asked how they felt, said this: *(Iris makes a gesture. Radio falls silent.)*

IRIS. Must be why they put the radio in the tv — you can't throw it out the window. *(We hear Dan's voice from the street.)*

DAN. *(Off.)* Iris? Iris? *(He enters.)* Good — you're here.

IRIS. How was your day?

DAN. Fabulous. I vomited in the parking lot.

IRIS. Oh.

DAN. You would not believe what that man's done.

IRIS. I know what he's done. *(Dan exits directly into the bathroom.)*

DAN. *(Off. Over the sound of running water.)* To know is not to hear him say it.

IRIS. I've heard him say a lot of things.

DAN. *(Off.)* You did not hear Melanie Bryce. *(At this point Reach — not Dan — enters from the bathroom. Reach does not seem visible to Iris, though he smiles shyly at her. He's still in handcuffs. Reach moves to the window and looks out. Iris continues talking to Dan.)*

IRIS. Must've been pretty bad.

DAN. *(Off.)* Pretty bad. *(Reentering from the bathroom.)* Come on, we're going out to eat.

IRIS. You're hungry?

DAN. I have an empty stomach, remember? Besides, we'll be driving a long time.

IRIS. How come?

DAN. Because we're not stopping till we get to a four-star restaurant.

IRIS. There isn't one in the state.

DAN. So what?

IRIS. So how far do you intend to go? All the way back to New York?

DAN. Why not?

IRIS. Are you serious?

DAN. I could give it up, if you could. Honest, today I could.

IRIS. I know how you feel. Come here, give me a hug.

DAN. A hug doesn't speak to the —

IRIS. Give me a hug. I'm pregnant.

DAN. You're what?

IRIS. Congratulations. You've just uttered the most inevitable line in the history of conversation. "You're what?". I'm pregnant. Now you say:

DAN. That's wonderful.

IRIS. And I say, "Isn't it?!". And we hug. Hug me. *(Dan does so.)* And then I say, "Aside from the fact that we'd never work for Scanlon again, and lose all our credibility in the business, *and* run away from something we've started — there is now this. We can't quit our day job. Not now. *(Dan sighs, releases her. He sits in a chair. Reach — still apparently not visible to either Dan or Iris, turns and watches them.)*

DAN. What are we doing here?

72

IRIS. What do you mean?

DAN. With Reach. Maybe there are some kinds of murderers.... Well, you've said it yourself — sometimes you're embarrassed to walk by the "True Crime" shelf in a bookstore. You wonder, "Who *is* that reading my book? Why are they interested?"

IRIS. Dan —

DAN. Why *are* they interested?

IRIS. If we leave this project, Scanlon will go out and get someone who can listen to Bill Reach. He won't have to look very far. The book will get written and published. Inevitably.

DAN. As inevitably as those girls got murdered?

IRIS. We can make sure the job is accurate, and as objective as possible. If we leave — *(Dan sighs resignedly.)* How about if we just try to get through the next group? After Melanie Bryce they won't seem so bad. When that's done, we can change subjects with him for awhile. Do background stuff: school, childhood. I've been getting more interested in that angle anyway.

DAN. I don't know what it is. I feel ... abandoned out here. I feel like we're out in the open.

IRIS. We're not abandoned, we're together. Ok? *(She kisses his cheek, rises, moves toward the bathroom.)*

DAN. Is it a girl?

IRIS. If there's any hope in science. *(She exits into the bathroom. After a moment, Reach rises and surveys the room. Dan hasn't moved and doesn't seem to see Reach.)*

REACH. Must be hard to sleep in a room like this. Right off the highway. Must be loud. You have a good marriage? Motel life'll kill any relationship, that's my experience. I've stayed in this chain. Rooms are terrible. Closets never have enough hangers, bathmats feel like they're alive. And that view of yours. I worried when I heard this was where you were staying. It's not good enough. Not if you're working with me. *(Reach kneels down a few feet in front of Dan.)* Does your wife still excite you? *(Dan shifts his gaze to Reach. Lights crossfade to interview room as Reach turns and moves directly there.)*

Scene 13

Reach sits. Iris turns on the tape.

IRIS. Bill, I know we planned to talk about victims today, but instead I'd like to go into some of your background.
REACH. How come?
IRIS. Change of pace. I want to ask you about college today. Dan will cover your childhood later.
REACH. I had a bad childhood. My mother was married three times.
IRIS. Dan'll ask about that. Let's see — you went into college straight from high school, right? Then took your BA in four years?
REACH. Yeah.
IRIS. You changed majors a few times. Any reason?
REACH. I liked it all. I was a good student.
IRIS. You settled on English — not the most practical, I can tell you. Then you got into a master's program in business management, right?
REACH. That's right.
IRIS. You were in this program a little more than a year and a half. Then suddenly you quit. With — what? — one quarter to go? Why?
REACH. I don't know why. I was already ... *(Trails off.)*
IRIS. You were already raping women.
REACH. Yeah.
IRIS. Still, nobody knew that. Not at the time. Why didn't you finish? Were you out of money, or — ?
REACH. I was a criminal.
IRIS. You weren't picked up till the following fall. Did you actually say, "I'm raping women now, I'll have to stop school"? *(He stares at her.)* Sorry, is this making you uncomfortable? I'm just trying to give you the chance to say in your own words why you did certain things. *(He stares at her.)* Let's go on to something during the killings.

REACH. Fine.

IRIS. You had a lot of jobs, right? The vending machine job, then you quit that and picked up a job in telephone sales — why?

REACH. I could make my own hours.

IRIS. But just a few months later you left to clerk in a sporting goods store.

REACH. What's wrong with that?

IRIS. All these jobs just seem so unambitious. You nearly had a Master's degree. *(A beat.)* A year after that you went to work for an advertising firm, but you were really little more than a gofer.

REACH. They said I'd move up.

IRIS. But you didn't.

REACH. *(With sudden force.)* I'm not here to talk about jobs! *(A sharp rapping — sound of a nightstick on the metal door. They both look towards the door. Iris waves, calls out.)*

IRIS. Everything's fine. *(Reach relaxes somewhat, smiles and waves at the door. His smile disappears when he looks at her.)*

REACH. I kill women, you know.

IRIS. Not anymore. *(A beat.)*

REACH. I changed jobs because of the killings. I didn't want people I worked with getting suspicious.

IRIS. You never changed where you lived. What about your neighbors?

REACH. What's going on here? Why are you harping on this?

IRIS. I'm just puzzled —

REACH. There's nothing puzzling. *Nothing puzzling.* Understand? *(A beat.)* Does Scanlon know you're asking me a bunch of irrelevant questions? Do you want me to call him?

IRIS. No, I don't want you to call him, Bill. I'm sorry if I've offended you.

REACH. We're through talking about jobs.

IRIS. All right. I honestly do apologize if I hit a nerve.

REACH. You didn't hit a nerve. Move on to something else.

IRIS. Sure, um ... I really do want to cover things in this period. Ok, let's talk about your fiancee.

REACH. She was not my fiancee.

IRIS. I thought she was.

REACH. *I only gave her a ring! (Lights shift to the motel.)*

Scene 14

Day. Dan stares out the window, talks into the tape recorder.

DAN. I talk to Bill about his childhood tomorrow — taking a vacation from his ... road trips. The scariest thing is that his upbringing wasn't scary. Couple stepfathers, but no abuse, beatings, molestation. Only child — so are millions. In a juvenile center for awhile — so are thousands. Didn't like his mother much, but she was no monster. His home life was marked by what you'd have to call — in this country at least — the usual emptiness. *(Dan rises, goes closer to the window.)* I've started dreaming about the Interstate. Mile after mile, every night. Utterly familiar by now, but ... featureless. Where's it come from? Everywhere. Where's it go? Everywhere. The other day, driving to work, I caught myself fantasizing about just going on: ignoring the exit, following the next bend in the highway, the next. Getting lost on the largest engineering project in the history of the world. Floating there. No set destination, no limit to where you go. Parallel universe. If someone wants a ride ... give 'em a ride. Nothing matters. Newspaper, tv, radio — it's their state, not yours; their problem, not yours; their daughter, not — *(Dan shuts off the tape, rewinds it briefly, plays it back to "... their problem, not yours ..." and stops it there. He starts recording again.)* In the decade of the 1950's, before completion of the Interstate, there was only one case of serial murder reported in the United States. In the whole decade, just one. Now — one a month. *(Lights shift back to the interview room.)*

Scene 15

Iris and Reach are as before.

IRIS. So. Donna was your girlfriend, not your fiancee. Her father owned a successful trucking firm. Ever think of going into that?

REACH. They wanted me to.

IRIS. Were you interested?

REACH. It could've been a lot of money, but —

IRIS. But what?

REACH. We're talking about jobs again.

IRIS. Oh, I'm sorry. Let's —

REACH. I'm definitely calling Scanlon.

IRIS. That's your right. I hope you don't. Donna and you broke up — for the first time, anyway — not long before you killed your first victim, Cindy Lauterber. Is that right?

REACH. So?

IRIS. Some people theorize that the trigger for the first time you went beyond rape and killed was Donna's rejection of you.

REACH. Who thinks that?

IRIS. A number of people. Is it wrong?

REACH. A.) She did not reject me; I rejected her. B.) Only after I rejected her did she reject me. C.) After we rejected each other, she crawled back to me and not vice-versa. And this happened several times.

IRIS. So it has no relationship to any of these crimes?

REACH. Why should it? She was just my girlfriend.

IRIS. You had a college degree — could've had a Master's. Career opportunities if you wanted them, a relationship with a woman — whom you loved?

REACH. I loved her.

IRIS. Yet essentially you rejected every chance to succeed. Why? *(A beat.)* What do you think of the theory that your killings were the acts of a man who hadn't formed a complete identity? A man who needed to kill people in order to be anyone at all. *(Reach is silent.)* Do you agree with that?

REACH. Who are you?

IRIS. Iris Henniman.

REACH. And in a hundred years, who are you going to be?

IRIS. Dead — that's who I'm going to be.

REACH. That's right. But I'll still be William Reach. Why do you think you're not writing about the guy who killed his family anymore? Or the guy who went berserk with his M-16? Don't talk to me about identities. You've got a chance — just a chance — to be somebody here. Stick to what Scanlon pays you for.

IRIS. What Scanlon pays me for —

REACH. What Scanlon pays you for is to write my book! Mine! Why doesn't matter. I did it — other men didn't. Besides, your theory is shit. I killed someone before Cindy Lauterber. She wasn't the first.

IRIS. Who else did you kill? *(Reach is silent.)* How do I know you're not just trying to undermine these theories? *(Reach is silent.)* The victim's family would like to know. *(Reach is silent.)* It should be in the book. If we're collaborators —

REACH. *It's for the sequel, bitch! (Sharp rapping on the door, which continues as lights fade to black.)*

Scene 16

In the darkness, we hear the sound of a Donohuesque Talk-Show Host on the motel tv. The tv's glow rises, followed by lights on the motel. Watching tv are Dan and Reach. Dan's on the edge of the bed, Reach sits on the floor.

HOST. ... but how do we recognize them? What do we know about them? What do they want? Is it only to kill? Is it sex? Is it sex *and* killing? Doctor? *(We hear the monotone of an expert guest.)*

GUEST. It's hard to say. Mass slayers often want sex, but the killing is what gives them the real sense of satisfaction.

HOST. A very distorted sense.

GUEST. But maybe the only real satisfaction they can achieve.
(Iris enters from the street. She carries the briefcase.)
IRIS. Hi.
HOST. How do we identify them? That's what's really important here, isn't it?
IRIS. What's this?
DAN. They're doing serial killers.
HOST. We can theorize all we want, but how can I tell, walking down the street, who's going to kill me and who's not?
IRIS. Oh, great.
GUEST. I don't think you can —
HOST. I've got to! It's life or death! One clue — anyone. *(Iris moves to the tv.)* Any of our guests. Some of you have been attacked. What did you notice? What do these men have in common? *(She turns the sound off. The glow remains.)*
REACH. Hey. *(Iris ignores Reach, who keeps watching the tv.)*
IRIS. *(To Dan.)* Hope you don't mind.
DAN. Are you kidding? That guy asks three hundred questions in twenty-two minutes, doesn't get an answer to one. "People being slaughtered like cattle? Who cares? Am I still on?" Keeps asking what men like Bill Reach want.
IRIS. To be him; that's what they want.
DAN. *(His arm going around her waist.)* It is, eh? It's not what I want.
IRIS. What do you want?
DAN. *(Suddenly pulling her down on the bed with him.)* I want to talk baby names!
IRIS. Dan — !
DAN. *(Kissing her.)* I thought of many valuable new baby names today. Can't wait to try them out on you.
IRIS. Such as?
DAN. Bitzy.
IRIS. Bitzy?
DAN. It'll be cute. She'll be little —
IRIS. Dan.
DAN. Ok, ok — how about Chloe?
IRIS. *Dan —*
DAN. Give it a chance, it grows on you.

IRIS. Chloe will never grow on me.

DAN. Scarlet? Hildegarde? Fawn?

IRIS. Are these old girlfriends?

DAN. How about Rachel?

IRIS. Rachel. That's a possibility. What's it mean?

DAN. Um ... patient in suffering.

IRIS. *(Rising, crossing to the window.)* Maybe not.

DAN. So. How was your day?

IRIS. Actually, I think I found something out.

DAN. What?

IRIS. Something about Reach. His jobs, school record — even Donna. It all really haunted him. He didn't want to talk about any of it. He seemed afraid of what he might say. I think it could be the pivotal issue in his life.

DAN. School?

IRIS. Failure.

DAN. He wasn't a failure. He was an educated, middle-class person.

IRIS. Not in his eyes. He thought he was nobody.

DAN. Why would he think that?

IRIS. Because he was nobody special. Look at the jobs he had: all beneath him. That's no accident.

DAN. I don't know.

IRIS. What about this? He hasn't shown the slightest regret over killing and mutilating people, right? But he's utterly ashamed his girlfriend dropped him, he never had a real career, he quit school —

DAN. He quit grad school.

IRIS. He quit. At all. At any point. Somewhere along the line Reach got the idea that unless you succeed — *really* succeed, become famous — you don't exist. Don't you see? It explains his choice of victim. Young, middle-class women. For him they weren't even real — just society's prizes. He grabs the prize, kills her, and has his revenge. On society, not on her.

REACH. *(Quietly, to himself.)* Bullshit.

DAN. And that's why he rejected killing Gina Miller? She was too poor? Didn't represent the right social group?

IRIS. Exactly.

REACH. *(Suddenly standing.) Bullshit! (Reach strides into the interview room. They pay no attention to him. Lights don't shift with him.)*
IRIS. Before he started killing women, there was no Bill Reach. There was, "Hey, you." There was, "Hurry up on your route today." "You don't understand me," from his lover and, "You'll get a business degree like fifty thousand other people." Each day he felt a little more of himself step into an emptiness that someone else might not even notice, but that to him was so complete, so inescapable, that the only way out — the only way not to be dead himself — was to become a monster.
DAN. Does this really make sense, though? He kills women 'cause he doesn't think he's a success? By that criterion, almost anyone could become Bill Reach.
IRIS. Maybe anyone could.
DAN. He kills women out of sexual anger.
IRIS. Men rape out of sexual anger. They abuse. They don't do what Reach does.
DAN. How do you know? How does anyone know how deep that goes?
IRIS. How do you?
DAN. One thing I do know: if this bothers Reach as much as you say, there's no way we'll get it in the book.
IRIS. Why not? We can phrase things, shade them —
DAN. How? Between Reach and Scanlon? We can't even get our own title. We can't prove this theory. So where's that leave us? We're here to write down what Reach did. In his own words. That's it, that's our brief: report it. Make it vivid, compelling —
IRIS. Stupid —
DAN. Whatever. It's not for us to decide. Our job's to be a good pair of journalists. Write the book, get the money, get another book —
IRIS. And another book, and another —
DAN. And support ourselves. There's nothing wrong with that.
IRIS. Iris and Dan Henniman — crime-writing couple.
DAN. Exactly.
IRIS. Watching our names grow on the covers: first half the size of the title, then the same size, twice the —

DAN. It's a business. It's marketing.

IRIS. Henniman crimes! Henniman criminals — better than other criminals, grislier —

DAN. *Iris* —

IRIS. Somewhere, somehow Bill Reach — a man with no identity, but a real gift for the twentieth century — found a goal: to become unforgettable, at any price. Because *something* taught him that nothing else matters. Don't you want to know what that something is?

DAN. It's not our job. *(A silence.)* What kind of shape did all this leave Reach in?

IRIS. A little ruffled.

DAN. How ruffled?

IRIS. It got to him — I said. Even made him a little desperate to disprove it. He claimed he'd killed someone before Cindy Lauterber.

DAN. Who?

IRIS. He wouldn't say. I don't even think it's true.

DAN. Was it one? Two?

IRIS. It?

DAN. The victim. How many?

IRIS. I think it's just a lie.

DAN. But if it isn't?

IRIS. If it isn't, he's saving it for a sequel.

DAN. He said that?

IRIS. He said that. *(Dan moves into the interview room. Lights shift with him.)*

Scene 17

Dan sets up the tape in the interview room as Reach watches.

DAN. How are you doing today?

REACH. Fine.

DAN. Nothing bothering you?

REACH. Nope.

82

DAN. Good. That's good. *(Dan turns on the tape.)* May seventh, 11:30 am. Bill, I was going to start with some childhood recollections today, but — *(Reach suddenly turns off the tape. He stares at Dan, then turns the tape back on.)*

REACH. May seventh. Today we're going to listen to Bill Reach for once, instead of all this crap!

DAN. Bill —

REACH. We're going to *listen.* *(Dan is silent.)* No more questions about college or childhood or jobs or — *No more.* What I did can't be explained. People don't want explanations anyway — they just want to know how it felt.

DAN. How did it feel before Cindy Lauterber?

REACH. What?

DAN. With your first victim. Your real first one.

REACH. You think you're being funny?

DAN. I'm only —

REACH. *We talk about what I want to talk about — understand!?* *(Sharp rapping on the door. Dan waves calmly. Reach rubs his temples.)* You want to know how it feels? I'll tell you. It feels like ... the middle of space. Floating. Alone. Driving late at night on a deserted road. Headed directly into a perfect dark that somehow gets darker. And the road and woods and sky all roll up together into a huge gateway that's always opening — just opening as you get there. The feeling of the steering wheel and the dashboard is so familiar, so ... owned by you. The girl — the victim — is in the seat beside you. And you're more alone than if she wasn't there. You understand? *(A beat.)* A lot of guys would try to deny this. But I feel we can be honest here, don't you? *(A beat.)* That victim owes you her breath. It's not hers anymore — from the time she trusted you. From the time she failed to protect herself. If you don't want her to breathe, if it gets to you, at any point — what do you do? Dan?

DAN. You kill her.

REACH. That's logic. Then you get out of the car, and stand there on the road, in the absolute dark. And you feel a silence, a stillness, that sounds better to you than any human voice you've ever heard. You can't even remember your own

83

voice — or that you ever had one. Then you think about that body, and the clothes still on it, and her bag on the floor of the car, and the things in that bag — and you decide what you want to keep, and what you want to throw away. *(A beat.)* You open the car door — the only light's the little courtesy light in the door — and you go through that bag, and through those clothes and through that body. And anything you want is yours. *(A beat.)* You print that. That's what they want to read. *(Reach turns off the tape. Dan rises, puts the tape into the briefcase and moves into the motel. Lights shift with him.)*

Scene 18

Iris sits looking out the window as Dan enters.

IRIS. Why are you back so early?

DAN. I'm all done for today. Bill said so.

IRIS. He what?

DAN. He generously provided me with a glimpse into yet a lower circle of hell, then informed me we were through. Till tomorrow, anyway. You he doesn't want to see ever again.

IRIS. That's impossible.

DAN. You were right when you said you ruffled him. Today he was very ruffled. What the hell did you say to him?

IRIS. I told you, just a few direct questions.

DAN. I guess that's what it takes. Did Scanlon call here to-day? Reach said he talked to him last night.

IRIS. Yes, he called. He was ... reasonably supportive. He said we should work the way we needed to.

DAN. Right up until he fires us. He didn't suggest how we might keep Reach talking?

IRIS. That won't be a problem.

DAN. You're already banned. I could go any time.

IRIS. Reach'll get over this. He needs us.

DAN. He needs writers, not necessarily us. Scanlon can't do anything if Reach won't talk to us — we'll have to be replaced.

IRIS. I just wanted the book to have some truth.

DAN. It's *got* the truth. It's fucking inundated with truth. I heard so much truth today I don't think I'll ever forgive myself. *(A beat.)* Tomorrow you need to go in there and apologize to Bill. That's if he'll even see you.

IRIS. I can't do that.

DAN. Then you'll wind up sitting here all day, writing down questions for me to go ask him. Is that what you want? *(A beat.)*

IRIS. What did Reach tell you, anyway?

DAN. What do you mean?

IRIS. What was the lower circle of hell?

DAN. Oh. It's on the tape. *(Lights shift to the interview room as she takes the briefcase and moves there.)*

Scene 19

Iris sits and turns on the tape. Reach is already sitting there.

IRIS. Today I'd like to talk about your fourteenth, fifteenth and sixteenth victims. You killed them all the same night — is that right?

REACH. *(Sing-song.)* Say I'm sorry.

IRIS. In a period of about six hours. You drove all night that night?

REACH. Put on a lot of miles. Say I'm sorry.

IRIS. You know how I feel.

REACH. But you don't say it. Say it. *(A beat.)*

IRIS. I'm sorry.

REACH. Apology accepted.

IRIS. I'm sorry you don't want to talk about some very interesting material. Because God knows other people have, and will. Your point of view on this will never be heard.

REACH. That's right.

IRIS. Your fourteenth murder —

REACH. Killing.

IRIS. Killing?

REACH. Murders have motives.

IRIS. Took place early in the evening. You were on the road.

REACH. Stopped at a carnival. Saw a girl there —

IRIS. Diane McCusick.

REACH. I suppose. She was there with friends, but she'd lost track of 'em. Offered to walk around with her, look for 'em.

IRIS. She was twenty. College student? *(Reach stares at her.)*

REACH. We got out near the parking lot. I told her I had something that could alter her mood in my car, and ...

IRIS. How did you kill her?

REACH. Hit her, as soon as we were in the car.

IRIS. With what?

REACH. Hammer. Did them all with a hammer that night. It was an efficient evening.

IRIS. You didn't leave the bodies at Sugar Lake, even though it was close by. Why not?

REACH. It's kind of personal. Awhile before that, after I dumped the tenth one ... um, shit, um —

IRIS. Roberta Anson.

REACH. I realized I forgot something. A bracelet — ankle bracelet. I always took things like that, threw them somewhere else. Why make it easy? So one day I went back.

IRIS. In daylight?

REACH. It was raining. Figured it'd be safe. I got to the hillside and looked down. She was lying there, but a lot further down. Animals had, you know, dragged her. I started down. It was slippery, and there was this smell. The rain kept it under control, but it was still ... I went down this slope —

IRIS. Past bodies?

REACH. Not there. Anyhow, I slipped. Slid all the way down, maybe thirty feet — covered in mud. Ended up right next to her body. Um, Roberta. And right there by my hand was her leg with the ankle bracelet. I tore it off and stood up, looked around — and all around me, everywhere, were these bodies. These parts of ... you know. And suddenly I saw this place for the first time. A place that I'd made. Sculpted. And I had this urge. I didn't do it, but ... No. No, I did do it. I did do it. This would be good in a movie, too. I had this incredible urge to howl. To just ... *(He trails off. We almost expect him to howl.)*

IRIS. You howled?

REACH. Yes. It was like a howl.

IRIS. Did you howl or didn't you? *(He stares at her.)*

REACH. I howled. *(A beat.)* I switched sites after that — got worried about losing control. *(Iris takes the tape and briefcase and moves into the motel. Lights shift with her.)*

Scene 20

Dan sits looking out the motel window. Iris throws the brief-case on the bed. Afternoon.

DAN. How was he?

IRIS. The usual unspeakable. We talked about Diane McCusick, Beverly Flemming, Mary Lander.

DAN. Fourteen, fifteen, sixteen. Sounds like he accepted your apology. *(She stares at him.)* Did he say anything about his mystery victim?

IRIS. I really don't want to talk about it right now. *(Picking up Dan's tape recorder.)* What did you do all day?

DAN. Oh — don't touch that. It's at a special place.

IRIS. Good. I'm dying to be at a special place. *(She turns it on. He reaches for it.)*

DAN. No —

IRIS. *(Pulling it away.)* Share your day. *(On the tape we hear the sound of vehicles roaring by on the Interstate.)* What is this?

DAN. Turn it off.

IRIS. *(Still listening to it.)* Did you record this?

DAN. It doesn't matter —

IRIS. What's it supposed to mean?

DAN. Nothing. I was bored.

IRIS. How much did you do?

DAN. Give it to me. *(He reaches for the tape, she avoids him, fast-*

forwards the tape.) Iris. (She turns it on again. Same sounds of vehicles rushing along.)

IRIS. I don't believe this.

DAN. There's nothing to believe —

IRIS. *(Fast-forwarding again, turning it on to hear the same sounds.)* Did you just go out by the highway and — ?

DAN. *(Finally taking the tape recorder away.) It doesn't matter!!? All right!? (He turns it off.)*

IRIS. How long did you do this?

DAN. Just today.

IRIS. You spent a whole day on this?

DAN. I wasted time. Yes, I wasted time. Take me out and shoot me!

IRIS. I only mean —

DAN. *It is not easy to look out this window!* I have a right to think about what I choose to think about! And I do not choose to think about four million cubic yards of concrete overpass. I do not choose to think about a shitpile of a house, and most of all — most of all, Iris — I do not choose to think about a fucking water heater!

IRIS. Don't look at it, then! Don't look out this window, and you won't see a — *(She stops short, looking out the window.)* It's not there.

DAN. Very good!

IRIS. What did you do?

DAN. I got rid of it.

IRIS. How?

DAN. I bought it. I went over there, said hi to Mrs. Pearson — that's her name, by the way — and asked how much she wanted for such an incomparable water heater. To which she replied — and I could kiss her for this — "That piece of junk? You can have it for the the price of hauling it away." Then I used my investigative skills to find a junk-dealer in the phone book, and lo and behold in twenty-three minutes he was there with two fine, strapping assistants. And for less than the cost of a day's parking in Manhattan, that water heater was in the back of a truck, traveling deep into the dark folds of history.

IRIS. You got rid of it.

DAN. *I got rid of it!* And then I missed it. And I spent all day sitting here trying not to feel more oppressed by its absence than by its presence. And I started thinking about you, and feeling regret — recalling that not really since the night you did the travelogue have we — *(He stops himself.)* Which oddly enough made me decide not to think about anything today, so instead I taped some nearby authentic ambient sounds. And I got carried away and ... spent all afternoon.

IRIS. Well. I'm glad you've had such a full, emotional day.

DAN. I'm being honest here.

IRIS. Fuck you.

DAN. Iris —

IRIS. I *liked* that water heater.

DAN. You were obsessed with it —

IRIS. *So what!?* At least I was obsessed with something harmless! Not like you, with all your lame notes about the highway and coming to understand how a man can get sick enough to kill nineteen perfect strangers —

DAN. Iris —

IRIS. *You sympathize with him!! It's in your notes!!* *(A beat.)* Is this who I'm married to? Is this who I'm going to have a child with?

DAN. *Maybe not!* *(A beat.)* This is getting to us. We wouldn't be normal if this didn't get to us.

IRIS. We'll never be normal again. *(A beat.)* He's starting to lie.

DAN. What?

IRIS. Reach. I caught him embellishing today. Making a detail a little bit more terrible than it really was. I think he's starting to figure something out.

DAN. What?

IRIS. That people want more. It makes him afraid.

DAN. Afraid?

IRIS. That he wasn't horrible enough.

DAN. I don't know what you're talking about.

IRIS. He's in prison. He reads the paper, sees movies-of-the-week about men who kill thirty, forty — God knows how many people. Who torture, mutilate with style. I think he's lying just

to keep up. *(A beat.)*
DAN. It doesn't matter.
IRIS. Doesn't matter?
DAN. It's his book. If he lies, and someday people uncover those lies, that's just another fact to know about him. Whatever comes out of his mouth, he's the primary source.
IRIS. And what are we? *(Lights fade to black.)*

Scene 21

Lights rise slowly on Iris and Reach, asleep on the bed. They're clothed, nuzzled together on top of the covers. They embrace and slowly kiss each other awake. The instant Iris realizes it's Reach, she jumps up.

IRIS. *(Hesitating, staring at Reach.)* I wanted to prove ... I wanted to prove that I could listen to the worst crimes. That I could hear what killers did from the killers themselves. That I could face ... *(Moving away from Reach, looking out the window.)* That I could work with you, write the story without becoming.... *(A beat.)* I thought I could look at you for what you are: both a cause and a result, both human and ... something else. A final judgment, and a warning of something even more final. *(She looks at Reach.)* Part of me — as you were once, part of a woman — and part of nothing. That's all I wanted: to record each detail, one after another, no matter how ... foreign — without getting lost. And I could, once.
REACH. Before me.
IRIS. Before you. *(Lights fade to black.)*

Scene 22

Lights up to very bright on the interview room. Reach sits across the table from both Iris and Dan. The tape is running. Reach can't conceal a grin.

IRIS. Jeannette Perry was ten.
REACH. That's right.
DAN. Wasn't that unusual for you?
REACH. Her age? Yeah.
IRIS. Where did you find her? *(Reach laughs.)*
DAN. Bill, what's wrong?
REACH. What do you mean?
DAN. Why are you laughing?
REACH. Feels strange having you both here. Don't get me wrong, you look cute. But why the switch? Safety in numbers?
IRIS. Bill, where did you find Jeannette Perry?
REACH. At her school. There was a convenience store about a block away. Kids went back and forth.
DAN. She was alone?
REACH. Yeah.
DAN. And you —
REACH. Grabbed her.
IRIS. Didn't she yell?
REACH. Sure. Couple kids heard, but they were pretty far off. Everyone else was in the store. I pulled her around the corner, threw her in my car, drove off. The way I went, no one could see the car. You guys look exactly like a couple I knew in high school.
IRIS. Grabbing her like that seems reckless.
REACH. I broke every rule in the book. Should've been caught. That couple — what the hell were they voted? Most likely to have a baby or something, I can't remember. *(Iris looks at Dan, who hurries to the next question.)*
DAN. Why a little girl?
REACH. What? Oh — I couldn't go any longer.
DAN. You mean the compulsion — ?

91

REACH. That's right.

IRIS. So, anybody — any woman, girl — ?

REACH. Hey, what are you going to call it?

DAN. Bill —

IRIS. Call what?

DAN. We're not here to talk about —

REACH. You guys'll make great parents.

IRIS. *(To Dan.)* You told him?

DAN. It slipped out one day. I'm sorry.

IRIS. It slipped out?

REACH. I hope it's a girl. Women like girls.

IRIS. Shut up.

DAN. Iris — !

IRIS. How could you — ?!

DAN. I said I'm sorry!

IRIS. That's not good enough!

REACH. It's just a baby —

IRIS. *Why did you kill a ten-year-old!?*

REACH. *I felt like it! (Sharp rapping at the door. All three wave it away simultaneously.)* I didn't like killing her that way. Don't like being that out of control. It's nothing I'm proud of.

IRIS. It's nothing you're proud of? *(A beat.)* So, you weren't functioning as a human being then, right?

REACH. What?

IRIS. I mean, there wouldn't've been any higher brain function connected with this sort of activity, would there?

DAN. Iris —

IRIS. Any animal, any species that preys on the untended young of its own kind would be capable of doing what you did. *(Reach suddenly turns off the tape.)*

REACH. What kind of comment is that?

DAN. She doesn't mean it.

REACH. Are you calling me subhuman? Is that how you're going to explain things? That I'm subhuman?

DAN. We're not going to explain things at all. That's not our job.

REACH. Damn right it's not. *(To Iris.)* Right? *(A beat. Dan turns on the tape.)*

IRIS. Why are you subhuman?

REACH. *GODDAMMIT — !!* (*Reach rises threateningly. Sharp rapping at the door. Reach shouts furiously.*) *EVERYTHING'S FUCK-ING GREAT!!* (*The rapping suddenly stops. Reach speaks in a normal tone.*) It's because it's a kid, isn't it? Take six or seven years off a victim and you can't hear about it. I'll tell you something — it's the same life. Ten, twenty, boy, girl — same life. We've all got one, and right now people want to hear about mine. Jeannette Perry's part of my life. It didn't have to be her, but it had to be someone. Finally, there had to be a girl. And I had to kill her.

IRIS. So you could tell your story?

REACH. You know how many kids are born in this country every minute? Let's say one was born right ... (*Pointing at Dan's watch.*) ... now — ok? Then the next one would be born right about — (*Pointing at the watch each time he says "now."*) ... now. And the next one — would come along right ... now. And it goes on like this — here comes the next one right ...

DAN. Jeannette Perry.

REACH. ... Now — twenty-four hours a day, seven days a week, twelve months a year —

DAN. You killed her.

REACH. Now.

DAN. Right away?

REACH. No.

DAN. No? But the court record said —

REACH. I lied. Made the case simpler. Easier on everybody. (*Reach moves into the motel. Lights are up on both rooms.*)

DAN. You buried Jeannette's body and covered it with quick-lime. It was quite ... decomposed when it was found. Are you saying that you — ?

REACH. I put a loop around her neck.

DAN. To choke her?

REACH. Her breath was coming real fast. I didn't look at her face. Just listened to her breath. It was like the air was forcing itself into her, whether she wanted it to or not.

IRIS. (*Quietly.*) He's lying.

DAN. Then what did you do?

REACH. I confessed. I told her what I'd done. Victim by victim.

DAN. How many were there?

IRIS. He's *lying*.

REACH. I was looking past her, out the car window. There was a little brown bird sitting real close, on a stump. The kind of bird you'd never notice in a whole lifetime. And I held on to that loop, and told my story, and the air was roaring in and out of her by now, so loud that.... And then it touched me. On my neck — I felt her breath, it.... And I looked up, and I pulled on the loop hard — like I was trying to pull someone up over a cliff, and ... her eyes were all I could see. They looked grateful. They got bluer and bluer, until finally they went the deep blue the sky turns just before it's night. *(Iris takes a small piece of paper from the briefcase and puts it in her pocket. She moves into the motel room.)*

IRIS. Eventually you gave yourself up. You walked into a county sheriff's office and confessed. Why?

REACH. It was time.

IRIS. Time to quit? Or announce what you'd done?

REACH. Both. *(Iris pulls the piece of paper from her pocket.)*

IRIS. This is a picture of Jeannette Perry. Her fifth-grade school photo. Scanlon wants to use it in the book. Any problems with it?

REACH. *(Looking at it.)* No.

IRIS. Her eyes are brown. *(She tears the picture in two, throws the pieces at Reach. Dan rushes into the motel room.)*

DAN. *Iris* — !

REACH. So I forgot. It doesn't prove anything. *(Smiling, Reach moves away from them.)*

DAN. We agreed. We agreed to try this.

IRIS. Why? To give him a voice? *Him?*

DAN. He has a right to tell his story.

IRIS. The right to tell any story — that's what we're giving him. You know what else we're giving him? The right to cover-art. On a million paperbacks, all over the country. It'll be just his eyes — staring out from over the title: *Blood Sport* or *Blood For Me*, or —

REACH. *Blood Hunger.* I've decided. *(Reach is by now lying on his back on the bed. He has removed his handcuffs — simply taken them off — and idly plays with them as Dan and Iris argue.)*

IRIS. Staring out from the shelves of every drugstore and supermarket. Saying, "Look at me — Bill Reach. I'm more important than you."

DAN. He is. What he did is. It's more socially significant — it deserves to be studied.

IRIS. It isn't studied, it's consumed.

DAN. So what?! That's how we do it here. He kills people — we put him on the news. He's fascinating — we write about him.

REACH. That's true.

DAN. When someone like him is discovered —

IRIS. *Chooses* to be discovered.

DAN. We discuss him in as broad a forum as possible. Learnedly, scientifically, foolishly, crassly, pervertedly — every way. Every way. That's what this culture does.

IRIS. Nineteen slaughtered girls: that's what this culture does. And it does one more thing. It charges admission.

DAN. Iris —

IRIS. We promote it! We do. We make it more likely — not less — that this'll happen to someone else's daughter. To *our* daughter —

DAN. For Christ's sake, you're not even discussing this anymore.

IRIS. What are you doing? Apologizing for — apologizing *to* — Bill Reach, trying to understand Bill Reach, for all I know trying to become Bill Reach —

REACH. There's only one Bill Reach.

DAN. I'm *trying* to finish what I start. I'm trying not to walk away from the book of my career. *Our* career. I'm trying to stay with this long enough to find out who Reach's other victim is!

IRIS. I know who it is.

DAN. You do?! Who?

IRIS. It's you. *(A beat.)*

DAN. There's a dead woman out there. Somewhere. Only he

95

knows. Her parents, whoever they are, don't know what happened. They'll never know unless someone talks to Bill Reach — unless someone gives him a reason to talk. He may tell lies about her. He may feed our nightmares. He may like it. But only he can walk out into a field — *somewhere* — and give us back what's left of her.

IRIS. *(A beat.)* I'm going. *(She moves to leave.)*

DAN. Iris, don't.

IRIS. Come with me.

DAN. I can't do that.

IRIS. I can't stay. *(She starts out again.)*

DAN. Iris — !

REACH. She'll stay. All I've got to say is Renee Michaels. *(Reach locks the handcuffs back onto his wrists and sits up on the edge of the bed. Iris stops. They stare at Reach.)*

DAN. Who's that?

REACH. Someone I killed.

DAN. She's not one of the nineteen.

REACH. She's from before. She's extra. *(Dan hesitates, then moves to set up a tape recorder on the bed.)* You didn't think I'd leave you high and dry? I'll add a new killing. Got to sell this thing. There's plenty of competition out there.

DAN. Iris?

REACH. It's an exclusive.

DAN. *(Turning on the tape.)* This person's name was Renee Michaels?

REACH. Yes. No one's found her yet. I buried her.

DAN. Do you remember where?

REACH. Absolutely.

DAN. Iris? Iris? *(To Reach.)* So her family, for example, still doesn't know — for sure — even that she's dead?

REACH. Not until right now.

DAN. Iris? *(Slowly Iris moves to the interview room and sits. She stares at them in the motel room.)* How old was Renee Michaels?

REACH. Eighteen.

DAN. Where did you meet her?

REACH. In a bar.

DAN. Near your home? *(Lights on the motel room begin a slow fade.)*

REACH. Yeah, pretty close.

DAN. Was she someone you knew?

REACH. I'd never seen her before in my life. *(Lights fade out on Dan and Reach in the motel, but stay up on Iris. Her stare hasn't changed. After a moment a rapping is heard — steady, not sharp. She doesn't move. The rapping comes again. She doesn't move. Lights fade to black.)*

THE END

FORTINBRAS

For Jeanne

Fortinbras received its world premiere at the La Jolla Playhouse (Des McAnuff, Artistic Director; Alan Levey, Managing Director) in La Jolla, California, on June 18, 1991. It was directed by Des McAnuff; the scene design was by Robert Brill; the costume design was by Susan Hilferty; the lighting design was by Chris Parry; the music was composed and performed by Michael Roth; the sound design was by Kenneth Ted Bible and Michael Roth; and the stage manager was Andy Tighe. The cast was as follows:

HAMLET . . . . Don Reilly

OSRIC . . . . Jefferson Mays

HORATIO . . . . Ralph Bruneau

ENGLISH AMBASSADOR . . . . William Cain

FORTINBRAS . . . . Daniel Jenkins

CAPTAIN OF THE
NORWEGIAN ARMY . . . . Paul Gutrecht

MARCELLUS . . . . James Crawford

BARNARDO . . . . James Kiernan

POLISH MAIDENS . . . . Archer Martin, Kim C. Walsh

POLONIUS . . . . William Cain

OPHELIA . . . . Laura Linney

CLAUDIUS . . . . Jonathan Freeman

GERTRUDE . . . . Devon Allen

LAERTES . . . . Josh Sebers

CHARACTERS

LIVING

HAMLET, Prince of Denmark

OSRIC, member of the Danish court

HORATIO, friend of Hamlet

ENGLISH AMBASSADOR

FORTINBRAS, Prince of Norway

CAPTAIN of the Norwegian Army

MARCELLUS, a sentinel

BARNARDO, a sentinel

FIRST MAIDEN

SECOND MAIDEN

OTHER

POLONIUS, the Court Councillor

OPHELIA, his daughter

CLAUDIUS, King of Denmark

GERTRUDE, Queen of Denmark

LAERTES, Polonius' son

TIME

Immediately following the events of *Hamlet*

PLACE

The Castle at Elsinore, Denmark

ACT ONE

Scene 1

The final tableau from Hamlet. *Horatio kneels holding Hamlet, who's mortally wounded. Laertes, Gertrude and Claudius all lie dead. Osric is also present.*

HAMLET.
Oh God, Horatio, what a wounded name,
Things standing thus unknown, shall live
      behind me!
If thou didst ever hold me in thy heart,
Absent thee from felicity awhile,
And in this harsh world draw thy breath in
      pain,
To tell my story.
(A march afar off. Exit Osric.)
              What warlike noise is this?
OSRIC.   *(Reentering.)*
Young Fortinbras, with conquest come from
      Poland,
To th' ambassadors of England gives
This warlike volley.
HAMLET.
              Oh, I die, Horatio!
The potent poison quite o'ercrows my
      spirit.
I cannot live to hear the news from England,
But I do prophesy th' election lights

On Fortinbras. He has my dying voice.
So tell him, with th' occurrents, more and
      less,
Which have solicited — the rest is silence.
(Hamlet dies.)
HORATIO.
Now cracks a noble heart. Good night, sweet
      Prince,
And flights of angels sing thee to thy rest.
(Sound of a military drum. Enter an English Ambassador. He is fol-
lowed after a moment by Fortinbras and his Norwegian Captain.)
ENGLISH AMBASSADOR.
            The sight is dismal;
And our affairs from England come too late.
The ears are senseless that should give us
      hearing
To tell him his commandment is fulfilled,
That Rosencrantz and Guildenstern are —
FORTINBRAS. Excuse me. *(The Ambassador stops, surprised.)*
Could you please be quiet, please? In fact, could you wait
outside? Please? *(The Ambassador hesitates. The Captain takes a*
menacing step towards him. The Ambassador exits.) I never liked
English guys. You're Horatio, right? I remember you.
HORATIO.   Fortinbras?
FORTINBRAS.   Hi. So — God, what is all this?
HORATIO.   I beg of you, give order that these bodies
High on a stage be placed to the view —
FORTINBRAS.   Yeah, ok — but what happened?
HORATIO.   The people must know —
FORTINBRAS.   Well, sure ... everyone's going to know. You
can't keep something like this quiet. Captain, why don't you
take these, um — *(Indicates the bodies.)* and put them some-
place safe for now, ok? *(The Captain grabs the body of Laertes,*
looks around.) Is everyone dead? The whole family, I mean?
HORATIO.   Two families.
FORTINBRAS.   Two?! No one's left? Of the whole royal — ?
HORATIO.   No one. *(The Captain drags Laertes out.)*
FORTINBRAS.   *(Picking up Hamlet's foil.)* They all just kill

104

each other, or what?

HORATIO.   Yes, m'lord. I was here to see everything. *(Pointing to Osric.)* He was, too. So were others, but they all seem to have ... *(He trails off as he notices everyone at court but he and Osric are gone.)*

FORTINBRAS.   I don't blame them. Nobody likes being a witness. You stayed, though. That's good. What's your name?

OSRIC.   Osric, m'lord.

FORTINBRAS.   So what happened, Osric?

OSRIC.   I don't know, m'lord.

FORTINBRAS.   But he said you were here.

OSRIC.   I was — I mean I am, but —

FORTINBRAS.   Afraid to get involved, eh?

OSRIC.   Yes, m'lord.

FORTINBRAS.   Imagine how I feel. I'm on my way back from the wars against the Poles — just stopped in to say hi — and look at this. What are these foils for?

HORATIO.   There was a fencing contest — Hamlet and Laertes. But it was a trap. One of the sword tips was poisoned.

FORTINBRAS.   *(Who was about to touch the tip.)* Really? *(Fortinbras hands the foil to Osric. The Captain returns. The Captain drags out Gertrude's body.)* So where were we? The sword was poisoned — by who?

HORATIO.   Claudius.

FORTINBRAS.   The King?

HORATIO.   He also poisoned the wine in that chalice. He and Laertes conspired against my lord Hamlet. The Queen was innocent, but drank the wine by mistake and —

FORTINBRAS.   Hold it, hold it! I'm never going to follow all that. *(Picking up a pearl from the floor.)* What's this?

HORATIO.   A pearl, m'lord. It was in the wine.

FORTINBRAS.   In the wine?

OSRIC.   As a prize.

FORTINBRAS.   Yeah? Neat. Not much of a prize, though, if the wine's poisoned. This was Claudius's idea? *(The Captain returns, drags off Claudius's body.)*

HORATIO.   If you'll let me explain —

FORTINBRAS.   Say, who's in charge now, anyway?

HORATIO.   M'lord?

FORTINBRAS.   *(Nodding towards Hamlet's corpse.)* It's obviously none of these guys.

HORATIO.   I'm not sure ...

FORTINBRAS.   Nobody's left, eh? I'll tell you what we do in Norway. We find out who died last —

OSRIC.   Last, my lord?

FORTINBRAS.   They must've died in some order. So what was it?

HORATIO.   Um ... the Queen, Laertes —

OSRIC.   No, the King.

HORATIO.   The King first?

OSRIC.   *After* the Queen.

HORATIO.   Didn't Laertes — ?

FORTINBRAS.   *Who died last?*

OSRIC.   Hamlet.

HORATIO.   Hamlet. *(The Captain returns. He removes Hamlet's body.)*

FORTINBRAS.   So — when he died, he was the king, essentially. Did he say anything about who should succeed him?

OSRIC.   You, m'lord.

HORATIO.   He said he *assumed* it would be you.

OSRIC.   Definitely you. He said.

FORTINBRAS.   You're kidding me.

HORATIO.   Of course you must be chosen by the Electors.

OSRIC.   A mere formality. After all, who's left? *(Horatio shoots Osric an angry look. The Captain reenters.)*

FORTINBRAS.   Me? That is so hard to believe. Captain — go bring me the head of the Electors. *(The Captain exits.)* This is a real surprise. I had no idea you guys liked Norwegians this much. Of course, you don't really, do you? *(Horatio and Osric look at each other embarrassedly.)*

OSRIC.   *(Kneeling.)* I for one love Norwegians.

FORTINBRAS.   Yeah? Well, great. Osric — you look like a pretty bright guy. *(Horatio gives an incredulous laugh. Fortinbras gives Osric the pearl.)* Take this. I want you to gather up everything here: foils, chalices, pearls — everything, and give it all a good wash.

HORATIO.   M'lord — !

FORTINBRAS.   Wash the floor, too. Get rid of any ... wine stains.

HORATIO.   M'lord, we need the proof —

FORTINBRAS.   We have proof.

HORATIO.   The bodies, you mean?

FORTINBRAS.   No — you can get bodies anyplace. We've got much better proof than that. We've got testimony.

HORATIO.   Testimony?

FORTINBRAS.   Yeah. You. Osric. Testimony. Now, look — while Osric's cleaning up in here, I want you to go back to whatever room you're in and write down everything that happened here. I want a full report, ok? That's the only way I'm going to figure it out. Then maybe I can start to make up the truth.

HORATIO.   Make up?

FORTINBRAS.   That's a poor choice of words. What I mean is nothing's true until it's certified — right? You're in government, sort of. You know that. And nothing gets certified, except by the proper authorities. And I'm the proper authorities now. Right? *(With a look at Osric.)* I mean, right? *(Fortinbras smiles cheerfully. Lights fade to black.)*

Scene 2

The battlements of Elsinore. Fortinbras stands looking through a telescope. Osric is nearby, with Marcellus and Barnardo. They hold up a large tapestry for inspection. On the other side of Fortinbras, Horatio stands holding a parchment.

OSRIC.   *(As Fortinbras continues to scan the horizon.)* It used to hang in the Queen's chamber. She had it moved after the unfortunate —

FORTINBRAS.   Sure. I can understand that. *(With a quick glance at it.)* Looks pretty good, though.

OSRIC.   It is. Just this little ... rip here, you see, and —

FORTINBRAS.   No blood on the front of it?

OSRIC.   No, all on the back. A little sewing, and —

FORTINBRAS.   Great. I like it. Put it in my rooms.

OSRIC.   Which will be?

FORTINBRAS.   The King's chambers. *(Osric nods.)*

HORATIO.   You haven't been elected yet, m'lord.

FORTINBRAS.   Ok. Just put it outside the King's chambers for now. What else is there?

OSRIC.   *(Searching through a pile of regal objects with Marcellus and Barnardo.)* Let me see ...

FORTINBRAS.   *(Looking through the telescope again.)* Where were we, Horatio?

HORATIO.   My lord Hamlet's ship had just been set upon by ... pirates.

FORTINBRAS.   Pirates? Get out of here.

HORATIO.   It happened, m'lord.

FORTINBRAS.   Did you see these pirates?

HORATIO.   No, m'lord.

FORTINBRAS.   Right. Go on.

HORATIO.   *(Reading from the parchment.)* "The pirates, on learning Prince Hamlet's identity, immediately released him — "

FORTINBRAS.   Released him? Why?

HORATIO.   He promised to do them a favor ... sometime. *(Fortinbras looks incredulous.)* It happened, m'lord.

FORTINBRAS.   Go on.

HORATIO.   "Hamlet then sent for me — "

OSRIC.   *(Holding up a bouquet of dried flowers.)* Dead flowers, m'lord.

FORTINBRAS.   Dead flowers?

OSRIC.   They were Lady Ophelia's — from her unfortunate period. After she died, the Queen kept them.

FORTINBRAS.   *(Finding this morbid.)* Oh. Keep them anyway. Put them on the wall or something.

HORATIO.   May I continue?

FORTINBRAS.   I wish you wouldn't, Horatio. This was all pretty unbelievable when I read it last night. I thought maybe if you read it to me yourself, but —

HORATIO.   It's what happened.

FORTINBRAS. I can't help that.

HORATIO. I was in a unique position to *know.*

FORTINBRAS. So what? I mean, who can understand all this stuff? A ghost appears to Hamlet and tells him his uncle killed his father, so Hamlet pretends to go crazy — or maybe he really does, who cares? — and he decides to kill his uncle. But he stalls around for a long time instead, kills a guy who's *not* his uncle, gets sent to England, gets rescued by pirates, comes back and kills everybody — including himself. I mean, come *on.*

HORATIO. *(As the others hold up a small, wooden prayer bench.)* The King's prayer bench, m'lord. It's hardly been used.

FORTINBRAS. Yeah, great — for my chambers. *(To Horatio, with disbelief.)* You really saw a ghost?

HORATIO. Yes. Old King Hamlet.

FORTINBRAS. And Hamlet saw this ghost?

HORATIO. And Marcellus, and Barnardo.

FORTINBRAS. *(To them.)* You did?

MARCELLUS. We think we did.

BARNARDO. It was dark.

HORATIO. They stood here with me, on this very battlement, and saw Hamlet's father's ghost.

FORTINBRAS. My father's dead; I've never seen *his* ghost.

HORATIO. Your father was killed in fair and equal combat.

FORTINBRAS. My father was killed, as you well know, by Hamlet's father. Old Hamlet killed Old Fortinbras — in a duel, of all things — on the day Hamlet was born. I was just an infant myself. Made me kind of an orphan.

HORATIO. Forgive me, lord. I merely —

FORTINBRAS. And because my father was an even worse gambler than he was a swordsman, he'd agreed to give certain lands to Denmark if he lost. *(Looking though the telescope.)* Those lands, over there. My father's ghost doesn't come back because he'd be ashamed to face me. Wish he could, though. It'd be nice to see what he looked like. For once. *(A beat.)* Well, they'll be my lands again soon enough, providing my captain ever brings me the *head of the Electors!* Osric, why is he having so much trouble?

OSRIC.   The Electors are ... a bit reluctant about coming to see you, m'lord.

FORTINBRAS.   Why?

OSRIC.   The phrase you've been using, "Bring me the *head* of the Electors." It seems to make them nervous.

FORTINBRAS.   You're kidding. Oh, God. I'm so sorry — that's really funny. I never heard it that way till right now. No wonder they don't want to come. *(The Captain enters and bows. He has a sealed parchment and a cloth bag, weighted down by something the shape and heft of a human head. He hands Fortinbras the parchment. Fortinbras reads it.)* Good. Good, good, good. I've been elected. *(To Osric.)* Take all these things and put them in the King's chambers. We'll go through them later.

OSRIC.   Yes, m'lor — *(Correcting himself, with a deep bow.)* Yes, my *sovereign* lord. And may I be the first to say —

FORTINBRAS.   *(Taking the sack from the Captain.)* Is this for me, too? *(Osric, Marcellus and Barnardo instantly bundle up everything.)* What were you saying, Osric?

OSRIC.   It'll keep. *(Osric, Marcellus and Barnardo hurry out with the objects.)*

FORTINBRAS.   Horatio, we've got to have a new story.

HORATIO.   But there's only the truth.

FORTINBRAS.   That's the problem. You want to tell everyone in Denmark that their entire royal family killed itself, plus a family of reasonably innocent nobles, *plus* two attendant lords? Good God, Horatio — how much do you think people can take? No one wants to hear their whole royal family's incompetent. Personally, I think we should just replace the whole story.

HORATIO.   Replace it?

FORTINBRAS.   We need a story that'll do something for us: explain the bodies, preserve the monarchy, give the people some kind of focus for all their — I don't know — anger, loss, what*ever*. And most of all, something that'll show people that everything that's happened up till now had to happen so that I could become king. I know how I'd like to explain it.

HORATIO.   How?

FORTINBRAS.   A Polish spy.

110

HORATIO. A Polish — ?!

FORTINBRAS. Exactly! It's the perfect idea. Look — the Poles, bitter at Claudius's pact with my uncle to grant me and my troops free passage through Denmark so that I can kick their Polish butts, send a spy to the court here in Elsinore. His job is to destroy the entire Danish royal family. You know, as a lesson to all who would conspire against the Polish crown — all that crap. Anyhow, he successfully sabotages the fencing match, bares the swordtip, poisons the weapon, the wine — see how easy this is, all one guy — sets the unsuspecting participants against each other in a sort of frenzy of sudden rage and paranoia, and executes the most extraordinary mass-regicide in the history of Europe.

HORATIO. But —

FORTINBRAS. *And* we can even add a lot of stuff about the horror when the royal Danes, each mortally wounded and/or poisoned, suddenly realized that Poland had achieved its ultimate revenge — blah, blah, blah.

HORATIO. That's not what happened.

FORTINBRAS. I bet it will be. It's just so much better. Anyone can understand it. And the best thing is, it gives me that historical reason-for-being that's so important to a new king. You see? I'm here to save Denmark from an imminent attack by Poland. *(Horatio looks incredibly dubious.)* Of course, if you want to tell people that ridiculous story of yours, be my guest. But I'll bet mine's the one that catches on. In fact, Captain, I want you to promulgate the true story you've just heard.

CAPTAIN. Which true story?

FORTINBRAS. The Polish —

CAPTAIN. Yes, my liege.

FORTINBRAS. Make it known throughout Denmark. And begin the amalgamation of Danish and Norwegian forces, preparatory to a full invasion.

CAPTAIN. Of — ?

FORTINBRAS. *Po*land.

CAPTAIN. Yes, my liege.

HORATIO. Invasion — !?

111

FORTINBRAS.   Relax. If people believe your story we won't invade anywhere. Then again, if they believe my story — well — I'll *have* to invade Poland. *(Sighs.)* And of course I'll have to find a Polish spy.

HORATIO.   But there is none!

FORTINBRAS.   That'll make it harder. But maybe we don't even need to catch him. Maybe just looking's the best. This story's going to work out great. Get going, Captain. *(The Captain exits.)*

HORATIO.   Sire, what you're suggesting is infamous.

FORTINBRAS.   What? The invasion? That won't really happen. We'll just march the army to the Polish border, rattle the old swords for twenty minutes and come home. Nobody'll get hurt, and I'll prove to you that I'm right about this story thing and you're not. Hey — want to know what's in the sack?

HORATIO.   No, sire —

FORTINBRAS.   Come on — take a look. Closer. *Closer!* *(Horatio steps closer.)* What could it be, I wonder? My captain brings me a lot of stuff. He's ambitious. *(Fortinbras peers into the bag.)* Ooo — man! You want to see?

HORATIO.   No — ! *(Fortinbras pulls a melon out of the bag.)*

FORTINBRAS.   Is that a beauty? *(Horatio can't help but give a sigh of profound relief.)* I wondered what I was going to have for lunch. You got a knife? *(Horatio hands him a knife. Fortinbras slices the melon.)* That was a weird sigh, Horatio. What'd you think I had in here, the head of the Electors? *(Fortinbras laughs.)* You thought it was a head. Instead, it's going to feed us both. There's a lesson in that. *(Offering Horatio a slice.)* Eat it. *(Horatio starts to eat.)* You know, this is a lucky place, Elsinore.

HORATIO.   Lucky?

FORTINBRAS.   For me it is. How many people walk through the door and — boom, they're king? That's lucky. *(A beat.)* So what was Hamlet like, anyway?

HORATIO.   Sire?

FORTINBRAS.   He was complex or something, right? *(Horatio nods.)* Sorry he's gone. I was always going to talk to him. You know, about ... various matters. You went to Wittenberg with him?

HORATIO.   I did.

FORTINBRAS.   I wanted to go to college. My uncle wouldn't let me, though. Afraid I'd get too powerful. Hamlet read a lot, didn't he? Words, I mean?

HORATIO.   Yes, sire.

FORTINBRAS.   Good times at Wittenberg, eh? Yeah, college life.

HORATIO.   I could ... teach you.

FORTINBRAS.   Teach me?

HORATIO.   Tutor you. Give you the benefit of my years there.

FORTINBRAS.   You want to do that for me? How come?

HORATIO.   Every prince needs an education.

FORTINBRAS.   Right now I know how to win battles. What else is there?

HORATIO.   Diplomacy —

FORTINBRAS.   That's just battles without soldiers. I do that great.

HORATIO.   Ethics.

FORTINBRAS.   Oops. We're back to telling the truth again.

HORATIO.   My lord Hamlet's life requires the truth —

FORTINBRAS.   It's just a vicious circle with you, isn't it? Try to understand this, ok? I'm not here to finish their story. They were all here to begin mine. *(Hefting the remainder of the melon in his hand, giving it to Horatio.)* It's the new perspective. Master it.

HORATIO.   Yes, my liege. *(Horatio bows, exits with the melon. Fortinbras turns and stares through the telescope at the horizon. After a moment, the ghost of Polonius enters. Fortinbras doesn't notice him. Polonius carefully reaches out to touch the telescope and startles Fortinbras.)*

FORTINBRAS.   Jesus! You scared me. Who are you? *(Polonius smiles anxiously. Fortinbras looks closer.)* Do I know you? *(Polonius nods.)* Polonius? *(Polonius nods.)* But you're — *(Polonius gives an gentle shrug, reaches out for the telescope.)* What do you want? This? *(Fortinbras gives it to Polonius, who seems pleased to hold it. Polonius stares through it this way and that.)* Don't you get much of a view where you are? *(Polonius pays no attention.)* My new lands? Is that what you're looking at? *(Polonius, still looking through the telescope, nods.)* Is there something you want to tell me? Something I should know? *(Polonius nods.)* What is it? *(Polonius starts to answer, but somehow can't bring himself to speak. He waves his hand dismissively, as though it's not really worth saying.)* Is it complex? *(Polonius turns, hands Fortinbras the telescope and nods. Polonius exits. Fortinbras stares after him. Lights fade to black.)*

Scene 3

The castle. Horatio and Osric collide as they cross paths in a hurry. Osric holds some objects, including the foils from Scene 1. Some of these spill to the floor.

HORATIO.   Watch it!
OSRIC.   Oh — !
HORATIO.   Idiot. What's wrong with you?
OSRIC.   Nothing's wrong with me. *I'm* well-adjusted. *(Dropping another foil.)* Damn!
HORATIO.   Where are you taking these?
OSRIC.   The King's chambers. Fortin — *King* Fortinbras wants them for the wall.
HORATIO.   Those are from the duel!
OSRIC.   They've been washed.
HORATIO.   You're not taking them. *(Horatio takes the foils from him.)*
OSRIC.   Horatio — !
HORATIO.   *This is the sword that killed your Prince!* *(Looking at the other foil.)* Or this is!
OSRIC.   They're not swords anymore. They're decor. Now give them back. *(Horatio sighs, returns them.)*
HORATIO.   He says no one will believe us.
OSRIC.   Believe us what?
HORATIO.   When we tell what really happened.
OSRIC.   Why would we do that?

HORATIO.   For the sake of the truth!

OSRIC.   Horatio, get a grip on yourself. Monarchs change and we change with them. It's natural as the wind and rain. Do you want *your* head to end up in a sack?

HORATIO.   That wasn't a head; it was a melon. I saw it. I ate it.

OSRIC.   Then ... what happened to the Electors?

HORATIO.   They're probably running for the countryside.

OSRIC.   They were always nervous. I wouldn't be surprised if one of them was the Polish spy who — *(Horatio grabs Osric by the collar.)*

HORATIO.   *There is no Polish spy!*

OSRIC.   I know, I know!! But if there were one —

HORATIO.   *There's none!*

OSRIC.   But if there were — you're choking me — if there were — and we know there's not — one of the Electors might actually be — *(Horatio throws him to the floor in disgust.)*

HORATIO.   You're a fool.

OSRIC.   *(Getting his breath.)* Thank you, Horatio.

HORATIO.   So is Fortinbras. He's an absolute child. He makes Laertes look cultured.

OSRIC.   I like him. *(Horatio gives Osric a look.)* Well, he's cheerful. It's not like Hamlet — wandering around, looking morose all the time, wearing earth tones. Fortinbras does things. He gives orders we can follow. So what if he lies a little? Claudius lied a lot. Honestly, Horatio, I think you should just try to get on board for once.

HORATIO.   And that's as deeply as you want to examine things?

OSRIC.   Goodness, yes. I wouldn't examine them that deeply if I could avoid it. Oh, I know — they say the unexamined life is not worth living. But the examined life is also not worth living, and it's a great deal more painful. I'd've thought Prince Hamlet's experience would have shown you that. *(Osric starts to leave again.)*

HORATIO.   I'm going to tell the truth! To everyone I meet.

OSRIC.   I'll warn them. *(Osric exits. Lights fade to black.)*

Scene 4

*Fortinbras in the King's chambers. His royal bed is imposing.
The tapestry from Scene 2 now hangs on the wall. Likewise,
Claudius's prayer bench, Ophelia's dead flowers and the foils
from the duel have been worked into the decor. Fortinbras,
dressed for lounging, sits on the foot of the bed, talking with
the Captain and toying with the crown.*

FORTINBRAS.   So, when'll they be ready to march?

CAPTAIN.   In the morning, sire.

FORTINBRAS.   Great. Tell my generals to go right up to
Poland and stop, ok? This is not a real invasion or anything
— just some dancing around.

CAPTAIN.   Very good, sire. *(The Captain exits. Horatio enters.)*

FORTINBRAS.   Horatio — good! Come on in. How about
this room, eh? Finally got it the way I like it. So tell me,
what'd they do with those guys at the funeral today? The ones
that got unruly.

HORATIO.   They were chastened and sent home.

FORTINBRAS.   That Hamlet was a popular guy. Four graves,
and everybody's jumping into his. Hope a lot of people will
jump on my grave when I'm dead.

HORATIO.   I'm sure they will, sire.

FORTINBRAS.   You're funny, Horatio. I should like that
more than I do.

HORATIO.   About the issue of sacred ground.

FORTINBRAS.   Sorry — they all get sacred ground. End of
argument.

HORATIO.   But Claudius? He killed his brother.

FORTINBRAS.   So you say.

HORATIO.   He slept with his brother's wife.

FORTINBRAS.   Hey — he married her.

HORATIO.   *And* he killed her.

FORTINBRAS.   An accident.

HORATIO.   A murder plot gone awry is not an accident. He

116

usurped the throne from its rightful heir —

FORTINBRAS.　He was elected, same as me.

HORATIO.　Precisely.

FORTINBRAS.　He has to be buried in sacred ground, or the Polish spy story doesn't work. I wish you'd get a sense of priorities. Come here and sit down. Come on, come on — sit. *(Horatio sits uncomfortably next to Fortinbras on the bed.)* How you doing on that story of yours? Anybody believe you yet?

HORATIO.　One or two have ... come close.

FORTINBRAS.　It's not easy, I know. I used to tell the truth all the time. People would get incredibly disappointed. I'd say, "But that's what really happened." *(Sighs.)* I was so unpopular. Then I thought, "Wait a minute — I'm a prince. And some-day, a king." And it's far more important for a king to be popular than to recount a bunch of random events the way they actually happened. You see what I'm saying? If the truth distances me from my people, then how can it be the truth? *(A beat.)* You know what I saw through my telescope? Up on the battlements?

HORATIO.　No, sire.

FORTINBRAS.　I saw the future. I saw a lot of farmers, cows, trees — but I also saw the future. And the future, Horatio, is that this kingdom gets more and more powerful.

HORATIO.　How?

FORTINBRAS.　First we get the army back from Poland, once we've made the spy story look good. Then we take it up to Norway and break off a few of my uncle's legs. Then, we turn around to the rest of Europe and say — and this is the great part, we only have to *say* it — "Watch out for Denway."

HORATIO.　Denway?

FORTINBRAS.　Or Normark — it doesn't matter. The point is, the combined power of our two countries will be over-whelming. Horatio, we are on the brink of the great Norween-ish age of Europe!

HORATIO.　Norween — ?

FORTINBRAS.　Or Daneweegian — it doesn't matter.

HORATIO.　Sire —

FORTINBRAS.　Think of it! Anywhere a Daneweegian goes,

he'll be safe. With military power like this, we can sit and polish our weapons till the end of time.

HORATIO. I gave my oath to Hamlet —

FORTINBRAS. Hamlet's dead now. I'm your King. You have wonderful loyalty, Horatio. You just have to learn how to point it in different directions. Think of it! For the first time in your life you could be proud to be Norweenish!

HORATIO. No! No, sire — strike off my head if you must, but do not ask me to renounce my oath. An oath is larger than a kingship, and a kingship is larger, may I say, than you! You can never tempt me with petty conquests!

FORTINBRAS. Petty? It's all of Norway.

HORATIO. A kingdom is not a plaything, and we are not boys! A king rules to serve his people, not himself. If you learn nothing from the tragic reign of Claudius, learn that.

FORTINBRAS. Hey, hey, hey! No need to get rigid about this. I just wanted to get you in on the ground-floor of the myth thing. The reign of Fortinbras needs one small, tidy conquest. Then we can relax and nourish our new nation on the very myth we've created. That's how a real leader leads. And it's how a leader's friend is his friend. I could use a friend, Horatio. Not like Osric. Someone ... like Hamlet had.

HORATIO. Hamlet earned his friends.

FORTINBRAS. That's fine, if you've got the time. But if you're going places like me, friendships have to be efficient.

HORATIO. Hamlet would never have said that.

FORTINBRAS. "Hamlet would never have said that." Loosen up! There's room for more than one philosophy in the world. Is that the right word? Philosophy?

HORATIO. *May I go, sire!?*

FORTINBRAS. Sure, go on. I'm not a tyrant.

HORATIO. *(Starting out, stopping.)* The truth goes beyond death. It can't be changed.

FORTINBRAS. But it can be ignored. Good night, Horatio. *(Horatio exits. As he does so, he passes Osric, entering.)*

OSRIC. My liege —

FORTINBRAS. What is it?

OSRIC. I'm here with tonight's alternatives.

FORTINBRAS.   Tonight's alternatives? I totally forgot. Well ... fine, all right. Where are they? *(Osric beckons, and two young Maidens enter. They are clean, but humbly dressed. They stare wide-eyed at the splendors of Elsinore. Fortinbras quickly puts on his crown.)*
OSRIC.   Tonight's alternatives.
FORTINBRAS.   Is it true, what I've been told?
OSRIC.   It is, my liege. They are Polish. *(Nudging them forward.)* Your soldiers brought them back after your last incursion there.
FORTINBRAS.   I tell them not to do that. So, do they speak any Danish or Norwegian?
OSRIC.   Not a syllable.
FORTINBRAS.   How'm I supposed to make them like me?
OSRIC.   I really don't know, sire.
FORTINBRAS.   Well ... go prepare them.
OSRIC.   Both, sire?
FORTINBRAS.   Why should I penalize one? *(Osric and the Maidens exit.)* What am I going to do about Horatio? Why won't he *like* me?! Show a guy a little vision, and wham — he seizes up on you. He doesn't even want to talk to me now. Can't get his head out of the past. I hate the past, it's pointless, it's so ... stiff. *(Looking around, to the audience.)* Something about this castle makes me want to talk to myself. Don't know why — I've spent my whole life *not* talking. Out on the battlefield, worried about spies behind every tentflap — all of them working for my uncle. I didn't dare say a word out loud. But here, the minute I'm alone I just ... jabber. *(Suddenly calling out anxiously.)* Osric, where are my alternatives! *(To the audience again.)* I hope you don't think I'm callous, just because of those maidens. They really will have as good a time as can be expected. Under the circumstances. Given the point in history. I'm not known as Fortinbras the Particularly Cruel or anything. I never used to do this sort of thing on my campaigns, but now that I'm King, it's sort of ... expected. And it *has* been a long time. Honest. Not to get too personal. Anyway, I really will try to communicate with them. *(He hears shuffling in the hall.)* At last! *(Polonius appears.)* Not you again.

119

(Polonius stands attentively, smiles.) Are you going to speak to me tonight? Are you ever going to speak to me? *(Polonius doesn't respond.)* What good is it if you won't tell me anything? *(Polonius shrugs, smiles, moves to the tapestry. He runs his hand over it.)* We keep going through this. What do you want? Do you have a dire warning? Is there a foul injustice? *(At "foul injustice" Polonius becomes excited, as though he wants to speak.)* Yes? *(Polonius suddenly shrugs and waves it off with an "it's not that important" gesture.)* Damn it — ! *(The two Maidens enter in nightdress looking anxiously at Fortinbras.)* What do you want? Oh — sorry. In the bed. *(They follow Fortinbras's gesture and demurely jump into bed. Their wide eyes watch Fortinbras's every move. They do not see Polonius.)* I've got company now, you'll have to go. *(Polonius smiles, remains.)* I'm serious. The alternatives are here. *(No move by Polonius.)* You can't want to watch — you're dead! *(Polonius shrugs.)* This is nuts. *Who sent you?! Why do you appear to me!?* *(Ophelia enters. The Maidens can't see her.)*

OPHELIA.   He always appears where he's least wanted. It's his trademark.

FORTINBRAS.   My God! Lady Ophelia! *(Polonius too looks a bit surprised.)*

OPHELIA.   Yeah, yeah, yeah — Ophelia. Big deal. Who cares? No one did in life — right, Pop?

1st MAIDEN.   *(In Polish, to Fortinbras.)* Are you not well, your highness?

FORTINBRAS.   *(To the Maidens.)* Quiet! *(To Ophelia.)* You spoke.

OPHELIA.   Huzzah. Ring the bells. Ophelia spoke. Of course I spoke. What am I supposed to do? Stand around like him?

FORTINBRAS.   But I thought ghosts —

OPHELIA.   Ghosts do what they like — haven't you figured that out? We're supernatural. Super-natural. Got it? At least, compared to you. *(To Polonius, indicating Fortinbras, rolling her eyes.)* He's King.

2nd MAIDEN.   *(In Polish, worriedly.)* Come to bed, sire.

FORTINBRAS.   *(To the Maidens.)* Can't you see I'm talking?!

OPHELIA.   They can't see us. What on earth are they speaking?

FORTINBRAS.　Polish.

OPHELIA.　Oh. Wonderful.

FORTINBRAS.　Why are you here? Why have you come to me?

OPHELIA.　I haven't come to you. I'm just here to collect this old idiot.

FORTINBRAS.　But I want him to talk to me.

OPHELIA.　You do?

FORTINBRAS.　Sure. Ghosts ... know things.

OPHELIA.　I'll tell you what ghosts know. They know what they did wrong in life. It's all they can think about. That and a second chance — which never comes. Right, Dad? *(Polonius shrugs.)* Dad talked too much in life. You see where that got him. Now he's afraid to open his mouth. It's really the only good thing I can say about being dead. Hey, Dad — I think I'm still in love with Hamlet. What should I do? *(Polonius fairly burns to advise her, forces himself not to. Ophelia laughs. To Fortinbras.)* Do you really want to know what he's been yearning to say when he comes to see you? The truth — that's all. About anything. When he was alive he couldn't tell the truth even when he tried. Now he won't say anything until he can be absolutely sure it's true. Which, of course, is never. Isn't that right, Dad? *(Cowed, Polonius exits.)* I was the fool in life. Now it's him. Do you remember when we last met?

FORTINBRAS.　Yes. You were ... young and fair.

OPHELIA.　You saying I'm not now?

FORTINBRAS.　No, no. But I guess death is a ... pretty harrowing experience.

OPHELIA.　Harrowing. It's been hell on my looks, I'll admit it. *(Suddenly touching him lightly.)* You still look great.

FORTINBRAS.　Agh!

1st MAIDEN.　*(In Polish.)* Sire?

OPHELIA.　Didn't know you could feel me, eh? It usually comes as a shock. I can turn it on and off. Comes in handy. Say, why don't you get rid of them? We can, um ... talk.

FORTINBRAS.　Talk?

OPHELIA.　Mmm ... unless you're getting other ideas. *(Ophelia turns to the Maidens.)* Come on, girls — everybody up! Go crawl under some other noble. (*Ophelia pulls the cover off the bed. The Maidens scream and exit.*) That's better. (*Climbing onto the bed, pulling the bedcover up around her.*) Are you coming or not?

FORTINBRAS.   You want me to — ?

OPHELIA.   You got it.

FORTINBRAS.   Is it possible?

OPHELIA.   It's not only possible, it's terrific. Did you know women don't reach their sexual peak until after they're dead? (*Fortinbras still can't bring himself to move. Ophelia smiles.*) You're afraid you won't satisfy me, aren't you? Don't worry. You'll still be the only one who ever tried. (*She opens her arms. Fortinbras moves towards the bed. Lights fade to black.*)

Scene 5

Dawn, the next morning. Fortinbras is alone in bed. Kneeling on opposite sides of the bed in a posture of prayer are Gertrude and Claudius. Fortinbras suddenly wakes with a start.

FORTINBRAS.   Ophelia! Don't go, don't — ! (*Noting Claudius and Gertrude.*) Who are you?! (*Suddenly seeing his crown upon Claudius's head, snatching it off.*) Give me that!

CLAUDIUS.   Forgive me. I couldn't help putting it on.

GERTRUDE.   The sin of nostalgia.

CLAUDIUS.   I know. I'm heartily sorry.

GERTRUDE.   Pray with me. (*Gertrude and Claudius instantly fall once more to prayer.*)

FORTINBRAS.   Claudius — !? Gertrude — !? Where's Ophelia? *Where is Ophelia!?*

GERTRUDE.   (*Looking up.*) The sin of wrath.

FORTINBRAS.   Answer my question!

CLAUDIUS.   She left well before daylight. I believe she is a damned soul.

FORTINBRAS.   And you're not?

CLAUDIUS. I have sinned in the past. For which I'm heartily sorry.

GERTRUDE. An act of contrition.

CLAUDIUS. In death I am more virtuous.

FORTINBRAS. You have a choice?

GERTRUDE. Everyone has a choice. Dead or alive. I used to think with death would come some sort of final judgment. Then I could embrace my fate, either in heaven or hell, knowing that I had no choice.

CLAUDIUS. If only it were that easy!

GERTRUDE. Death is harder than life. The temptations we feel are almost irresistible. The lusts —

CLAUDIUS. Don't talk about it!

GERTRUDE. Are only more intense. If I so much as look at Claudius —

CLAUDIUS. Don't look at me!

GERTRUDE. I won't! *(They both avert their gaze.)*

CLAUDIUS. Pray to God!

GERTRUDE. I do!

CLAUDIUS. *(Rushing to his prayer bench.)* The sin of lust! Deliver us from it!

GERTRUDE. Deliver us!

CLAUDIUS. Save us from ourselves!

GERTRUDE. Oh, save us!

FORTINBRAS. *Shut up!! (They fall silent.)* What is wrong with you?!

CLAUDIUS. Everything.

GERTRUDE. We're hideous, hideous beasts. We admit it.

CLAUDIUS. The lust is so intense, but the *remorse* —

GERTRUDE. It's unbearable.

CLAUDIUS. We must be together!

GERTRUDE. But we've got to be apart!

CLAUDIUS. We've come to warn you.

FORTINBRAS. Of what?

GERTRUDE. Ophelia. You had relations with her last night, didn't you?

FORTINBRAS. None of your business.

CLAUDIUS. Fear her.

GERTRUDE.   She's a succuba.

FORTINBRAS.   And a pretty good one, too!

CLAUDIUS.   She will obsess you. She will leap into your heart. She will reach into your spine and travel along every nerve. Your only hunger will be for her. Your only fear will be of her. Your only hope will be in her eyes, and there will be no hope. When you wake in the morning, she will go before you in the day. Every face you see, every hand you touch, every sight, sound, taste, odor — it will all be her.

FORTINBRAS.   Have you really looked at Ophelia lately?

CLAUDIUS.   I'm not speaking of her appearance!

GERTRUDE.   She will mislead you!

CLAUDIUS.   She will compound your sin!

FORTINBRAS.   What sin?

GERTRUDE.   The sin of falsehood!

FORTINBRAS.   Falsehood?

GERTRUDE.   You buried us in sacred ground!

FORTINBRAS.   I thought you'd want to be —

CLAUDIUS.   We're sinners! How can we repent?

FORTINBRAS.   I don't know —

GERTRUDE.   Dig us up — please!!

CLAUDIUS.   Throw us on a dungheap!

FORTINBRAS.   I'm not listening to another word of this! Get out! Go on! Now!

GERTRUDE.   Reject Ophelia!

FORTINBRAS.   Now! *(Gertrude and Claudius scramble to their feet and make for an exit. They bump into each other, cry out with alarm and exit separately.)* Geez Louise — this place is overrun. *(Calling after them.)* And don't come back till you're invited! *(Osric enters.)*

OSRIC.   My liege.

FORTINBRAS.   Osric! You're here early.

OSRIC.   I came to fetch last night's alternatives.

FORTINBRAS.   Oh. Oh — yes. Well they disappeared. I think there was a ... maidens' meeting of some sort.

OSRIC.   I ... see. *(Osric notices the bouquet of dead flowers on the bed, picks them up with a quizzical look.)*

FORTINBRAS.   Oh. They wanted to see those. Yesterday

happened to be dead flower day in Poland.

OSRIC. *(Starting out.)* I'll go look for them.

FORTINBRAS. No! Um, no. *(Osric turns.)* Hang around awhile, ok? Make the bed or something. *(Osric does so, hesitantly.)* So, um ... I don't suppose you have any suspects yet? On that Polish spy thing?

OSRIC. No, sire.

FORTINBRAS. Osric — Have you seen any ghosts, ever?

OSRIC. I haven't had that dubious pleasure, sire.

FORTINBRAS. Why dubious? You think ghosts are bad?

OSRIC. Have you seen ghosts?

FORTINBRAS. Me? No. Why should I see ghosts? I mean, do they even exist?

OSRIC. Horatio thinks so.

FORTINBRAS. Well. Horatio.

OSRIC. Indeed.

FORTINBRAS. He and Hamlet saw ghosts everywhere: on the battlements, in the Queen's closet —

OSRIC. I believe they only saw one ghost.

FORTINBRAS. Right. Right — one ghost. That's what I meant. I just thought with so many reported sightings, that maybe you —

OSRIC. I never see ghosts, my liege. They have no need of me.

FORTINBRAS. Need?

OSRIC. Ghosts appear in order to destroy, sire. That's my experience, at least. And I am clearly not worth destroying.

FORTINBRAS. That's not the only reason they appear.

OSRIC. It is, as far as I can tell. Whenever a ghost appears, the next thing I know I'm cleaning up wine stains. *(Fortinbras suddenly grabs a foil from the wall, whirls and grabs Osric by the collar. He pins him to the bed, foil at his throat.)*

FORTINBRAS. *You'll clean up whatever I tell you! Whenever I tell you to, understand?!!*

OSRIC. *My lord Hamlet — !!*

FORTINBRAS. *What?!*

OSRIC. Sorry! Your majesty! Fortinbras! *(Fortinbras lets go of Osric, who falls back on the bed.)*

FORTINBRAS.   What's wrong with me? This isn't like me at all.
OSRIC.   You have seen a ghost!
FORTINBRAS.   Sorry, Osric. I was ... I was up all night. *(Fortinbras exits. Lights fade to black.)*

Scene 6

A cellar in the castle. In the darkness there is a sudden glow. It's a television screen. As it flickers to life, we see no one is onstage. The image on the tv gradually comes into focus. It's a very tight closeup of a man's face. We can see only an angry brow and eye. The eye looks left and right, as though in search of something. We hear the sound of men approaching. Marcellus, Barnardo — bearing torches — rush in, accompanied by Horatio.

MARCELLUS.   This way!
BARNARDO.   I see it! Over here! *(All three stop and stare at the tv from a safe distance. The eye looks in their direction. With great caution, they begin to circle behind it. As they do so, the tv turns with them, so that the eye can continue to watch them. The men make a complete orbit of the tv, and it turns with them the whole way.)*
MARCELLUS.   You see, Horatio. It's as we say.
HORATIO.   I'll speak to it.
BARNARDO.   No! Look what happened last time.
HORATIO.   Who are you? Speak! Reveal yourself! *(The shot on the tv pulls back, revealing the face of Hamlet.)* My lord!
MARCELLUS.   Hamlet!
HORATIO.   *(Falling to his knees.)* Good my lord, speak! Forgive this poor servant. I've failed you in everything. No one knows your story. Fortinbras has put forth a terrible lie —
HAMLET.   Swear.
HORATIO.   M'lord?
HAMLET.   Swear.

126

HORATIO.   Swear what?

HAMLET.   Swear you'll never touch that button.

HORATIO.   Button? *(Once again, we can see only Hamlet's eye. It jerks once or twice toward a switch on the tv set. Pointing.)* This?

HAMLET.   *DON'T TOUCH IT!!*

HORATIO.   What is it?

BARNARDO.   *(Reading puzzledly.)* "On/off."

HAMLET. *SWEAR!*

HORATIO.   I swear.

MARCELLUS and BARNARDO.   We swear.

HORATIO.   What do you want of us, lord?

HAMLET.   I want ... *(Trailing off.)*

HORATIO.   Yes?

HAMLET.   I want ...

HORATIO.   Anything.

HAMLET.   I want to look at you.

HORATIO.   That's all? Just look at us?

HAMLET.   That's all.

HORATIO.   Of course. For how long?

HAMLET.   *Does it matter!?*

HORATIO.   *(Fearfully.)* No, m'lord! Look at us, by all means. *(Horatio motions the others to kneel with him. They do so.)*

HAMLET.   It's so good to see you. It's all I can do, now: watch and think. I couldn't bring myself to act in life, at least not swiftly enough. Now ...

HORATIO.   Don't blame yourself, m'lord.

HAMLET.   *Who should I blame!?*

HORATIO.   I — I don't know!

HAMLET.   Bring me to Fortinbras.

HORATIO.   My lord?

HAMLET.   *Now. (The three men hurriedly trundle the tv out. Lights fade quickly to black.)*

Scene 7

The throne room. Fortinbras sits on the throne, receiving news from Osric. To one side of Fortinbras, apparently invisible to Osric, are Ophelia and Laertes.

FORTINBRAS.　　What do you mean we've taken Warsaw? I told the army not to attack.
OSRIC.　　They didn't, my liege. They were invited.
FORTINBRAS.　　Invited?
OPHELIA.　　I told you you were popular.
OSRIC.　　Apparently the Poles, seeing our combined armies on their border, decided to forestall further hostilities by surrendering unconditionally.
FORTINBRAS.　　But they don't even know what we want.
OPHELIA.　　*(To Laertes.)* What do we want?
OSRIC.　　We'll have to want something, sire.
FORTINBRAS.　　Well, I don't know — maybe we should have the troops stay in Warsaw for awhile and ... mingle.
OSRIC.　　Mingle?
FORTINBRAS.　　Not possible, eh? What's wrong with me? I used to be so decisive.
OPHELIA.　　Maybe you're not getting enough sleep.
LAERTES.　　Ophelia — !
OPHELIA.　　Oh, bite it, Laertes.
FORTINBRAS.　　Well ... have the army declare victory then, and ... just come back.
OSRIC.　　Yes, sire.
FORTINBRAS.　　And have them tell the Poles to ... watch it.
OSRIC.　　Very well, sire.
OPHELIA.　　*(To Fortinbras.)* I love it when you're stern. *(Osric turns to go. Before he can do so, the Captain enters and falls to one knee. He too is unable to see Ophelia or Laertes.)*
CAPTAIN.　　My liege.
FORTINBRAS.　　What is it?
CAPTAIN.　　The army's left Warsaw — they're pushing on.
FORTINBRAS.　　Pushing on?

CAPTAIN.   Yes, sire — towards Carpathia.

FORTINBRAS.   Carpathia?

OSRIC.   Just beyond Poland, quite mountainous — nice in the summer.

FORTINBRAS.   I know where it is! Why are they doing that?

CAPTAIN.   No one knows. But most of the Polish army has joined them.

FORTINBRAS.   I can't have this. This is all wrong. Get them back. Tell them to come home. Now!

CAPTAIN.   *(Exiting.)* Yes, sire.

FORTINBRAS.   *(To Ophelia and Laertes.)* Carpathia. The minute my generals get back, you guys are going to have company.

OSRIC.   Sire, to whom are you speaking?

FORTINBRAS.   *(Defensively.)* Nobody.

OSRIC.   Of course, sire.

FORTINBRAS.   What about the Polish spy?

OSRIC.   The — ? Oh ... no progress, I'm afraid.

FORTINBRAS.   Why not?

OSRIC.   I wasn't aware that you wanted progress. And then there's the fact that there is no actual ... spy.

FORTINBRAS.   We have to have a spy now. After a victory like this? With no shots being fired? We need a reason to have gone at all. A villain.

OSRIC.   But sire —

FORTINBRAS.   One Polish spy. An opponent. This is all about self-image, Osric. How can we be heroes if we can't even see who we've triumphed over? We need someone we can hate right here, right now. Someone palpable. A volunteer, maybe. What about you?

OSRIC.   Me?

FORTINBRAS.   Yeah, what are you doing?

OSRIC.   Well ... nothing, but —

FORTINBRAS.   That's a great idea! You'd be perfect! Believe me, I wouldn't ask if it wasn't important. The public needs this kind of image right now. You know? A human face we can all loathe and detest. Your face.

OSRIC.   I don't know ...

FORTINBRAS. What do you mean, you don't know? We need a Polish spy, and you're elected. It's simple as that. Understand?

OSRIC. But ... but ... *(Fortinbras stares at Osric.)* Very well.

FORTINBRAS. Good! Thanks. *(An awkward beat.)*

OSRIC. So ... I'll just ... go put myself ... in jail. *(Osric exits. Ophelia instantly kisses Fortinbras hard.)*

LAERTES. Ophelia — !

OPHELIA. *(Ending the kiss, to Laertes.)* Why are you hanging around, anyway? Did Claudius and Gertrude send you?

FORTINBRAS. Sometimes I wonder how well I'm running the government.

OPHELIA. You're doing fine. You just had a great victory. Let's celebrate. *(She snuggles up to Fortinbras.)*

FORTINBRAS. Stop that — we're in public.

OPHELIA. You mean *you're* in public.

FORTINBRAS. For God's sake — your brother's here.

OPHELIA. So what? He wants me too.

LAERTES. *Ophelia — !*

OPHELIA. Don't be such a phoney — admit it. Like it matters anymore. *(To Fortinbras.)* Sometimes I don't think he even knows he's dead.

LAERTES. It came as such a shock —

OPHELIA. That's what happens when you think you're immortal. You should've been raised as a girl. Then you'd have been ready. *(She reaches for Fortinbras again. He moves away.)*

FORTINBRAS. *Please* — ! I'm just feeling disoriented right now, ok? Having a ghost for a ...

OPHELIA. For a what? Say it. For a lover.

FORTINBRAS. I don't know what I'm feeling. Or if I'm feeling anything. Or if there's anything to *feel.*

OPHELIA. *(Placing Fortinbras's hand on a provocative part of her anatomy.)* Feel this.

LAERTES. *Ophelia — !*

OPHELIA. Oh, grab it while you can. Get 'em while they're living — that's what I say. *(She kisses Fortinbras again.)*

LAERTES. Fortinbras? Fortinbras — I appeal to you. If you don't respect the boundary between the living and the dead,

130

how can you expect us to?

OPHELIA. Boundaries are made to be broken. *(Fortinbras pulls away.)*

FORTINBRAS. Osric said all ghosts come to destroy.

OPHELIA. Osric? Osric the Wise?

FORTINBRAS. How do I know he's not right?

OPHELIA. Well, you did look pretty destroyed last night.

FORTINBRAS. That's not what I mean. How do I know you're not going to win me to my doom?

OPHELIA. Oh, that is *sweet!* Win you to your doom. You are so cute sometimes. *(She kisses him again.)*

LAERTES. Fortinbras? Wouldn't you rather go kick a ball around or something? It's a beautiful day. I feel athletic.

OPHELIA. *(Coming up for air.)* Me too. *(They go back into the clinch. Unnoticed by the three of them, Horatio wheels in the tv, complete with its image of Hamlet's eye. Horatio can't see Ophelia or Laertes.)*

HORATIO. Sire?

FORTINBRAS. What? Oh — Horatio!

HORATIO. Why did you have your tongue out, sire?

FORTINBRAS. Never mind! What's this?

HORATIO. I found it in the cellar, sire. It's Prince Hamlet.

FORTINBRAS. Hamlet?

HORATIO. Well ... his ghost.

FORTINBRAS. *Another* one?

HORATIO. Sire?

FORTINBRAS. *(Of the tv.)* What's he doing in there?

HORATIO. It's a minor inhibition. We're still working on it. If you'll just listen to what he —

FORTINBRAS. No! No — I refuse. No more ghosts! This is my castle now, my kingdom. It's my army in ... in ...

OPHELIA. Carpathia.

FORTINBRAS. Carpathia! I'm not going to be distracted or betrayed by any more ghosts!

HORATIO. *(Seeing only Hamlet.)* *More* ghosts? But there's only ...

FORTINBRAS. You're dead! You understand?! You're all

131

dead, and I'm free of you! From this moment on! You hear me? Free! *(Fortinbras storms out, with Laertes following.)*

LAERTES.   You want to kick a ball around?

FORTINBRAS.   *NO!! (Fortinbras and Laertes are gone.)*

HORATIO.   *(Looking around, puzzled.)* Carpathia? Who else does he see? *(To the tv.)* I'm sorry, m'lord — he's gone.

HAMLET.   You've done well. Leave me now.

HORATIO.   Leave you?

HAMLET.   *Go! (Horatio hurries out.)*

OPHELIA.   So. You found your way back.

HAMLET.   Is Claudius here?

OPHELIA.   Yeah, he didn't have any trouble. Funny, eh? Looks like you're in a fix.

HAMLET.   I want to be back. Among you.

OPHELIA.   So? Get out of the box.

HAMLET.   I don't know how! Please — I have so much to do.

OPHELIA.   Don't worry. I'm doing it for you. Fortinbras is completely under my control.

HAMLET.   He's not telling the truth!

OPHELIA.   He's been busy. Conquering Poland.

HAMLET.   Help me!

OPHELIA.   Do I look like I have a manual? I don't know how to help you. What's this? "On/off"?

HAMLET.   *Don't touch that! Free me, Ophelia!*

OPHELIA.   Why should I?

FORTINBRAS.   *Free me now, as you love me! Ophe — !! (Ophelia turns off the set.)*

OPHELIA.   Dream on. *(She starts out, stops.)* God, that felt good. *(Ophelia exits. Lights fade slowly to black. Just as they reach black, the tv turns on again, by itself. We see the brooding eye of Hamlet. Then darkness.)*

END OF ACT ONE

ACT TWO

Scene 1

A castle hall. Polonius appears. He carries with him the Queen's old tapestry. He stops, looks around to make sure no one's there. Satisfied, he spreads out the tapestry, finds the hole made by Hamlet's sword.

POLONIUS.   *(Touching it.)* Here. *(Touching his chest.)* Here. *(To the audience.)* It does something to a man's point of view when he suddenly feels a sword go through his heart. I was pinned like a bug against the wall. Where was all my good advice then? Stuck in my throat, where it's remained ever since. Oh, I still have plenty of advice, don't misunderstand. I could tell everybody in this castle, living and dead, what to do. But to hell with 'em, that's what I say. *(Sighing.)* If there were a hell. There doesn't seem to be, for me. No heaven either, that I've been able to discern. Only this — wandering around the scene of all my errors, watching everyone make the same old mistakes, *burning* to advise them — and hating myself for it. Death has been my greatest disappointment. It's too much like life. I thought there would be a great adventure, but there's no great adventure. I've asked the King, the Queen, the others — no one's had a great adventure. So far, there's been nothing to compare with that first moment, pinned against a wall, translated by a steel point — my face buried against the blank side of a tapestry — hoping that in a single instant all might finally be revealed. *(Tossing over the corner of the tapestry.)* What a hoax. Death has all the uncertainty of life, and twice the solitude. If you take my advice — and no one ever does — you'll avoid it. *(Polonius turns to go. As he does, Fortinbras steps into view. Polonius freezes.)*
FORTINBRAS.   You spoke! *(Polonius turns and hurries toward another exit. Fortinbras moves to block his way.)* No, you don't! Talk to me — now! *(Polonius tries another direction. Fortinbras*

blocks him again.) Can't you see how desperate I am?! *(Polonius tries yet another direction. Fortinbras doesn't move.)* Damn it, I need your *advice! (Polonius stops, fighting his urge to advise. Fortinbras falls to his knees.)* Please! Nothing makes sense anymore. I swore off ghosts, I even swore off Ophelia. But I can't make it stick! Every time I see her, I just crumble. I used to handle everything so well: battles, intrigues, women. I never even worked up a sweat. But here at Elsinore I've seen things — I've *done* things.... Give me advice, Polonius, please! One sentence, one phrase, one word.

POLONIUS.   Ophelia.

FORTINBRAS.   Ophelia?

POLONIUS.   Lay off her.

FORTINBRAS.   Ok — ok. I know I should. Why?

POLONIUS.   It's obvious. You're not suited to treat with the dead. Hamlet was fathoms deeper than you. Now look at him: locked in a box of light — and he only *talked* to a ghost.

FORTINBRAS.   What you're saying is, I'm in jeopardy here.

POLONIUS.   At least.

FORTINBRAS.   But I have these feelings about her. It's not like with any other girl.

POLONIUS.   I should hope not.

FORTINBRAS.   It's so *intense.* The minute I see her, the minute I touch her —

POLONIUS.   I *am* her father.

FORTINBRAS.   It's love. How can I resist that?

POLONIUS.   What you feel isn't love, it's nostalgia. For non-existence.

FORTINBRAS.   For non — ?

POLONIUS.   The moment we become aware of our own existence, we secretly begin to long for the time before: when we never were. And why not? It's attractive — utter oblivion, utter peace. *Non-being.* We think death will give us that again. No wonder we fall in love with it. But that's not what death gives us. Nothing can erase, completely, what has been.

FORTINBRAS.   So, um — how would I fit that into a plan of action?

POLONIUS.   Tell the truth! To thine own self be —

FORTINBRAS.   Nice?

POLONIUS.   *TRUE!!*

FORTINBRAS.   Right.

POLONIUS.   And get married!

FORTINBRAS.   To Ophelia?

POLONIUS.   No, not to Ophelia! To someone else.

FORTINBRAS.   Who?

POLONIUS.   It doesn't matter. Someone living, that's all.

FORTINBRAS.   Married? But there's no one.

POLONIUS.   What about those two I saw in your bed?

FORTINBRAS.   They were just — They don't even speak my language.

POLONIUS.   All the better! Find them. Marry one. Then maybe Ophelia will leave you alone, and you can gain the courage to tell the truth.

FORTINBRAS.   About *what*? What truth am I supposed to tell?

POLONIUS.   Hamlet's truth. My truth. Without it, nothing can go forward — all is held back.

FORTINBRAS.   But I've already told the Polish spy story —

POLONIUS.   *Tell the truth!!* What did I just tell you?!

FORTINBRAS.   But —

POLONIUS.   *You can't take advice! None of you! You never take advice!!* I'm leaving.

FORTINBRAS.   No — ! *(Polonius starts out, dragging the tapestry behind him. Fortinbras grabs a corner of it.)* What should I do about the army? They took Carpathia without a shot!

POLONIUS.   *(Tugging at the tapestry.)* I don't care!

FORTINBRAS.   Why's Hamlet in a box?

POLONIUS.   Let go!

FORTINBRAS.   Should I hang Osric?

POLONIUS.   *I don't care!! (Polonius tugs the arras free.)* Tell the truth. Tell it soon. There isn't much time — for either of us.

FORTINBRAS.   What do you mean? You're dead.

POLONIUS.   You think eternity's forever? *(Polonius exits. Fortinbras stares after him. Fortinbras exits the opposite way. A moment passes, then Horatio hurries in, pushing Osric ahead of him. Osric is in chains.)*

OSRIC.   Horatio, stop it! Where are you taking me!?

HORATIO.   Quiet.

OSRIC.   I won't be quiet! You're hurting me! Horatio — ! *(Managing to pull away.)* Put me back in my cell.

HORATIO.   No.

OSRIC.   I demand it!

HORATIO.   I'm trying to save your life!

OSRIC.   Why?

HORATIO.   *Why!?*

OSRIC.   It's none of your business. Besides, you don't even like me.

HORATIO.   I *need* you! We're the only ones who know the truth. Do you want to hang? *(Osric is silent. Horatio pushes him along again. Osric resists.)*

OSRIC.   Where is it we're going?

HORATIO.   I'm getting you out of the castle. *(Osric is stunned.)*

OSRIC.   Out of the — ? Out of — ?!

HORATIO.   What's wrong?

OSRIC.   I've never ... I've never ...

HORATIO.   What!?

OSRIC.   *Been* out of the castle. *(Now Horatio is stunned.)*

HORATIO.   Never?

OSRIC.   There was no need. Everything I wanted was right here. Out there it was all just ... Denmark.

HORATIO.   *(Pushing him again.)* You'll get used to it.

OSRIC.   No, no, no, no, no — Horatio — please! Just stop! Stop for a minute and *listen to me!* (Horatio stops.) I want to hang.

HORATIO.   What?

OSRIC.   That's overstated. But I would rather hang than have to go out into ... whatever that is. I've seen it from the ramparts, Horatio. No one looks happy out there. No one's well dressed —

HORATIO.   *(Pushing him yet again.)* Come on.

OSRIC.   *I'm a Polish spy!! Listen, everyone! I'm a spy! I really am!!*

HORATIO.   Shut up.

OSRIC.   *Long live Poland!*

HORATIO.   *(Clapping a hand over Osric's mouth.)* You're insane! Everyone in this castle is. *(Osric nods.)* How can you accept it? You've been falsely accused. Even you must feel some outrage.

OSRIC.   Outrage is a luxury best enjoyed by those who can do something about it. I must simply be patient and wait for the storm to pass over me.

HORATIO.   Or swallow you whole.

OSRIC.   No system's perfect. May I please go back to my cell now?

HORATIO.   All right. Till I can think of another way. But don't blame me if you're hanged in the meantime. Fair enough?

OSRIC.   You are good to me, Horatio.

HORATIO.   I'm just trying to do one honest thing.

OSRIC.   We all have our faults. *(Horatio pushes Osric off the way they came. Lights fade to black.)*

Scene 2

Lights slowly come up on the Queen's chambers. As they do, we hear the following, which starts in darkness.

CLAUDIUS.   My words fly up, my thoughts remain below —

HAMLET.   Kill him!

CLAUDIUS.   My words fly up —

HAMLET.   Kill him! Kill him now!

CLAUDIUS.   My words —

HAMLET.   *What are you waiting for? (By now lights are up. They reveal Claudius kneeling at his prayer bench. Laertes stands behind him with a drawn dagger. In the foreground Gertrude lies on the now-familiar tapestry, in an awkward — if alluring — posture. U., surveying all this, is Hamlet — or Hamlet's eye, rather — since he's still in the tv.)*

LAERTES.   I — I can't.

HAMLET. Why not?

CLAUDIUS. Am I facing the wrong way? Maybe if I —

LAERTES. No, no — it's just that this isn't what happened.

HAMLET. It's what should have happened. Go on — kill him! He won't feel a thing.

CLAUDIUS. Only remorse.

LAERTES. But it's so meaningless. I won't be sending him to heaven *or* hell. We're all just floating here. I don't understand why we had to carry all this stuff into the Queen's chamber in the first place. Feels weird.

HAMLET. Never mind that.

LAERTES. Besides, I'm not really a man of violence.

HAMLET. Neither was I. *(Claudius laughs.)* Quiet! As long as I'm confined to this box, I'll spend my time as I like! Now strike, Laertes! While the chance is there!

GERTRUDE. Please strike, Laertes. This is such a humiliating posture.

HAMLET. You be quiet, too! Claudius — again!

CLAUDIUS. My words fly up, my thoughts remain —

HAMLET. Now, Laertes! *(Laertes stabs Claudius, who gives a mortal groan.)* Yes! *(Claudius falls to the floor, dies.)* How easy it was! How exquisite! If only I'd really done it!

LAERTES. Why didn't you?

CLAUDIUS. *(Rising, kneeling at the bench.)* Yes, why didn't you?

GERTRUDE. Why didn't you?

HAMLET. Quiet! All of you! Laertes, stab him again.

LAERTES. But I just —

HAMLET. You heard me! I want to see it again!

CLAUDIUS. It's all right. I deserve it. A thousandfold, if you like.

GERTRUDE. This is so uncomfortable — can't we get to my part?

CLAUDIUS. Yes, do her part.

HAMLET. Very well. Begin.

GERTRUDE. Please forgive me my son, for all the wrongs I've committed.

HAMLET. Such as?

GERTRUDE.   Lusting after Claudius.

HAMLET.   And?

GERTRUDE.   Marrying him so soon after he murdered your father.

HAMLET.   And?

GERTRUDE.   Not giving you my whole support.

HAMLET.   *And?*

GERTRUDE.   Don't make me say it.

HAMLET.   Say it! It's the truth!

GERTRUDE.   And forgive me for lusting after you.

HAMLET.   *Yes!*

LAERTES.   She — !? I never knew that.

GERTRUDE.   It's not true.

HAMLET.   It is! You wanted me. Just as I wanted you. The unspeakable attraction. The root cause of all our sufferings.

CLAUDIUS.   I thought I was the root cause.

HAMLET.   *The root cause is what I say it is!! (They fall to arguing. Ophelia enters, topping all their voices.)*

OPHELIA.   *What is going on in here?* I can hear you from across the cas — *(Stopping short as she takes in the scene; with disgust.)* Oh, very nice.

HAMLET.   Get out of here.

OPHELIA.   *(To Hamlet.)* This was your idea, I suppose. You are such an infant.

HAMLET.   It's none of your business.

OPHELIA.   Your mother's bedroom. How old are you?

HAMLET.   What's between me and my mother —

OPHELIA.   Is really nauseating, I know.

HAMLET.   *Get thee to a — !*

OPHELIA.   *(Suddenly pointing a remote control at the tv.)* Shut up. *(Hamlet's mouth continues to move, but we hear no sound. To the others.)* Isn't that nice? *(She turns up the sound again.)*

HAMLET.   ... just a horny little lady-in-waiting with ambitions above her — *(She turns the sound off. Hamlet's mouth keeps working. After a moment she turns the sound on again.)* ... don't think you went mad at all. You probably *tripped* into the river —

OPHELIA.   *(Turning the sound off again.)* I could do this all day. *(She turns the sound back up.)*

HAMLET.   Where did you get that?

OPHELIA.   In the cellar. Neat, eh?

HAMLET.   Laertes — take it away from her!

OPHELIA.   Don't worry. I won't abuse it. Go ahead, show me what you're doing here. I could use the laugh.

HAMLET.   Yes! Yes — good idea. Let's show her. *(Claudius, Gertrude and Laertes all groan tiredly.)*

LAERTES.   *Hamlet ...*

HAMLET.   *Do it! Now! (They reluctantly resume their positions. Ophelia looks on.)* All right! Kill him again!

CLAUDIUS.   My words fly up —

HAMLET.   Kill him! Keep stabbing! And mother — writhe! *(Laertes stabs Claudius over and over. Claudius doesn't fall, but groans mightily each time. Gertrude writhes demurely on the tapestry.)*

GERTRUDE.   Hamlet, I want you! God forgive me, I want you so!

HAMLET.   *Yes! Yes!! Yes!!! YES!! YES!!!! (A sudden darkness, followed by an explosion of light and smoke. Almost immediately lights rise again to reveal the same scene. Hamlet stands beside an empty tv. The others are surprised.)*

GERTRUDE.   Hamlet!

HAMLET.   *(Smiling.)* I thought that might do the trick.

LAERTES.   Well ... um, welcome back.

HAMLET.   Thanks. I'm sorry for some of the things I've made you all do, but I thought if I could just let myself go —

GERTRUDE.   We don't mind.

CLAUDIUS.   Whatever works for you.

HAMLET.   No hard feelings?

CLAUDIUS.   No, no, no.

LAERTES.   *(Simultaneously.)* No problem.

GERTRUDE.   *(Simultaneously.)* Not at all. (Hamlet looks at Ophelia.)*

HAMLET.   And you? *(Ophelia approaches Hamlet slowly, aiming the remote control at him. Suddenly she lets it fall to the floor and melts into a deep romantic kiss with him. Lights fade to black.)*

Scene 3

The throne room. Fortinbras sits despondently on his throne as Horatio reads from a parchment.

HORATIO. After the conquest of Carpathia, the combined Danish and Norwegian ... and Polish and Carpathian forces have successfully placed Transylvania, Anatolia and the Trans-Caucasus under your control. *(Fortinbras gives little groans at each new name.)* No hand has been raised in anger. No battles have been fought. In each case, the swelling hordes were welcomed as heroes of liberation, ushering in peace, prosperity, enlightenment — etc., etc. Shall I go on?

FORTINBRAS. No.

HORATIO. *(With a glance at the parchment.)* Apparently they are.

FORTINBRAS. What's happening, Horatio? What's happening to me?

HORATIO. You're winning.

FORTINBRAS. Why don't I feel like I'm winning?

HORATIO. I'm sure it's hard for you to know, without —

FORTINBRAS. Without what?

HORATIO. I was going to say, without speaking to my lord Hamlet.

FORTINBRAS. I won't talk to Hamlet! That's final!

HORATIO. But his *story* —

FORTINBRAS. It's too late for his story! We're committed now. Troops are in the field. Troops are in *all* the fields.

HORATIO. But he could teach you —

FORTINBRAS. This is no time for an education! I can't get caught up in ethics, for God's sake.

HORATIO. We're beyond ethics now. More in the realm of first causes, the nature of being, phenomenology, metaphysics —

FORTINBRAS. Don't talk metaphysics to me! I've been sleeping with a dead woman!

HORATIO. Pardon?

FORTINBRAS.   Ophelia. She's back. So are the rest of them. Hamlet's not the only ghost — they're all here. Especially Ophelia.

HORATIO.   You and Ophelia are — ? *(Fortinbras nods.)* And you won't even *talk* to Hamlet?

FORTINBRAS.   I suppose you think it's unnatural. Decadent. Perverted.

HORATIO.   It's ... out of the ordinary.

FORTINBRAS.   Well, it's over. I'm not seeing her anymore. Satisfied?

HORATIO.   I ... I don't —

FORTINBRAS.   She used to affect my judgment. I can see it now. I lost my edge.

HORATIO.   Speaking of judgments — you've condemned Osric.

FORTINBRAS.   I had to; he's a spy.

HORATIO.   But — not really.

FORTINBRAS.   What do you mean, not really? Didn't you read the proclamation?

HORATIO.   Yes, sire. But you know and I know —

FORTINBRAS.   Besides, I commuted his sentence.

HORATIO.   I don't think a commutation from being whipped to death to hanging is really —

FORTINBRAS.   You want me to be *more* merciful?

HORATIO.   I think you should release him.

FORTINBRAS.   Release him?! What did I send him to prison for?

HORATIO.   I don't know, my liege. Perhaps this ghost of Lady Ophelia you describe —

FORTINBRAS.   You're saying my political judgment's being influenced by a woman?

HORATIO.   You just said so yourself.

FORTINBRAS.   I did? Right — I did. Well, don't worry. I'm taking steps to correct the situation. I'm getting married.

HORATIO.   Married? To whom?

FORTINBRAS.   To one of those Polish girls, if I can find them again. They seem to have gotten misplaced. And if they're still alive. Otherwise the wedding's off.

HORATIO. In any case, I think you should release Osric. Clearly you condemned him at a time when you were ... were ...

FORTINBRAS. Crazy? Is that what you're trying to say?

HORATIO. Actually, I'm trying *not* to say it —

FORTINBRAS. Well, consider it said. After Hamlet, you must think every Prince is crazy, but it's not true. I can function. I can make calm, rational judgments. Just watch: A.) I'm releasing Osric —

HORATIO. Thank you, my sovereign!

FORTINBRAS. Probably too late for a Polish spy by now, anyway. We'll start looking for a spy from wherever the army is at the moment.

HORATIO. *(Consulting his parchment.)* Umm — Persia.

FORTINBRAS. Persia?! Fine. B.) I'm ordering the army home again, not that they'll listen. And C.) I'm going to marry a living Polish woman as soon as possible in order to be no longer distracted by a ghost who was admittedly magnificent in bed.

HORATIO. This is very kingly.

FORTINBRAS. Thought you'd like that. It's not so hard to be regal. I could do it all the time, if I liked. So, go! Send word to the army!

HORATIO. Yes, sire! *(Horatio starts out, stops.)* Sire, this is not only kingly of you. It's very ... educated.

FORTINBRAS. *(Complemented.)* Yeah? Thanks. *(Horatio exits. The Captain rushes in, goes to one knee.)*

CAPTAIN. My liege.

FORTINBRAS. What is it?

CAPTAIN. There's been an explosion in the Queen's quarters.

FORTINBRAS. Explosion? Was anyone hurt?

CAPTAIN. No one was found at all. Only a strange sort of ... box.

FORTINBRAS. Box? *(Gesturing.)* Was it about ... this big?

CAPTAIN. Yes, my liege.

FORTINBRAS. And it was empty?

CAPTAIN. Quite empty.

FORTINBRAS. Oh, *great*. Hamlet's out!

CAPTAIN. My liege?

FORTINBRAS. Oh, nothing. Have you found the two Polish maidens?

CAPTAIN. Not yet, sire.

FORTINBRAS. Find them! I'm in constant danger until I marry one of them. Oh — and I almost forgot — release Osric from his suffering. At once!

CAPTAIN. Release — ? My liege! *(The Captain exits.)*

FORTINBRAS. I'm feeling a little better already. It's good to put some discipline into your life. If I can just get the army to tone it down.... But I'm more in control. More than ever. Horatio's right. There *is* something educated about not executing innocent people. It's not as workable, but it's ... more relaxed. Not to mention controlling your urges to sleep with the dead. Polonius was *really* right about that. *(With sudden, panicky fury.) Where are those Polish maidens?!! I can't wait forever!! (Regaining an intense calm.)* I have total control. Nothing bothers me. Not even Hamlet. Oh, I know the whispers'll start, now that he's out of that box. "Hamlet would've been a better king. Hamlet would've known what to do. Hamlet had more depth." *(Shouting, as before.) Well, Hamlet's dead, if anybody hasn't noticed!! Hamlet's dead and I'm alive — there's a big difference!! (Quieter.)* I wonder where he is? He could be anywhere. He could be here. Is that it? Are you here, watching me? Laughing at my mistakes? What if you are? Kings don't make mistakes, anyway. They reassess policies. *(A sudden realization.)* What if he's not here at all? What if he's promulgating his story? All over the castle? What if he's telling the truth, and people are ... *believing* it? No, no — stop. Just stop! Get hold of yourself. It's what the King says that matters. Just keep the story *straight*. A spy — of indeterminate nationality. A plot, mass-regicide, sacred ground. It's the only logical story. The only ... logical ... *(Unable to help himself, shouting running out of the room.)* Hamlet! *Hamlet!! (He exits. Lights fade to black.)*

Scene 4

The battlements. Hamlet and Ophelia sit together staring out over the landscape. She leans against him. They are holding hands. Behind them, at a distance, are Marcellus and Barnardo, quietly watching the two ghosts.

OPHELIA. Things seem so simple suddenly. Why do you think we had so much trouble before?

HAMLET. Who knows? We were just a pair of kids. Who had the perspective? *(She sighs, resting her head on his shoulder. He looks at Marcellus and Barnardo.)* Why are Marcellus and Barnardo over there?

OPHELIA. Fortinbras is trying to avoid me. He's assigned them to keep watch whenever I appear.

HAMLET. Oh. *(Marcellus and Barnardo smile.)*

OPHELIA. We could've been so happy. Married, children — waiting for Claudius and Gertrude to die.

HAMLET. Yeah, it sounds good, doesn't it? Well, it can't always work out, trying to make the best decision in life.

OPHELIA. You didn't make any. *(Hamlet looks at her.)* Hardly any. You finally managed to kill Claudius, but you had to clean out the whole castle to do it.

HAMLET. If by that you mean I was careful to examine all the moral ramifications of an act of personal revenge —

OPHELIA. I mean you stalled around, and acted like a lunatic, and generally let things get worse and worse, that's all. And you killed my father.

HAMLET. That was an accident.

OPHELIA. And my brother.

HAMLET. He killed me.

OPHELIA. Anyway, all I'm saying is, you took an awfully long time to do a very simple thing. Badly.

HAMLET. *(Starting to leave.)* If that's how you feel about it —

OPHELIA. No, no, no — oh, Hamlet, no! I didn't mean it! Hold me, please just hold —

HAMLET. *(Simultaneously, falling into an embrace with her.)*

145

Ophelia — !

OPHELIA. We've been through so much together; we can't fight anymore, we can't!

HAMLET. You're right!

OPHELIA. Say that again. Please?

HAMLET. Ophelia, you're right.

OPHELIA. *(With a sigh of pleasure.)* Oh! *(They kiss. Marcellus and Barnardo look on attentively. When the kiss ends, Hamlet looks at them. They avert their gaze. Ophelia and Hamlet stare off over the fields.)*

HAMLET. You know, it all began right here.

OPHELIA. What?

HAMLET. My father's ghost. This is where I saw him — promenading through the air at midnight, just beyond this wall.

OPHELIA. We could do that; would you like to?

HAMLET. No, that's all right. It makes me think about everything that's happened. I can hardly wait till Horatio convinces Fortinbras to let the real story come out.

OPHELIA. You ... think he will?

HAMLET. Of course. Inevitably. The truth will out.

OPHELIA. But would that really be good?

HAMLET. What do you mean? Of course — why wouldn't it be?

OPHELIA. I don't come off particularly well in the real story. I mean, I tend to look sort of like ... an idiot.

HAMLET. I was cruel, I admit. But —

OPHELIA. Does it really matter what people think?

HAMLET. Of course it matters. What do you think we all suffered and died for?

OPHELIA. Nothing, in my case. Please, Hamlet — let things stay as they are. We have each other, at last. We can be content with that.

HAMLET. Maybe you can, but ... not me.

OPHELIA. Hamlet — ! I can't believe you won't do this one little thing for me.

HAMLET. Little?! My whole reputation? My *story?* The mark I made in the world. The great lesson I have to teach.

OPHELIA.   What? Stab quicker?

HAMLET.   I might have expected you not to understand.

OPHELIA.   Because I'm a girl — right. You haven't changed a bit! I'm going back to Fortinbras.

HAMLET.   You don't love me at all, do you? This has simply been a contemptible ruse. You're trying to use me.

OPHELIA.   Oh, *there's* a shock! One of us trying to use the other. I wonder if that's ever happened before?

HAMLET.   The story will be told!

OPHELIA.   From whose point of view? Yours? Mr. Hamlet It's-All-About-Me the Dane? Oh, sure — your point of view is clearly the most rewarding, the most complex. No wonder it has a special right to exist.

HAMLET.   Ophelia —

OPHELIA.   *I will not ... be ... marginal!*

HAMLET.   I thought by now you'd understand. I thought when you committed suicide —

OPHELIA.   I didn't commit suicide, I was pushed!

HAMLET.   By whom?

OPHELIA.   By your mother.

HAMLET.   That's a disgraceful lie!

OPHELIA.   *Were you there?!* If Fortinbras can tell a new story, so can I. *(Fortinbras rushes in, stopping short when he sees Ophelia.)*

FORTINBRAS.   *Ophelia!!*

OPHELIA.   Fortinbras?!

FORTINBRAS.   I'll ... come back later.

OPHELIA.   No — *wait!* I haven't said hello yet. *(Clearly for Hamlet's benefit, Ophelia gives Fortinbras a very memorable kiss. Hamlet pulls out a dagger and moves to strike Fortinbras with it in the back. Barnardo and Marcellus stare horrified. But Hamlet can't bring himself to strike the blow, and instead stalks out of the room. Fortinbras breaks the kiss.)*

FORTINBRAS.   No ... no ... I — thank you, but — actually I just came to make sure that Hamlet's been behaving. You know — about everything.

OPHELIA.   He's not.

FORTINBRAS.   He's not? Oh. Well ... maybe I'd better go

find him, then. And about the kissing — I can't actually, any-more, because I'm about to get married.

OPHELIA. To whom?

FORTINBRAS. Uh ... someone Polish. I'll just be on my way now, ok? So ... 'bye. *(He starts out.)*

OPHELIA. *Wait right there! (Fortinbras stops.)* Are you saying my kiss doesn't do anything for you?

FORTINBRAS. Of course. It does too much! That's the whole problem.

OPHELIA. I'll tell you what the problem is. The problem is you and Hamlet. Sure, Ophelia's fine for a good time now and then, but the minute you have another priority, Ophelia goes right out the window!

FORTINBRAS. No, you don't...!

OPHELIA. Listen to me — don't get married!

FORTINBRAS. I have to.

OPHELIA. If you love me, you won't!

FORTINBRAS. *(Torn, but resolute.)* I'm sorry.

OPHELIA. *(Storming out.) Oh — why can't someone just kiss me and do what I want?!!!*

FORTINBRAS. *(With a look at Marcellus and Barnardo.)* You guys are a *great* help! *(He exits. Lights fade to black.)*

Scene 5

A hall in the castle. Claudius and Gertrude are on their knees praying silently, heads bowed, with the two Maidens. Fortinbras hurries in, looking behind him and muttering. Neither he nor the four praying notice each other at first.

FORTINBRAS. *(To himself.)* She had no right to yell at me. No right at all. I am through with ghosts forever, and that's — ! *(Fortinbras falls over Claudius.)* Agh!

MAIDENS. Oh!!

GERTRUDE. Your majesty — !

CLAUDIUS. *(Helping him up.)* Are you all right? I'm heartily sorry!

FORTINBRAS. *(Slapping his hand away.)* I'm fine! I'm fine! Leave me alone! *(With surprise.)* The maidens!!!

GERTRUDE. We asked them to pray with us.

CLAUDIUS. They seemed to need it.

FORTINBRAS. You let them see you? You could've terrorized them!

GERTRUDE. They don't know who we are.

CLAUDIUS. They don't even know we're dead.

FORTINBRAS. And no one's going to tell them! Get out!

GERTRUDE. Again?

FORTINBRAS. I have things to do!

CLAUDIUS. There's something you should know about these maidens —

FORTINBRAS. I know what I need to know. Go!

CLAUDIUS. You'll be surprised —

FORTINBRAS. Out! *(Gertrude and Claudius exit — separately. To the Maidens.)* So. Praying. That's lovely. That's very ... maidenlike. *(Suddenly remembering.)* Why am I talking to you? You don't speak a word.

1st MAIDEN. *(With a strong accent.)* You ... want it bad?

FORTINBRAS. What?

2nd MAIDEN. *(With an accent.)* Hot time ... my stud?

FORTINBRAS. How do you...? How can you...?

1st MAIDEN. I give you good gallop.

2nd MAIDEN. I can be naked in one minute.

FORTINBRAS. Who taught you to say this?

1st MAIDEN. I love a good soldier.

2nd MAIDEN. Let's do it on the horse!

FORTINBRAS. My *palace guard* — ?! Do you even know what you're saying?

1st MAIDEN. *(Kneeling, kissing his hand chastely.)* Give it to me hot and heavy.

FORTINBRAS. Those — ! I'll have them *whipped! (The Maidens look anxious, confused.)* Not you! Listen — I need you for something honorable. I need you to marry me. *(They don't understand.)* To marry? Understand? *(He mimes putting a wedding ring on and off his finger. They confuse this with a graphic gesture.)*

149

MAIDENS.   *(Shocked.) Oh — !*
FORTINBRAS.   No — a *wife!* To take my mind off — I can't go into it right now. *(Grabbing the 2nd Maiden, placing her at his side, putting his arm through hers.)* Husband? Wife? Understand?
2nd MAIDEN.   Have you ever seen such a big one?
FORTINBRAS.   *Damn it!* It doesn't matter. I'm the King, and I can do what I want. I can even marry myself. Now — which one of you? Who cares, as long as you're not Ophelia. *(He clasps the 2nd Maiden a bit tighter. To the 1st Maiden.)* You can be the witness.
1st MAIDEN.   Do you want me to watch?
FORTINBRAS.   Right! *(To the 2nd Maiden.)* Do you, um ... before God and everybody, um ... take me for your lord and master and husband? Say "I do." *(She stares at him blankly.)* "I — do." Say it: "I — do."
2nd MAIDEN.   *(Recognizing the phrase.) Ah!* I do it on the floor with you.
FORTINBRAS.   No —
1st MAIDEN.   I do it with everybody!
FORTINBRAS.   No, not you! Don't answer.
2nd MAIDEN.   I do whatever you say.
FORTINBRAS.   Close enough! Good! And I, King Fortinbras of Denmark — and apparently several other places — take you for my wife, and promise to, um ... do a lot of things for you when I have time. All right? We're married.
1st MAIDEN.   I will tickle you all night.
FORTINBRAS.   No, no — you're not my wife. She is. I'm making a few changes, ok? One wife at a time. It's not you — you're lovely. It's just these damned ghosts.
HAMLET.   *(Appearing behind them, carrying a book.)* We're not damned. We're not anything. *(They turn. All three see Hamlet.)*
FORTINBRAS.   What do you want?!
HAMLET.   Nothing. Just ... catching up on a little reading. *(The Maidens find Hamlet very impressive.)*
MAIDENS.   Ooo!
FORTINBRAS.   Hey — how come they can see you?
HAMLET.   It seems to be getting harder for us to turn it on and off.

FORTINBRAS. *(As the Maidens gravitate unavoidably to Hamlet.)* Well, try!

HAMLET. I'm trying. *(This only impresses them more.)*

MAIDENS. *Ooooo!*

FORTINBRAS. I'm *married* to one of them!

HAMLET. Really? Which one?

FORTINBRAS. Um ... her.

HAMLET. What's her name?

FORTINBRAS. It doesn't matter! Keep your hands off! *(Moving the Maidens away.)* What is it with you ghosts? Do you have a special musk, or what?

HAMLET. *(To the Maidens, in Polish.)* I wish you both could stay.

MAIDENS. *Ooooh!!!*

FORTINBRAS. Stop it! Stop it! Don't tell me you speak Polish — !

HAMLET. I picked up a little at Wittenberg. *(To the Maidens, in Polish.)* Would you like to take a stroll?

1st MAIDEN. *(In Polish.)* I'd love to!

2nd MAIDEN. *(In Polish.)* Me too! *(Hamlet starts to escort them out.)*

FORTINBRAS. *(Pulling them back, away from him.)* Stop it! Get back here! Now! Right now!

MAIDENS. *(Disappointedly.)* Oooo...!

FORTINBRAS. Why don't you wait for me in the King's chambers? I'll be right there. *(The Maidens look blank.)* The King's chambers. The bedroom — where I go to sleep? *(Making a sleeping gesture.)* Sleep? Sleep? To sleep, perchance to — *(Fortinbras stops. A cold shiver goes through him. The Maidens stare at him concernedly.)* Get out! Get out! *Go on! (Frightened by his tone, the Maidens rush off.)* What's happening to me?

HAMLET. Could be a lot of things. The northerly climate, the disorder of the world, the elusiveness of your opponent.

FORTINBRAS. Which is?

HAMLET. Which is death.

FORTINBRAS. Polonius said I was in love with death.

HAMLET. He's entitled to his opinion. I never found him that well-read, myself. You seem awfully tense.

FORTINBRAS.   Well, why not? I finally get my kingdom, and I can't even rule it, it's so plagued with ghosts.

HAMLET.   I suspect it's pretty much like any kingdom — only here, we're more visible. When I was locked up in that box, I saw countless ghosts. All around me. Speaking innumerable languages. Dressed in fashions I'd never seen. Crowds of them. Multitudes.

FORTINBRAS.   What is wrong with my army?

HAMLET.   I'd only be guessing. I was never that much of a soldier. I spent most of my time at court, wondering what was wrong here. Maybe if you told my story.

FORTINBRAS.   That story Horatio told me? With all the ridiculous — ?

HAMLET.   It's true.

FORTINBRAS.   It is? Even about the pirates? *(Hamlet nods.)* It doesn't matter. It's not what the people want to hear.

HAMLET.   How do you know, unless you try?

FORTINBRAS.   What do you care, anyway? You're dead.

HAMLET.   If you pass through a desert, wandering, lost, you might leave a little cairn of stones. No one will ever find it. You yourself will die miles away, your body will disappear. Even the cairn will be buried, in time, by the sand. But somehow you want it to be there, the little mark, deep in the enormous heart of that wasteland. It may never be found, but it exists. Because you existed. That is how the truth works. *(Offering Fortinbras the book, which has no title on the cover.)* Hey, this is good — you want to read it?

FORTINBRAS.   Not at the moment.

HAMLET.   Well ... keep it anyway. Never know when the mood will strike. *(Hamlet hands Fortinbras the book. Fortinbras doesn't open it. Hamlet exits. Fortinbras looks at the book, opens it. He casually flips through a few pages, then something catches his eye. He starts reading more closely. He exits as he reads. Lights fade to black.)*

Scene 6

The courtyard. We see a man's legs dangling lifelessly at least ten feet above the ground. No more than the legs are visible. Horatio strides across the courtyard hurriedly. He doesn't see the legs. Horatio calls out loudly.

HORATIO.   Captain! Come here! *(The Captain appears.)* I've sent the King's message to our forces in the field. Tell me, has Osric been released?

CAPTAIN.   Released?

HORATIO.   Yes, released!

CAPTAIN.   From his suffering, you mean?

HORATIO.   Exactly.

CAPTAIN.   Oh. Absolutely. He's been released, all right. *(The Captain exits with a sidelong look at the legs. Horatio doesn't catch this. Instead, he breathes a great sigh of relief. He bends at the waist, letting his arms dangle. He straightens up, continuing this relaxing regimen into a stretch of his arms high above his head — at which point he sees the legs for the first time. He falls to the ground, shocked.)*

HORATIO.   My God! Osric! How could he?! How — !? You were innocent!! *You were innocent! (Osric enters from upstage.)*

OSRIC.   Relax. It wasn't anyone's fault. The Captain misunderstood.

HORATIO.   Osric! But ... aren't you...!?

OSRIC.   Yes. Very. "Release Osric from his suffering." That's how he put it. A rhetorical disaster.

HORATIO.   Then ... you're a — ?

OSRIC.   What else is new? There's more of us than you by now. You can't float down a corridor without bumping into two or three of us.

HORATIO.   How does it ... how does it feel?

OSRIC.   Oh, don't be a tourist. You'll find out soon enough. We all do.

HORATIO.   Can't you tell me anything?

OSRIC.   Only this: whatever you're doing to prepare for it,

153

don't bother.

HORATIO. Why have you come back?

OSRIC. Come back? I never left. Look at me — I was just hanged. *(They stare up at the lifeless legs.)* Don't know where I'm supposed to go. Just the same old faces, the same old walls. The only thing different is the way I feel.

HORATIO. What do you mean?

OSRIC. Suddenly I don't feel like pleasing everyone. I used to get so much satisfaction out of being of service. Now, I ... rather resent things.

HORATIO. You have reason.

OSRIC. Oh, drop that eternally earnest tone, will you?! *(Catching himself.)* There — you see? Resentment. Criticism. I don't know what's wrong with me. I should be looking for somebody to toady up to. Instead, I'm being ... abrasive.

HORATIO. I'm sure it's in the service of some higher end.

OSRIC. I don't think so. To be honest, I feel sort of ... on my own. *(Looking up at the legs again.)* It's not how I thought it would be. Then again, I'm not sure I ever thought of how it would be. Maybe it's different for everyone. Millions of different deaths. Just as there are millions of different lives. *(Turning suddenly to Horatio.)* Did that sound philosophical?

HORATIO. A little.

OSRIC. I've never been philosophical. *(Osric looks at the legs once more, then exits thoughtfully. Horatio stares after him. Suddenly Horatio draws his dagger and rushes out a different way.)*

HORATIO. Fortinbras! Fortinbras!! *(Lights fade.)*

Scene 7

The King's chamber. The two Maidens are sitting in Fortinbras's bed, much as in Act One, Scene 4. Fortinbras enters, reading the book. He's startled to see the Maidens.

FORTINBRAS. Oh! Yes ... you're here. The consummation! I completely forgot. *(The Maidens watch him a bit warily. The 1st*

154

Maiden puts her arm in front of the 2nd Maiden protectively.)
1st MAIDEN.   Bring on the regiment!
FORTINBRAS.   No, no — let's not talk. Shh, please? It's better if you don't ... talk. In fact ... *(Delicately taking the 1st Maiden by the hand and guiding her from the bed.)* It's better if you aren't in the bed at all.
1st MAIDEN.   *(Disappointedly.)* Oooo....
FORTINBRAS.   *(To the 1st Maiden.)* I'm afraid you'll have to wait out in the hall. *(The Maidens look at each other, worried about being separated.)*
1st MAIDEN.   *(Anxiously.)* Oooo...!
FORTINBRAS.   It's just for the night —
2nd MAIDEN.   Ooooo...!
FORTINBRAS.   *(To 2nd Maiden.)* Now, don't you start — !
MAIDENS.   *Ooooooo...!!!* *(The 1st Maiden slips out of his grasp and hurries back to the bed. Fortinbras sighs.)*
FORTINBRAS.   Ok. Ok. Why should anything be easy? *(Escorting the 1st Maiden out of the bed once more and towards a place to sit.)* You sit here. All right? And look the other way. Just ... the other way. *(As she does so.)* Good. Good enough. So, um ... wife — having exchanged our vows, pretty much — it's time that we ... um ... *(He sighs hopelessly, gets on the bed. He stares at her a moment, then raises the book that's still in his hand.)* Do you mind if I read a book? I know it may seem like an odd request, but actually I've gotten kind of ... involved ... *(He becomes engrossed in the book. She looks along with him.)* I feel so many things when I read it. Sensations. It's like I'm on the battlefield again. I can almost hear the sounds. You know, the way the men sound ... when they die. I wonder if this is what Horatio meant by an education. *(With a quick look to her.)* It's not about my battles — don't misunderstand. *(Thoughtfully.)* It's not really about me at all. *(The 2nd Maiden gently places her hand on his, stops him turning the pages. He stares at her. She hugs him comfortingly. At first he can't respond. Then he suddenly takes her in his arms and holds her tightly — almost desperately. Claudius and Gertrude enter. They rush to the bed. The Maidens can see them just fine.)*
CLAUDIUS.   It's true!

FORTINBRAS.   What — ?!

GERTRUDE.   Ophelia said you were getting married.

FORTINBRAS.   What are you doing here?!

GERTRUDE.   We've come to bless your union.

CLAUDIUS.   Is this the consummation? We didn't want to be late. *(To Gertrude, of the bride.)* Isn't she lovely as a bride?

FORTINBRAS.   Please — *go!*

CLAUDIUS.   *(To the 1st Maiden.)* You're lovely, too. I hope I won't feel lust.

GERTRUDE.   Don't speak of lust.

CLAUDIUS.   How can I avoid it?

GERTRUDE.   Think of the remorse!

FORTINBRAS.   Get out of here! *Now!*

CLAUDIUS.   We can't.

GERTRUDE.   We're still in sacred ground.

CLAUDIUS.   Please, unbury us. Hurry!

FORTINBRAS.   Have you no sense of decorum? This is is my wedding night.

CLAUDIUS.   We're heartily sorry, but we have no choice.

GERTRUDE.   You must do it now — or you'll run out of time!

FORTINBRAS.   *(Struck by her comment.)* What?!

CLAUDIUS.   ... In your busy day.

FORTINBRAS.   What's going on here?

GERTRUDE.   Nothing.

CLAUDIUS.   A minor disinterment — that's all we ask.

FORTINBRAS.   *No!* Leave us! *(Claudius and Gertrude look at each other, then suddenly make a gesture. Instantly, the two Maidens can't see them. The Maidens look confused, fearful.)*

MAIDENS.   Ooooooo...??! *(Gertrude and Claudius make another gesture.)*

CLAUDIUS.   Hello again. *(The Maidens see them again.)*

MAIDENS.   *Ooooooooo....!!!* *(The Maidens run from the room.)*

FORTINBRAS.   I don't care how many maidens you scare away. I *won't* dig you up — understand?!

CLAUDIUS.   Please.

GERTRUDE.   Oh, please.

CLAUDIUS.   *Please.*

FORTINBRAS.   Get out! *Get out, get out, get out, get out!!* *(Fortinbras closes his eyes as he pleads. During his speech, Hamlet, Ophelia, Polonius and Laertes enter to join the others around the bed.)* Just *go!* All of you — every ghost! I can't fight you anymore! What do you want from me? I know I didn't tell the truth, but who ever does?! Why won't you *depart!*? Why won't you let me be ... alive?! *(Fortinbras opens his eyes, sees them all.)*
LAERTES.   We can't go.
POLONIUS.   We need to be near you.
HAMLET.   At least, in spirit.
FORTINBRAS.   Ophelia — please! Get them to leave!
OPHELIA.   Oh — now you want a favor? Tell me, how's the consummation going?
FORTINBRAS.   Slow. Please, Ophelia. I'll do anything. I'm sorry I wanted to get married. I just thought you and Hamlet would be so much better suited —
OPHELIA.   I admit, he had me charmed for awhile. There's something about all that negativity. But I'm over it now. And I'm willing to forgive you. *If* you swear never to tell Hamlet's story.
CLAUDIUS.   He'll tell it.
LAERTES.   He must.
HAMLET.   All will come out.
OPHELIA.   *(To the ghosts.)* No, it won't! Why should it? Do you want to be remembered as a bunch of murderers, lechers, liars and fools?
POLONIUS.   If we must.
GERTRUDE.   It's our choice.
OPHELIA.   *It's not mine!* You were worse than me — all of you!
HAMLET.   We admit that.
OPHELIA.   Not enough! *(Quietly.)* Never enough.
CLAUDIUS.   It's over now.
GERTRUDE.   The time's up.
OPHELIA.   There's always time!
POLONIUS.   Not anymore.
FORTINBRAS.   What are you talking about?
POLONIUS.   Rest well, Fortinbras.

GERTRUDE. Rest well.

HAMLET. Rest, my friend.

LAERTES. Rest. *(The other ghosts all look at Ophelia expectantly. She fights having to join this chorus, but something inside her is defeated, and she does so through clenched teeth.)*

OPHELIA. *Rest, damn it!* (All the ghosts make the gesture Claudius and Gertrude made earlier in the scene. Now Fortinbras can't see them. He searches frantically as they all exit. He has the book.)*

FORTINBRAS. Where are you? Where *are* you!? What's going on? *What's going on!?* (Horatio rushes in, his dagger ready.)* Horatio?!

HORATIO. You villain! Osric is hanged!

FORTINBRAS. Hanged? That's ridiculous — I freed him.

HORATIO. He's hanging in the courtyard. Look for yourself! *(Fortinbras peers out a window. His eyes widen.)*

FORTINBRAS. It's a mistake. My Captain must've —

HORATIO. You killed him!

FORTINBRAS. I didn't mean to —

HORATIO. Prepare to die!

FORTINBRAS. To die!? What are you — !

HORATIO. *Someone, somewhere* is going to die for what they've done! Efficiently! At the appropriate time!

FORTINBRAS. Just because I killed Osric? By mistake?

HORATIO. Because someone's dead, and you're responsible. If my lord Hamlet had done what I'm about to do — *(He thrusts the dagger at Fortinbras, who dodges and tumbles over the bed.)*

FORTINBRAS. *Horatio — !*

HORATIO. Take death like a man!

FORTINBRAS. *You* take death like a man! *(Horatio thrusts again, misses.)* Horatio ... Horatio — ! I'll tell the truth! Hamlet's true story!! I was going to do it anyway! I'll tell the truth!!

HORATIO. *I'm sick of the truth!!* You know how many people I've tried to tell that story? You know how far I get?! Right up to the part where Hamlet walked *directly past Claudius* at prayer and didn't kill him! *(Missing again.)* I try to explain the religious underpinnings of his decision, the whole problem of

letting Claudius die shriven of his sins —
FORTINBRAS.   Of course —
HORATIO.   You think anyone believes me!? *(Fortinbras knocks the dagger from Horatio's hand and bolts. Horatio grabs him and pulls him back. Both men simultaneously reach for the foils on the wall. They fight briefly, Horatio nearly running Fortinbras through at one point.)*
FORTINBRAS.   Careful — ! *(Fortinbras trips and his foil goes flying. He scrabbles to his feet and Horatio stalks him.)* Horatio —
HORATIO.   "Would've killed him," they say! "The Hamlet we knew would've killed Claudius then and there! *Any* man would!!" *(Fortinbras makes a move for his sword, but Horatio grabs him and pushes him back on the bed, sword at his breast.)* You see?! They understand Elsinore better than we do! They know that here there's only one chance — one *split-second* — to take revenge! *If that!!*
FORTINBRAS.   Someone save me!! Ophelia! *OPHELIA!!!* *(Horatio pulls back to strike the death blow.)* NO!!!! *(Swift blackout.)*

Scene 8

The battlements. Fortinbras stands looking through a telescope. Arrayed behind him are Osric, Claudius and Gertrude with the same pile of regal objects. Ophelia and Laertes stand over to one side, Hamlet to the other. Polonius stands next to Fortinbras.

OSRIC.   *(As Gertrude and Claudius raise up the tapestry from the pile.)* What about this, Fortinbras?
FORTINBRAS.   Throw it in the moat.
GERTRUDE.   In the moat?
CLAUDIUS.   Are you sure?
FORTINBRAS.   *In the moat. (Looking through the telescope again, as the arras is thrown into the moat.)* Where's the army? They should be back by now.
POLONIUS.   It's a long and uncertain road. You've learned

that.

OPHELIA. *(Exasperatedly, to Polonius.)* Oh, please.

OSRIC. *(Holding up the chalice.)* Chalice?

FORTINBRAS. Moat.

OSRIC. Prayer bench?

FORTINBRAS. Moat.

CLAUDIUS. Moat?

OPHELIA. *(As these are thrown in.)* Why not toss it all in the moat?

FORTINBRAS. I intend to.

OPHELIA. And just how do you plan to revenge yourself on the living, if you leave them no reminders?

FORTINBRAS. I don't.

OPHELIA. But you were murdered.

FORTINBRAS. Not everything can work out. Oh, and thanks, everyone, for that great warning about my imminent death.

LAERTES. We gave you hints.

FORTINBRAS. Hints? "Rest well, Fortinbras"? It was bedtime! *(Looking through his telescope again.)* Why don't I know where my army is?! *(Horatio enters with a parchment.)*

HORATIO. I know where it is.

FORTINBRAS. You do? Excellent. Where?

HORATIO. *(Unrolling the parchment, reading.)* "A Summary of the Latest Events. The combined Danish-Norwegian-Polish-Carpathian-Transylvanian-Anatolian-Trans Caucasian-Persian-Afghan and Baluchistani forces under the supreme command of Fortinbras have reached the banks of the Indus River."

FORTINBRAS. So that's where they are.

HORATIO. "There they stood for a long time, staring across into that profound and endless universe of mysteries known as India."

FORTINBRAS. I distinctly told them to turn around.

HORATIO. "Poised for the final, inevitable conquest this proud array of forces, such as the world has never seen — the army of Fortinbras — "

OPHELIA. Get to the point.

HORATIO. "Laid down their arms — "

160

FORTINBRAS. And started home?

HORATIO. "And walked into the roiling Indus River, and drowned."

FORTINBRAS. Drowned?

HORATIO. To a man.

FORTINBRAS. To a man? *(Horatio nods, reads on.)*

HORATIO. There's one more item. "Horatio, having failed one prince and murdered another, today took his own life, in the Roman fashion. He can now — at last — be counted in the ranks of the dead. A distinction he holds in common with practically everyone he knew. Certainly everyone he cared about." *(Horatio looks first at Hamlet, then at Fortinbras, then reads on.)* "No one can fully explain the recent spate of untimely death within the walls of Elsinore — a seat of power and enlightenment once widely envied. Some have put forth the theory that death somehow became the fashion at court for a short time. Others think that a spiral of revenge more vicious and personal than ever before seen reigned here briefly. Still others think that the dead, having discovered that there is no final judgment, and sensing that they would soon dissipate into nothingness, forever — occupied themselves with the torture of the living. This manner of amusement sufficed only until so many had died that there was, in fact, no one worth taking revenge on any longer." *(Horatio rolls up the parchment, hands it to Osric.)* For the moat. *(Gently taking the telescope from Fortinbras.)* This too. *(Looking out over the battlement.)* When I first rode toward Elsinore, I thought, "What magnificence. How bright the future must be, if men have progressed so far as to build this." *(Horatio exits.)*

FORTINBRAS. *(To Polonius.)* Was Horatio right about the army? *(Polonius starts to answer, decides against it, touches Fortinbras gently on the cheek, exits. To Hamlet.)* Was he? *(Ophelia moves to Fortinbras.)*

OPHELIA. Why should you care? You're dead.

FORTINBRAS. I was responsible. My whole army.

OPHELIA. Oh, lighten up. Just means they'll get back here that much faster. Place is really going to be crowded.

FORTINBRAS. We're going to disappear forever.

OPHELIA.   *Will you stop talking like that!!?* Maybe those of you who had lives will disappear, since you don't need afterlives. But ... people like me —

LAERTES.   *(Moving to Ophelia.)* Come on, Sis.

OPHELIA.   *People like me ... ! (She can't finish.)*

LAERTES.   Let's take a walk.

OPHELIA.   With you? You can't even believe you're dead yet.

LAERTES.   It's sinking in. *(Laertes escorts her out. Gertrude picks up the bouquet of dead flowers and drops them into the moat. She and Claudius exit as well.)*

FORTINBRAS.   I'm sorry I killed you, Osric.

OSRIC.   You ought to be. It was a dreadful mistake.

FORTINBRAS.   Can you forgive me?

OSRIC.   *(Making the bold choice.)* No. *(Osric smiles, pleased with himself, and exits. Fortinbras and Hamlet are alone. Hamlet bends down and picks up the only remaining object: the book.)*

HAMLET.   For the moat? *(A beat. Hamlet moves towards the moat.)*

FORTINBRAS.   No! Um ...

HAMLET.   Yes?

FORTINBRAS.   I ... can't decide.

HAMLET.   Well, when you read it, how did you like it?

FORTINBRAS.   I was ... captivated. Is that the right word?

HAMLET.   Yes. *(With a look around.)* They'll tell a story about this place, no matter what we do. It could still be this one. *(Fortinbras hesitates, then reaches for the book. Hamlet hands it to him. Fortinbras holds it a moment, takes in the view one last time, then sets the book down on the battlement. The two men exit together, smiling. After a moment, Marcellus and Barnardo enter quickly — each of them arm in arm with one of the Maidens. They stare out over the battlement.)*

MARCELLUS.   *(Pointing.)* There! There's where we saw it!

1st MAIDEN.   *(Not understanding, but catching his mood.)* Oooo!

BARNARDO.   The ghost of Hamlet's father!

2nd MAIDEN.   Ooooo.

MARCELLUS.   *(Picking up the book.)* What's this?

BARNARDO.   I don't know. *(Barnardo prepares to throw it over the battlement. The Maidens quickly reach for it.)*

MAIDENS. *Ooooooo* — *!*

BARNARDO. You want it? *(The Maidens nod. The 2nd Maiden opens the book, turns to a page at random. She starts to sound out the words with her usual strong accent.)*

2nd MAIDEN. "For in ... For in dat —

MARCELLUS. *(Looking over her shoulder.)* That.

2nd MAIDEN. "That ... Sleep? Sleep of ... "

BARNARDO. Death.

2nd MAIDEN. "Death. For in that sleep of death, what ... um — "

MARCELLUS. Dreams may come.

2nd MAIDEN. "Dreams".

1st MAIDEN. *(Also starting to read.)* "Venn ve haf ... haf —"

BARNARDO. "When. When we have shuffled off — "

1st MAIDEN. *(Eager to continue by herself.)* "Shuffled off ... dis ... mortal ... um —"

2nd MAIDEN. "Mortal ... ?"

MARCELLUS. "Coil."

MAIDENS. *(Together, nodding and smiling with accomplishment.)* *Ah!* "Coil."

MARCELLUS. That's right — coil. *(The Maidens beam at their book. Barnardo looks uncertainly at Marcellus.)*

BARNARDO. Coil? *(Marcellus shrugs. The Maidens look at the book. The men too are drawn back to its pages. Lights fade to black.)*

THE END

LAKE STREET EXTENSION

To Jeanne Blake

Lake Street Extension was produced by Ensemble Theatre of Cincinnati (David A. White III, Artistic Director), in Cincinnati, Ohio, on May 13, 1992. It was directed by Jeanne Blake; the set design was by Michael J. Blankenship; the costume design was by Gretchen H. Sears; the lighting design was by Jeff Gress; and the stage manager was Terri L. Wilson. The cast was as follows:

FULLER . . . . Gordon C. Greene

TRACE . . . . Keith A. Brush

GREGORIO . . . . Enrique Munoz

Lake Street Extension was produced by Signature Theatre Company (James Houghton, Artistic Director; Thomas C. Proehl, Managing Director), in New York City, on November 27, 1992. It was directed by Jeanne Blake; the set design was by E. David Cosier; the costume design was by Teresa Snider-Stein; the lighting design was by Jeffrey S. Koger; and the production stage manager was Dean Gray. The cast was as follows:

FULLER . . . . Joe Sharkey

TRACE . . . . Keith A. Brush

GREGORIO . . . . Rick Telles

CHARACTERS

FULLER, 50, recovering, religious
TRACE, 19, thin, dangerous
GREGORIO, mid 20s, illegal

TIME

1982 and 1992

PLACE

A basement room in a northern city

SCENE ONE

FULLER

*The room is nearly bare. There's a twin bed covered with a
fitted sheet and a pillow. On the pillowcase is a large picture of a cartoon duck. Fuller enters. He looks at the bed for
a moment. As he speaks, he moves slowly around the room.
He runs his hand over the bed, then over what seem to be
other pieces of furniture, though none are there.*

FULLER.   People appeared — almost by magic. Central
American peasants in the back of someone's station wagon.
Five-foot Latinos standing next to six-foot snowdrifts — this
lost look in their eyes. They just stood there — their old lives
dead, born into a new world that was empty of everything but
snow.

At first they all stayed in the church basement, but it got
crowded, and they didn't want to give the INS any excuses, so
some of us volunteered to take them in. I got Gregorio. Reverend Hagen said if I did a very, very good job — made
Gregorio comfortable, learned from him, taught him, really
showed my commitment — then the church would help me
get to El Salvador. I really wanted to go. I wanted to be
there, to help. He said I wouldn't have to come back till I
wanted, if ever.

Every night I dreamed of it — of the soft, green mountains. Of the frightened and the dead, and of what I could
do.

169

SCENE TWO

BED

Trace sits in the middle of the bed. He wears black jeans, no shirt. He has on boots, which he slowly slides back and forth over the sheet. Fuller stands at the foot of the bed, staring at Trace.

TRACE.   I always loved this bed. This bed has been a partner.

FULLER.   Trace — ! You're getting it dirty.

TRACE.   You ever sleep on it?

FULLER.   No.

TRACE.   Not even to sleep one off? *(Trace begins to bounce more and more on the bed as he speaks. Fuller doesn't move.)* Still bounces. This bed always had great bounce. Look at that. Eh? Great bounce? We could all use a better fucking bounce.

FULLER.   You haven't come at a good time.

TRACE.   Yeah, I know. So tell me: what's this guy like, anyway?

FULLER.   He's quiet. His English is good.

TRACE.   So's mine. How long's he staying?

FULLER.   We're not sure.

TRACE.   This all you give him? One sheet?

FULLER.   I was starting to make his bed.

TRACE.   You wash his sheets? *(Trace curls up with the pillow, holding it like a lover. Trace begins a slow humping motion with the pillow — more nostalgic than comic.)*

FULLER.   Stop that.

TRACE.   Pillows are better than humans. No heads.

FULLER.   That's not your pillow.

TRACE.   I'm playing the field.

FULLER.   *(Pulling the pillow away.)* Stop it!

TRACE.   Why's he wear a handkerchief over his face?

FULLER.   He doesn't want to be recognized.

TRACE.   Is he a bandito?

170

FULLER.   Trace — You need coffee.

TRACE.   What country's he from?

FULLER.   El Salvador.

TRACE.   That's a shit pile. Isn't it? Why's he in my room? I grew up in this room. What if I want it back?

FULLER.   You don't want it back.

TRACE.   Never know. Things aren't going so well right now.

FULLER.   That doesn't mean you can —

TRACE.   *It's my fucking room!* He sleeps somewhere else.

FULLER.   There's only my room and this room.

TRACE.   Then he sleeps with you.

FULLER.   No one sleeps with me. *(Trace smiles, rolls over and starts humping the duck picture on the pillowcase.)*

TRACE.   Oh, baby. Baby, have I missed you. Great beak. This is great fucking beak. *(Rolling over, a little woozily.)* Whoo, getting dizzy.

FULLER.   Are you all right? You want some coffee?

TRACE.   No coffee. I'm giving up caffeine.

FULLER.   Just a cup. It'll make you feel —

TRACE.   No fucking coffee! I'm trying to take care of myself! Where's my blanket? I'm cold. *(Fuller hesitates.)* I'm *cold*. *(Fuller exits. Trace spread-eagles on the bed, face down. He starts to hump the bed slowly. The humping gets faster and faster as he emits a low groan that grows into a loud, rageful scream. The lights shift to the spot outside the room, as his voice too fades.)*

SCENE THREE

FULLER

FULLER.   *(In a spot outside the room.)* When Trace was ... nine, I think — just after his ninth birthday — he came to me and asked me to take him to the park. In school they were studying trees, and everyone was supposed to get leaves to bring to class. All sorts of leaves.

I took him to the park, and we walked around and got the usual: maples, elms, oaks. He kept wanting to find the best specimen of each leaf, so it took some time. I didn't mind. Beautiful morning. May. Finally, we had everything the park could offer.

He didn't want to stop. Normally he didn't like to spend that much time with me, but this particular morning he didn't want to stop.

I took him to the arboretum. I said there were lots more kinds of trees there — we could look all day if we liked. And we did. We sneaked around, even took leaves right off the trees sometimes. Palm trees, live oaks, magnolias, trees from rain forests with names — you couldn't even tell what language. That night he went to bed at seven. Completely tired out. I just sat and looked at all the leaves. Never had a drink, all night. Never went to his room. *(Lights shift.)*

SCENE FOUR

DRESSER

The bed is as it was. A knotty-pine dresser has now appeared in the room. Trace sits on top of the dresser. The top drawer of the dresser is open. Trace rummages around in it, pulls out a T-shirt and puts it on. He pulls out another T-shirt, then takes a scissors and cuts the second shirt in two. He pulls out a pair of jockey shorts, cuts them in half as well. Gregorio appears. He looks as though he's recently been dressed at K-Mart. He's surprised to see Trace, and stands uncertain what to do. Trace continues cutting up the underwear.

TRACE. Stuff's a real mess, isn't it? *(No response.)* Looks new, too. Is it? They just buy you all this stuff? Take you down to Underwear America, some place like that? *(No response.)* I'm doing you a favor. This stuff's trash. You get no respect wearing this. *(No response.)* Hey, Greg. *(No response.)* Greg. *(No response.)* Greg-or-io. What's wrong? You not talking to me? *(Trace jumps down, stands close to him.)* Seriously. Something the matter? I don't want to get off on the wrong foot here.

GREGORIO.   Where is...? Where is — ?

TRACE.   Fuller? I think he's in the laundry room. *(Gregorio turns to leave.)* Hey! Put on your handkerchief again.

GREGORIO.   What?

TRACE.   I saw you on the news, man. Yesterday. I was — kind of at a friend's. You were great: sitting in that press conference wearing that handkerchief. Why do you do that shit?

GREGORIO.   I don't want to be recognized.

TRACE.   Who's gonna recognize you? Only guy in the state with a handkerchief on his face. *(Trace starts cutting up another T-shirt.)*

GREGORIO.   At home. The television. They can see.

TRACE.   We beaming the noon news down to Central America now?

GREGORIO.   If they see, they can kill ... family.

TRACE.   So? *(As it occurs on him.)* Oh, you mean *your* family. Huh. So where are you going tonight?

GREGORIO.   Tonight?

TRACE.   Yeah. This is my room. Fuller says you can't sleep with him. You gotta go somewhere. Where're you going?

GREGORIO.   Fuller said I live here.

TRACE.   *I* live here.

GREGORIO.   Fuller said —

TRACE.   This is my room. You understand? *My* room. That's my bed. This is my dresser. *(Trace sits again.)* Fuller keeps a place for me. I'm not always around, but the place is here. He's got a spot for me. I'm his little fucking boy.

GREGORIO.   Fuller said —

TRACE.   Look, Greg — what you need — you need to live on the street for a while. That's how to become a real American. You need to go downtown, meet a few people. You know what you need? You need to get a room in the Russell Hotel. You need to find a way into the Russell. Climb up an old

fire escape, break in through a basement window. It's only half-inch plywood — you can break through it. Then you got to find a room. Look for one that's padlocked, then you might not get attacked so much. Sometimes there's a hole in the wall that's not just recreational. Or you can make a hole. You know, to get in and out of your room. 'Course, there's no light at the Russell, so do all this before night or bring a shitload of matches. Once you're settled in, you got to climb back out for water — or money, if you're doing any business. Don't work during the day, though. Not enough customers. They'll just bust you. Ok? You got it? The Russell Hotel. Downtown. Take the number six bus. Oh — and if you need a mattress, look for one in a dumpster someplace and haul it up to your room. Or if there's not too much shit in the dumpster, just sack out there and skip the hauling. But find out when they collect the garbage, or you'll end up like when you're wearing the handkerchief. We won't recognize you. *(Picking up the pillow, stripping off the pillowcase.)* Look — you can even have my pillowcase. *(Stuffing scraps of underwear into it.)* What do you say? Keep you warm at night when business is slow. Say goodbye to Fuller on your way out. *(Gregorio hesitates, then drops the pillowcase on the floor.)* This is *my room!* Get it!? *My room!* You're a visitor to this whole damn country! You're not *even fucking legal! (Fuller appears, with clean bedding.)*
FULLER.   What's going on? When did you get back?
GREGORIO.   A few minutes ago.
TRACE.   I'm helping him get oriented. *(Fuller sets the bedding on the dresser, notices the pillowcase on the floor.)*
FULLER.   What's that? *(Pulling underwear scraps from it.)* What happened to these?
TRACE.   They wore out.
FULLER.   These weren't yours.
TRACE.   They were in my dresser.
FULLER.   I'll just buy new ones. *(Fuller reaches for the scissors on the dresser. Trace grabs them first.)* Those are my scissors.
TRACE.   Come and get 'em. *(Fuller makes no move.)* I better keep 'em. This guy might be violent.
FULLER.   He's here because he's *not* violent. *(To Gregorio.)*

174

Did everything go all right today? *(Gregorio nods.)*
TRACE.   Where's he been?
FULLER.   Doing an interview with a reporter. My minister took him.
TRACE.   Oh, right. Reverend Fuckhead. You religious, Greg?
FULLER.   Just give me the scissors.
TRACE.   Why don't you come and stick me with 'em? *(To Gregorio.)* Fuller's got religion now. Didn't use to. *(To Fuller.)* You shouldn't be a Protestant, though. You should be a Catholic. Then you'd have to confess — everything. Just jam it right in the old priest's ear. *(Suddenly Trace drops the scissors near Fuller's feet.)*
FULLER.   Hey!
TRACE.   Come on, introduce us. Does this guy even know who I am? *(Trace reaches his hand out to Gregorio to shake.)* Trace. It's not my real name. Come on — shake. *(Gregorio does so. Fuller picks up the scissors.)* Hey — you want to see something? I just thought of it. *(Trace pulls the dresser out so he can get at the back of it. He squats behind it as though looking for something.)* Hope Fuller didn't erase it or something.
FULLER.   Erase what?
TRACE.   It's here! Right where I wrote it. Listen. *(Reading aloud.)* "No one will ever know who wrote this. No one will ever know what the person who wrote this thought. No one will know anything about him. Everything is hidden." *(Rising.)* Guess how old I was when I wrote that. Ten. I was ten. *(Fuller shoves the dresser back into position, almost hitting Trace.)* Hey! *(Fuller strips the duck sheet off the bed.)* That was clean.
FULLER.   *It's dirty! (As he continues making the bed.)* I'm giving you a cot.
TRACE.   A cot?!
FULLER.   This is Gregorio's bed. You get a cot.
TRACE.   I'm not sleeping on a cot in here.
FULLER.   Then leave.
TRACE.   Fuck you.
FULLER.   If you stay, you're on a cot.
TRACE.   That's the rule, eh?
FULLER.   That's the rule. *(Trace suddenly pushes Fuller back*

onto the bed, at the same time picking up the scissors from where Fuller set them down. Trace holds the scissors to Fuller's throat.)

TRACE.   What are you saying to me!? What the fuck do you think you're saying!? *(Gregorio takes a step towards them. Fuller motions him back.)*

FULLER.   No! It's all right.

TRACE.   Yeah, Greg — it's just great. You familiar with the phrase, "family shit?" That's all this is. I haven't seen Dad here in a long time. So there's family shit we got to go through. That's why you might like the Russell Hotel better. Isn't that a good idea, Fuller? For Greg? The Russell?

FULLER.   You wouldn't like the Russell.

TRACE.   He would! I stay there all the time.

FULLER.   Why don't you stay there now?

TRACE.   I'm home for the holidays.

FULLER.   It's March.

TRACE.   St. Patrick's. *(To Gregorio.)* You'll love it — whole country throws up green.

GREGORIO.   I'll get someone.

FULLER.   *No* — no, it's all right.

TRACE.   You don't understand what's going on here. If you did, you'd want to go to the Russell Hotel.

FULLER.   He's not a whore.

TRACE.   *(Threatening with the scissors.)* What!?

FULLER.   He's not a whore. Get out of here. Now.

TRACE.   You're in no position to —

FULLER.   *You can't stay!* Not even on a cot.

TRACE.   I can kill you. *I can fucking kill you!*

FULLER.   Kill me. *(Trace slowly smiles. He bends his face close to Fuller's, and kisses him on the lips. He lets Fuller up. He offers the scissors to Fuller, who reaches for them. Trace pulls the scissors away again. Fuller looks nervously at Gregorio and exits. Trace smiles at Gregorio.)*

TRACE.   We love each other. *(Lights shift to spot outside the room.)*

SCENE FIVE

TOY BOX

FULLER.   *(In spot.)* I told Gregorio Trace was my son, and that he'd been on the street — on his own — for years. I told him all Trace wanted was to stay a few days — that's all he ever wanted. That he wasn't dangerous, that soon he'd leave, go back to the Russell Hotel and disappear. We simply had to be patient. *(Fuller moves back into the area of the room. As he does so, the spot widens until the whole room is visible. It's the same, except a toy box — knotty-pine like the dresser — now sits near one end of the bed. The bed is made up, complete with blanket. Gregorio sits on the bed, staring at the toy box. He doesn't acknowledge Fuller's presence in the room. As Fuller continues, Gregorio opens the box and extracts different toys, examining them silently.)* Gregorio noticed Trace's old toy box. I had to explain that I'd kept the room just the way Trace left it when he ran off. *(Gregorio pulls out a toy bayonet.)* They were war toys — that's all Trace ever liked. *(Gregorio takes out a toy pistol. It has a very real look. He continues taking out toy weapons as Fuller speaks: another pistol, an ammo belt, a toy assault rifle, helmet, grenades, etc. One by one he sets them on the floor. Fuller watches him throughout. Gregorio continues to take no notice of Fuller.)* Kids love guns. Something to hold onto. He used to point them at me. They blame the father for everything, don't they? Dad's fault. Whole life long. We take it on our shoulders, into our hearts.... We don't complain, we just take it. And that's a good thing, of course. They need someone to focus on. Someone to — a lightning rod, that's what we say up here. For the storm. *(Suddenly Fuller kneels and grabs the toys, piling them back into the box. Gregorio shows surprise, but only as if he's been listening to Fuller all along. The scene shifts smoothly into a realistic style.)* I haven't missed a Sunday in three years. You know that? I'm the *most* faithful. Trace may say things. He may try to tell you things. They're not real. Not — *(Shutting the toy box, sitting on it, smiling, sud-*

177

denly relaxed again.) Reverend Hagen came to me. He said, "I have someone special for you, Fuller. Speaks English wonderfully — a real spokesman." You are, too. It's a tremendous thing, speaking out for your people. *(Smiling nervously.)* How did you get up here? Did someone drive you up from — where? Texas? Arizona?

GREGORIO.   Arizona.

FULLER.   And getting across the border?

GREGORIO.   Some of us paid a man to take us at night. The next day, we all waited in the desert. The truck they sent to pick us up broke down. A woman almost died in the heat. Finally the truck came. It took us to a church.

FULLER.   I can't imagine it — what you've gone through. Do you have family?   Back in...? *(Gregorio is silent.)* You're right. It's better I don't know. That's what Reverend Hagen says. You can't tell Immigration what you don't know. Right?

GREGORIO.   Right.

FULLER.   You're going to love it here. You really are. Things'll quiet down the minute Trace goes.

GREGORIO.   You think he will?

FULLER.   He's got to. I mean, he always does.

GREGORIO.   I can stay with someone else.

FULLER.   No. Just — it'll be all right. You'll see. Tomorrow, the next day, he'll be gone. Just a dream. I promise. *(Trace enters. He carries a cot under one arm, a pillow and sleeping bag with the other.)* I'll let you two get some sleep.

TRACE.   Hang on. I'm gonna set up the cot. *(Trace drops everything, starts setting up the cot. Trace speaks exclusively to Gregorio.)* Fuller and me used to set up cots all the time. When we went camping. You ever go camping down there, in the world's butt? We do up here. I never knew when it was gonna be. Fuller'd come home from work and say, "Time to hit the trees," and by God we'd get in his truck and hit those trees. Didn't matter what I thought. We'd slam the doors on the old pickup and head up to the biggest, darkest, most dangerous damn woods Fuller could find — never the same place twice, never anybody around, always somewhere colder'n shit. And we'd always get there with about twelve minutes of light left, and he'd shout "Tent or die!" — which meant we had to get the goddamn tent up before we froze to death — which was possible, since he never packed any warm clothes for us. And so there we'd be — stomping around trying to find the right kind of almost-flat ground for this fuckmonkey tent that was ten years old and too small and leaked anyway. And once we found it, our hands would be too fucking cold to put any of the shit-eating stuff together, and it'd take *an hour* to put up a tent you could assemble in three minutes in the store. Then we got to put together the motherfucking *cots* and shove 'em in. And after all that — after the cots were up in the tent from hell, and the fucking sleeping bags were on the fucking cots, and the pillows were all soft on top of the sleeping bags, you know what that cocksucking fuckface asshole wanted to do then?

FULLER.   *(To Gregorio.)* Go upstairs.

TRACE.   Every goddamn time?

FULLER.   *I mean it! Out! Now!! (Gregorio hurries out.)* What are you doing?

TRACE.   Just talking.

FULLER.   Why are you here? Why'd you come back?

TRACE.   You always want me back.

FULLER.   Not now — with him here.

TRACE.   This is my home, isn't it? I just thought this guy had a right to know who he's staying with.

FULLER.   Leave him alone! He's innocent.

TRACE.   The other night you know what some guy said to me? We were having sort of a — business meeting — and he said in Japan women pay doctors like a hundred thousand bucks to get their virginity *put back*. For their weddings. That innocence, man. That's valuable stuff.

FULLER.   Do you want money? There's money for you. You know that. As soon as you agree to —

TRACE.   *(Laughs.)* I'm not here to agree, Fuller. I don't agree. You can get all the Reverend Hagens in the world to buy your line of shit, but *I don't*. If I want to drop by and give Gregorio the news at noon, there's nothing you can do about it. *(Fuller is silent.)* Except one thing.

FULLER.   What?

TRACE.   There was a guy. When I was — I don't know — eight or nine. There was a guy. Remember?

FULLER.   I'm ... not sure I —

TRACE.   You remember. You took me to his house.

FULLER.   That was ten years —

TRACE.   *Shut up! You remember!* His name was Ray. Or Roy. His house was nice. You took me there. You left me there. Overnight. It was the only time I was ever there. His name was Ray. Or Roy. *(A beat.)* I want to see him again.

FULLER.   Why?

TRACE.   He liked me.

FULLER.   You only saw him once.

TRACE.   He liked me a lot.

FULLER.   I'm not even sure who you're —

TRACE.   Don't shit me! He was some guy you worked for. You were doing some kind of job for him or something. And you had to go someplace that day, and you left me with him. I remember his face, I remember his house, I remember everything but his goddamn address! What is it, Fuller?

FULLER.   I don't know.

TRACE.   We had a great time that night. Want to hear about it?

FULLER.   No.

TRACE.   He was real smooth. I didn't even know what was happening to me. He gave me money too, to stay quiet. It was the first time anybody ever gave me money.

FULLER.   Shut up!!

TRACE.   You guessed, didn't you? I hardly said a word for a week. You could tell by the way I looked, though. You knew what he did.

FULLER.   Trace, believe me — I never would've left you if I'd known that he was going to —

TRACE.   Do what you did? At least he paid. And like I say, he liked me. He was sorry to see me go. You know the last thing he said, while you were coming up the driveway? He said, "Anytime you want anything, Trace, come to me. Just come on back to good old Roy." Or Ray. I want to come back now. Give me his name.

FULLER.   You don't want to see him.

TRACE.   What's his address? Tell me, and I'll get out now. I'm gone.

FULLER.   I can't help you.

TRACE.   Why not?

FULLER.   He's dangerous. If that's what he did to you, there's no telling what he'd do if you suddenly —

TRACE.   That's my problem!

FULLER.   No. It's not.... It's not moral.

TRACE.   *(Trace gives a sharp laugh.)* That's an interesting word.

FULLER.   Everyone has a moral journey to take, and —

TRACE.   I'll have to burn this house down, won't I? Someday. Where do you want to be when I do it. What room? This one? *(Suddenly noticing something on the floor near the bed.)* What the hell's this? *(Picking up a toy pistol which Fuller missed.)* You and Greg *playing* down here?

FULLER.   He was just looking through your —

TRACE.   That's right. We've still got the Trace museum here, don't we? Everything just the way it was — like for a dead kid. *(Trace suddenly pushes the toy gun against Fuller's crotch.)*

FULLER.   Take that away.

TRACE.   Does God grant prayers, Fuller? Does He?

FULLER.   Yes.

TRACE.   God, I wish this was real. When I think of killing you, I think, "Right here. Start right here." *(Sliding the toy gun back and forth over Fuller's groin.)* I could pay you, Fuller. I could give you something. I could.

FULLER.   No.

TRACE.   Don't you want to be close to me?

FULLER.   *Stop it! (Fuller bats the toy gun away, rushes from the room. Trace laughs.)*

TRACE.   Fuller, come back! I'm not done playing! *(Smiling, pointing the gun at the door.)* I'm not. *(Lights shift to spot outside room.)*

SCENE SIX

FULLER

FULLER.   *(In spot.)* My father's hands. When I was little —
before I was five, I think — I tried believing that his hands
were different from each other. That one hand was bad and
one was good. The right hand, the bad hand, would hit and
... do the other things. The left hand was good. Whenever the
left hand hit me I tried to believe that somehow it was ... for
the best, and if the right hand did something I liked, I knew
it was a trap.

Then I tried believing my father's hands were separate
from him. I decided my father was born without hands, and
then was forced by magic to accept two hands he didn't want.
He was too proud to admit this to his own son.

Eventually I had to admit my father's hands were his
own. That there was no difference between them, that he
used them as he wished.

I hated him, wanted to kill him. I loved him, wanted to
feel him. I followed his voice into the deepest silence I ever
knew. *(The spot fades as dim light rises on the room.)*

SCENE SEVEN

WINDOW

*Gregorio is asleep on the bed, Trace on the cot. We see morn-
ing light enter the dim room from a basement window high
up on the wall. This window was not visible before. Trace
wakes. He sits up, stares at Gregorio. After a few moments,
Trace stands. He wears a T-shirt and jockey shorts. Trace
pulls a flashlight out from under his cot. He moves next to
the bed, stares down at Gregorio. Trace aims the flashlight*

182

in Gregorio's face and turns it on. Gregorio wakes with a start.

TRACE.   *(In a fierce, 'official' voice.) Who the hell are you!? What are you doing here!? Where're you from!? (Trace sits on top of the dresser, watching as Gregorio collects himself. Trace shines the flashlight on his own face from below, creating a ghostly image.)* Morning. *(He flicks off the flashlight.)*
GREGORIO.   What time is it?
TRACE.   Early. Did I scare you? Think I was the cops? That's how they wake me up. Flashlight in the face. "Who the hell are you?" *(A beat.)* Who the hell are you?
GREGORIO.   Gregorio.
TRACE.   What's your last name?
GREGORIO.   It's not important.
TRACE.   *Hey! We're roommates!*
GREGORIO.   Hernandez.
TRACE.   I know a Spanish guy. His name is ... shit, Rico or something. Works at Happy Jose's. Totally illegal. Sometimes he tosses me stuff out the back door. You know, shit to eat. Stupid Mexican. Just pleased to be here. You pleased to be here? *(Gregorio turns away.)* New land. Million possibilities. That's why you came, isn't it? Hang out awhile, earn some bucks, go back home and live it up.
GREGORIO.   If I go back, they'll kill me.
TRACE.   You're here for bucks, like everybody. Got a job lined up yet? I could help you. You good with your hands?
GREGORIO.   I didn't come for money —
TRACE.   Come on — anyone can tie a handkerchief around his head. As far as I'm concerned, if you're from Mexico on down, you're a fucking liar until proven worse. You're up here to mow somebody's lawn. Period.
GREGORIO.   I knew a man in El Salvador.
TRACE.   Can he mow lawns?
GREGORIO.   Alberto. They put him in prison. The army. They tortured him.
TRACE.   You could tell me anything.
GREGORIO.   Alberto helped people look for relatives. The

ones who disappeared. He didn't break the laws. But in El Salvador ...

TRACE.   Hey — I don't care.

GREGORIO.   When he was in prison, his wife came to see him. They arrested her, too. They held her three days. Raped her. Killed her. A week before Alberto left prison, his son disappeared. He looked for his son, but.... Then one morning he found his son's body. In front of his door. The head was cut off.

TRACE.   You work for the Tourist Office or what?

GREGORIO.   He came here, to the U.S.

TRACE.   Genius. What's the point?

GREGORIO.   They sent him back. They don't think he's in danger.

TRACE.   (*Clearly impressed.*) Man, you'd be a natural in my business. Clients always want to hear the story, you know? I gotta make up all kinds of shit for 'em. Can I borrow that one?

GREGORIO.   You don't believe me?

TRACE.   Do I look pitiful? God, I can't wait till Immigration gets some balls and sends you back home.

GREGORIO.   I won't go.

TRACE.   You won't have a choice.

GREGORIO.   Maybe I'll hide.

TRACE.   Where?

GREGORIO.   Maybe I'll go to Canada.

TRACE.   Canada? That's a bigger joke than El Salvador. A hundred percent of Canadians live within five miles of the border — you know that? They're bunching. They're all bunching together like lemmings. They're gonna break. Someday when we're not looking, all of 'em — millions — are gonna run clawing and screaming down here — right across the border. They're gonna fall on their knees and shout, "Please — don't make us be Canadians anymore! We hate it! We fucking hate it!" (*Suddenly kneeling on the dresser, looking out the window.*) Hey — you like this window? I used to look out all the time. Not bad, for a basement. You can see the river, kind of. Through the trees. You can see the road, too. The

Great River Road. You know what that is? The Great-fucking-
River Road? It's this little two-lane piece of shit that runs
down the Mississippi River all the way from Minnesota to Ant-
arctica or someplace. The worst road in America. Built about
a thousand years ago. Nobody fixes it. Just sits rotting on the
floodplain. Like driving on railroad ties. You know our road
right here, in front of the house — Lake Street Extension? It
used to be part of the Great River Road. When I was a kid,
we had this big sign out front and everything, with this stupid steamboat wheel on it — and it said, "Great River Road."
Like there was something great right there at our house.
'Course, it was just this butt-killing piece of crapped-out as-
phalt, but *I* didn't know. Later they blocked the street off for
a park and shifted the Great River Road down there. Took
the sign away. Now we're just Lake Street Extension. Not anything. Just here.
GREGORIO.   I'm sorry.
TRACE.   Eat my shit, Gregorio. If you knew what it was like
to live here, you'd jump in the river and swim home.
GREGORIO.   Is your mother dead?
TRACE.   What?
GREGORIO.   Where is your mother? Is she — ?
TRACE.   Don't ask about my goddamn family — ok?! Christ,
fucking wetback. *(Looking out the window again.)* You know I
used to dream this river was alive? Like a big snake or some-
thing. Like at night it'd get up and slither all over, you know?
Killing people or something. I used to dream of it sliding up
the hill, into the window, around Fuller's neck. Choking him
to death. Then slipping back down into the riverbed, in the
dark. Perfect crime. *(Suddenly moving from the window, sitting on
the dresser.)* You smoke? *(No response.)* Hey, alien. You smoke?
GREGORIO.   What?
TRACE.   What are you, retarded? Do — you — smoke?
GREGORIO.   Yes.
TRACE.   Give me a cigarette. *(A beat.)* Give me a butt,
fuckhead, or I'll rip your arm off!
GREGORIO.   I don't think I have any.
TRACE.   Bullshit.

GREGORIO.   Maybe I ran out.

TRACE.   You people practice lying three times a day? Where you got 'em, in the dresser? That's where I always kept mine. *(Trace rifles through the dresser.)*

GREGORIO.   There's nothing in there.

TRACE.   Don't lie to me, Greg.

GREGORIO.   I'm not lying! *(Trace leans over him threateningly.)*

TRACE.   Are you losing your temper? *(No response.)* Just tell me if you are. *(Going back to the drawers, throwing clothes on the floor, finding no cigarettes.)* I'm starting to get pissed, Gregorio. I'm very bad in the morning.

GREGORIO.   So go back to bed.

TRACE.   You think this place is yours now, don't you? Think you'll be making peanut-butter sandwiches up in the kitchen for the next thirty years. I'll tell you something: I'll be smoking cigarettes here long after they send you back home for a bullet in the head. *(Emptying the final drawer.)* Where are they!!?

GREGORIO.   Maybe you should quit.

TRACE.   *You fucking greaser!* You come crawling up to my country, to my *street*, I give you my my bed — you won't even give me a cigarette?! *(A beat.)* I'm going to break your arm. *(Trace angrily grabs Gregorio. Instantly Gregorio reacts, taking hold of Trace's wrists and controlling him quickly with a practiced movement. Gregorio holds him in a headlock. Trace struggles, but Gregorio gives a quick twist and Trace yells in pain. Trace is silent. Gregorio stands as Trace sinks to the floor, holding his neck.)* What the fuck was that? What was that? *(Gregorio reaches under the bed, pulls out a carton of cigarettes.)*

GREGORIO.   You like filters?

TRACE.   You sonofabitch. *(Gregorio reaches down and gives Trace a cigarette.)* Does Fuller know you can do that? Does anybody?

GREGORIO.   *(Lighting it for him.)* It's not important.

TRACE.   Not important? You're lethal. Where'd you learn that? *(A beat.)* Can I get up?

GREGORIO.   Do what you like. Keep the carton. *(He hands it to Trace. Trace moves back to the cot and sits. Gregorio reaches*

186

under his bed, pulls out more cigarettes, lights one.)
TRACE.   That's a barbaric move, man. Would you teach it to me? *(No response.)* No one who can do that should be allowed in this country.
GREGORIO.   What I can do is not your business. Forget what I can do.
TRACE.   Is that an order?
GREGORIO.   Yes. *(A beat. Trace shrugs.)*
TRACE.   What do I care what you can do? *(A moment passes. They smoke.)*
GREGORIO.   *(Quietly.)* Why are you here?
TRACE.   What?
GREGORIO.   Why did you come? Why are you staying? What do you want?
TRACE.   You gonna make me tell you?
GREGORIO.   Yes. *(The two men smoke. Lights shift to Fuller, outside the room.)*

SCENE EIGHT

PHONE

FULLER.   *(In spot.)* There used to be Indians — American Indians — who thought they could make themselves invulnerable. They thought if they had a certain religion, did a certain dance, the soldiers' bullets somehow miraculously wouldn't harm them. It's like keeping a secret. You think you won't be discovered. You feel more and more ... perfect. Invisible. And every year that no one finds out, was another year that it never happened at all. You have secret rules. You're safe if you just keep them. *(Lights come up on Trace, now sitting in the room with a phone and phonebook. Trace dials the phone.)*
TRACE.   *(On the phone.)* Hello? Is this ... *(A quick look at the phone book.)* Ray Branagan? And you live on, um ... Harrison Avenue? I was just wondering, Mr. ... Branagan, if you might happen to know or remember a man named Fuller? This

would have been several years ago. Fuller. You're absolutely sure? Ok, fine. Sorry to bother you. *(Trace hangs up, looks in the book, and freezes.)*

FULLER.   I kept my rules for years. And I kept my secret. Until Trace was nine. I'm a subcontractor — electrical. When Trace was nine, I was working for a particular man, a builder. He asked me once about my family. I told him about Trace, how much I loved him, what a beautiful boy ... what a beautiful boy he was. I didn't think I said anything that ... but maybe, somehow.... Not long after that, he arranged things so I had to go away overnight. "Let Trace stay with us," he said, "Trace'll be right at home with my wife and me." But his wife wasn't there. *(Trace unfreezes and punches a new number.)*

TRACE.   Hello, Mr. ... um, Mr. Brandt? Mr. Roy Brandt? On Summit? Hi, um ... could you tell me if you might happen to know or remember a man named Fuller? Fuller. F-u-l-l-e-r. A few years ago. It doesn't matter who I am. Just do you know — *(Trace has been hung up on. He punches the same number.)* His name was Fuller, Mr. Brandt. About ten years ago. Just do you know him, that's all. I — Why are you so nervous? Just answer when I — *Don't worry who this is! Just answer the question, fuckhead!* Mr. Brandt? *(He's been hung up on. Trace takes out a cigarette, lights up, looks at the phone book, freezes.)*

FULLER.   You get a feeling with some people. Or maybe just I do. Somehow you know. When I picked Trace up the next morning, I could tell. Something in the man's face, something in Trace's. What do you say? What do you accuse him of? He was a powerful man — still is. The deals he puts through — he's dangerous. He looked at me like I was picking up the laundry. He smiled, said he and Trace had a great time. In that moment I think all three of us knew everything there was to know. But ... what was there to do? Trace never said a word about it. Neither did I.

TRACE.   *(Unfreezing, on the phone again.)* Hello, Mr. ... um, Mr. Ray Brauer? Right. Do you know a man named Fuller? Yeah — Fuller. It was awhile ago. He had a little boy. The boy stayed with you one night ten years ago. Yeah, ten years. Don't you have a memory? What are you, a stroke victim?

Come *on!!* (*Trace bangs the phone down and angrily slams the phone book shut. He throws the phone book at the cot.*)

FULLER. It never happened again. Never. I made sure of that. But we had a new secret. I always said I'd never let a stranger do that to him. But I broke my rule, and the bullets didn't go through my body. They went through Trace. (*Lights shift with Fuller as he moves into the room.*)

SCENE NINE

RUG

Afternoon. The room's unchanged, although now next to the bed we see an oval braid rug. Fuller sits alone on the bed, staring at the rug. Trace enters, towel in hand, wearing his father's bathrobe. He's just showered.

TRACE. What are you doing here? (*Fuller is silent.*) What are you staring at? The rug? This fabulous rug? (*Kneeling down at the edge of the rug.*) The rug of my youth?

FULLER. Let's talk.

TRACE. (*Running his hands over the rug.*) What about? Ray? Or Roy? Gonna tell me his name?

FULLER. You have to go.

TRACE. I do, eh? (*Stretching out on the rug, burying his nose in it.*) Still smells the same. Remember what I used to do with it? (*Drawing himself into a fetal position on the rug.*) I'd lie like this — just this way — and I'd say, "You can't come in. You can't touch me. I'm on the rug." Like it was my little country. You even let me get away with it.

FULLER. You can't stay here.

TRACE. If I could get to this rug in time, you'd leave me alone. 'Course, I'd get tired eventually, and go to bed. No rules there. But on my rug I was safe. For hours, sometimes. Whole evenings. My braid rug.

189

FULLER. I'll give you money. I won't make any demands.

TRACE. Demands? What — no reform? No forgiveness? This *is* progress.

FULLER. I'll drive you wherever you want.

TRACE. Ray's house? *(Fuller's silent.)* Roy's house? *(Fuller's silent.)* My rug. I had a nightmare once, sleeping on it. I ever tell you? I dreamed you took a knife, and you cut the rug up, right in front of me. I mean, you cut all around the edge — you know? So it unbraided. Just turned into a long piece of nothing. And when you got done you said, "See, Trace? The rug's not real. I can make it disappear."

FULLER. I would never have done that.

TRACE. I said it was a dream. I woke up, the rug was there. Everything was just as great as usual. *(Sitting up.)* Hey, let's get loaded — maybe then you'll tell me what I want to know. Is there beer upstairs?

FULLER. There's no alcohol in the house.

TRACE. Fuller Reform. Year three. What am I gonna do? If I can't get you stinking —

FULLER. Trace.

TRACE. You know where I get loaded now? That railroad bridge behind the Russell. There's a wooden walkway right under the tracks. Probably not even for walking. Just a foot wide. You can look straight down into the river. Hundred feet. I walk out there and load up. Train comes. The bridge starts shaking —

FULLER. I don't want to —

TRACE. And I hold on for dear life, and I let go with one hand and I'm hanging, whipping around like I'm in a tornado, and that train's roaring over me and *God, I want to let go!! (Suddenly still.)* I almost do. *(Shrugs.)* Then I walk back in, go on with things. *(Trace moves to the dresser, takes off the robe, throws it on the bed. He wears only a dingy pair of jockey shorts. Fuller averts his eyes. Trace opens the dresser drawer.)* I'm gonna borrow some of this Pride-of-K-Mart crap, if you can handle it. Meanwhile you think hard about that name. *(Looking at Fuller.)* Hey — look at me. *(Fuller looks.)* Something wrong? I keep myself in shape. Considering. Keep my weight down. Don't

190

skin-pop. You should be glad I still let you look.

FULLER. You look fine.

TRACE. I look beautiful. That's what you used to say. *(Fuller looks away. Trace puts on new underwear, continues dressing.)* Young men are beautiful. Old men look like shit. Everything else is lies. What's the name, Fuller? Roy, Ray — what is it?

FULLER. Once you're dressed, you have to go.

TRACE. This is my room. You want me to find more stuff I wrote?

FULLER. I own this house.

TRACE. Just legally.

FULLER. What if I sold it? Have you ever thought of that? I could sell it. I could move.

TRACE. *(Dressed, of the new clothes.)* Hey — what do you think? Is this a look? Maybe I should go to work this way.

FULLER. I could leave you!

TRACE. Yeah, and snakes could fly. Ok, Fuller, quit fucking around. What's his name?

FULLER. I'm not going to give you — *(Trace starts dialing the phone.)* Who are you calling?

TRACE. Hello? Do you have a listing for Reverend Anthony Hagen? *(Trace writes the number on the phonebook.)*

FULLER. What are you doing?

TRACE. *(Starting to dial the number.)* I've never really had a good talk with the old Rev. You know? About me, about you — *(Fuller rushes to the phone, breaks the connection.)*

FULLER. *Stop it!!* What the hell's wrong with you?!

TRACE. Maybe the phone upstairs'd be better.

FULLER. I don't know what you are. You don't love, you don't care, you don't think — you don't know half the harm you do.

TRACE. Just give me his name, Fuller. I'm gone.

FULLER. You don't listen, you don't understand, you don't plan —

TRACE. I plan.

FULLER. *You don't plan! You don't plan!* Your life's a mistake. *You* let it stay that way, not me. I pray for you every day. Every minute.

TRACE.   Every second?

FULLER.   You live on the moon. Your whole world is ten city blocks on the moon. I've asked you to forgive me. I've begged you. My God, what does it take?

TRACE.   What would it take for me to forgive you — even a little bit? What would I need to hear you say? "Trace please kill me for everything I did to you?" Maybe. "Please cut off my arms and legs and we'll call it even." Or I know: "Trace, please haul me down to the police station, make me get down on my knees — no, on my fat, fucking belly — and say everything I ever did to you. Then drag me away to prison and tattoo what I am on my goddamn face, so everybody *knows*. Then cut my fucking nuts off." That might do it. *(Fuller is silent. Trace starts out.)*

FULLER.   I'm leaving you. *(Trace continues toward the door.)* I'm going to El Salvador. *(Trace stops.)* I've been thinking how to tell you. I'm going to sell the house. People are dying in the streets there. I'm going to help.

TRACE.   What are you talking about?

FULLER.   *(Sitting back on the bed.)* I'll be gone a year or two. At least.

TRACE.   What the fuck are you talking about?

FULLER.   I need a new life, Trace —

TRACE.   You don't have a life!! You have me!!

FULLER.   There's a whole country of people suffering and dying. Gregorio's only one —

TRACE.   Are you kidding!? Don't you know what Gregorio is?!

FULLER.   Trace, I can't be here anymore.

TRACE.   You have to be! This is where you are!

FULLER.   No.

TRACE.   You're not going to a fucking foreign country.

FULLER.   Reverend Hagen says —

TRACE.   Gregorio was a fucking soldier! Don't you know that?

FULLER.   A soldier?

TRACE.   He almost killed me. Got me in a hold — could've broke my neck.

192

FULLER. He's not a soldier.

TRACE. *Damn it, he is!* I've been with fucking Marines — you think they haven't tried shit out on me?! Gregorio's some AWOL asshole who's probably killed more people than you've ever met, and you're hiding him in your goddamn basement!

FULLER. That's a lie.

TRACE. Should we see what Hagen thinks?

FULLER. Whatever you tell him, I'm still going.

TRACE. You're never leaving this house! I'll kill you first!

FULLER. You won't kill me —

TRACE. *I'LL KILL YOU!! (Fuller stands.)*

FULLER. You won't kill me. *(Fuller walks out of the room.)*

TRACE. *(Shouting after him.)* I will!! I'll kill you before you ever — I'll fucking — ! I'll — ! *(Fuller is gone. A wave of pain overcomes Trace. He sinks to the rug, one hand covering his face.)* You can't go! You can't — You are not excused! You understand? You're not — *(Trace lies on the rug, almost unconsciously curling into a fetal position. A beat. Trace breathes more calmly.)* I really miss you, Dad. *(Lights shift.)*

SCENE TEN

ATLAS

A day later, evening. The room's the same, save that now an oversized, hard cover book — an atlas — leans against the downstage side of the toy box. Fuller and Gregorio enter.

FULLER. Trace? Trace, you around? He's not here. *(As they move into the room, Fuller seems excited, happy. Gregorio is more thoughtful.)* Wonder where he is? When did he leave today?

GREGORIO. Morning sometime.

FULLER. Well. We'll try to get along without him. It's still early — if you'd rather go for some food, we could —

GREGORIO. No, thanks.

FULLER. Something to drink? Soda? I can go around the

corner for a beer —

GREGORIO. I'm fine. Just tired.

FULLER. I'm not surprised. That interview was wonderful!

GREGORIO. It was just talking.

FULLER. Even Reverend Hagen — did you see his face? He was glowing when he looked at you. I've never seen anyone prouder. When's it on the radio? The day after tomorrow? We'll listen together. Maybe all of us, down at the church. How 'bout that? (*Gregorio stares at him, shrugs. Fuller looks around the room.*) I feel so — I don't know — free, all of a sudden. I knew this would happen — that he'd just pick up and go. Trace never sticks to a plan of attack. It's great to be alone with you.

GREGORIO. It is?

FULLER. You were ... I felt — I shouldn't say this, but tonight you were, for me, like a son — or the dream of a son. The ideal, that I dreamed of, when Trace was born. You know — young, confident, answering questions, speaking out about what's really important — in a global sense. What's ... what's got to change. I was so excited. It brought my son back, it really did.

GREGORIO. Fuller, I don't think —

FULLER. 'Course, you have only the worst idea. What you've seen of Trace — He was such a beautiful boy, he really was. I'd show you pictures, but ... he took 'em once, and I'm pretty sure burned them. But I do have other things. I do. Um ... well this, for example. (*Fuller goes to the toy box.*)

GREGORIO. Maybe tomorrow —

FULLER. No, no — this'll only take a moment. You'll see. (*Fuller retrieves the atlas from behind the toy box.*) This. We still have this. Here, take a look. (*He sits next to Gregorio on the bed.*) An atlas. We have an atlas. From when he was seven. Look. Look at all the roads. 'Course, I shouldn't talk to you about roads, but look — they're all colored in. All the roads we ever drove on. Around here, where we went on vacation — all of them. Every road. So we'd remember.

GREGORIO. Fuller —

FULLER. That's not all. Look here. The world section?

These are the roads that we wanted to travel. They're colored in, too. All over the world. Where we dreamed of going, when Trace was seven.

GREGORIO.   Trace told me. He told me everything about you and him. *(Fuller looks stunned. He slowly closes the book.)*

FULLER.   It's not true.

GREGORIO.   I know when men are lying. What Trace told me is true.

FULLER.   *(Rising, setting the atlas down.)* Did he talk about his mother?

GREGORIO.   Yes.

FULLER.   She left. *She left us!* He was three! I never left him. Brought him halfway across the country with me. I never hit him. Raised him alone. How many fathers...? Reason and patience. And he responded.

GREGORIO.   What else did you do?

FULLER.   Nothing! I was of value to him. I made sure he got a good education. Made sure he behaved at school.

GREGORIO.   Trace says —

FULLER.   Trace is lying! He ran out on me — did he tell you that? One day he was gone. Just gone.

GREGORIO.   Why did he go?

FULLER.   He called that night, said I shouldn't look for him, that he'd be all right — that he'd get in touch now and then.

GREGORIO.   How old was he?

FULLER.   Fourteen. I looked for him everywhere. I heard what he'd started doing — for money, that is. The few times I spotted him, he always ran. Finally, I went to the police. You can imagine how terrified I was. They found him and brought him home, but he ran away again. A few months later, he showed up. Things'd gotten rougher on the street — I don't know, he wouldn't say. I was trying to stop drinking by then. And he'd stopped ... being young. I pleaded with him to stay, whoever — whatever — he was. I told him he could just be my son, nothing else — that's all. He ate my food for a week and left.

GREGORIO.   Does Reverend Hagen know about you?

195

FULLER. You can't tell Hagen what Trace said! It's lies! If Hagen believed that, it would ruin everything.

GREGORIO. Ruin what?

FULLER. My plan, my — everything I stand for now. Everything I want to do. Hagen's going to send me to your country. To El Salvador.

GREGORIO. To my — ?

FULLER. It's my chance to be new. You see? My chance to do the same kind of good you do. Only you'll be here helping, and I'll be there. But Hagen'd never understand. I'd never be able to go.

GREGORIO. *Habla espanol?*

FULLER. I started a class last week —

GREGORIO. A man who's done what you have done? You're coming to my country?

FULLER. I haven't done any — !

GREGORIO. You can't even tell your minister who you are.

FULLER. I have a new life now! God has come into me.

GREGORIO. God? God is in you now?

FULLER. Yes.

GREGORIO. Let me speak to him.

FULLER. Gregorio —

GREGORIO. I mean it.

FULLER. That's not how it works —

GREGORIO. It better be how it works, because in El Salvador, if God doesn't speak straight out of your mouth, you'll be dead before you know enough Spanish to order eggs in the morning. A man like you. What can you do? How can you help?

FULLER. Just by being there — speaking out, getting attention —

GREGORIO. They killed Romero. How much attention can you get? You're a fool. A criminal and a fool. In El Salvador, you'll lie in your own blood.

FULLER. You can't know that.

GREGORIO. In El Salvador, you'll be killed by a gun made in your own country. By soldiers who trained with your army. They may torture you first. Later, maybe they'll cut your body

196

into pieces. But you will die, a man like you.

FULLER. Even if I did die, if it was for the cause —

GREGORIO. Cause? What cause?

FULLER. The one you keep giving interviews for — or don't you care about that?

GREGORIO. *(Gregorio laughs.)* How far are you willing to go, Fuller? Eh? To keep your secret?

FULLER. Gregorio —

GREGORIO. How many miles? How many miles can you go and never confess? You talk about the 'cause' in my country. You pretend it's yours. But there's no cause. There's only living and dying. Right now you are alive. If you go there, you will die — a man like you.

FULLER. How can you know that?

GREGORIO. Because I *am* a man like you. How do you think I know English so well? To make me such a 'spokesman?' Where do you think I learned? Why do you think I learned?

FULLER. Why ... did you?

GREGORIO. Do you want to know? Do you want to know about me? Why not — at least someone can tell the truth. *(A beat.)* I come from a good family. My father was a factory manager — important man. Above him was the owner. Rich, confident, safe. He was the man I watched. Every day he swam through us all like a shark. We were the ocean around him, nothing more. I wanted to be like him someday: strong, in charge. He spoke English, the language of money, so I studied English, very hard. I joined the army. I studied English there, too. I didn't want to fight anyone. I only wanted to work, translate, become an officer. Then I would retire, go into business — the way you do it here. I would be a gentleman. In El Salvador. *(A beat.)* But they decided I should work with some Americans. USA. CIA. I didn't want to. They ordered me. I said to myself, "It's only training. Only for a while." I helped the men from the CIA teach our officers.

FULLER. Teach them what?

GREGORIO. I think you know. I kept telling myself it wouldn't be that, but it was. I translated techniques in questioning prisoners.

FULLER. Techniques?

GREGORIO. They didn't need much translation. Car batteries, handcuffs, bedsprings — you could watch and see. But they liked to talk while they did it. I translated the jokes.

FULLER. I don't believe you.

GREGORIO. Why not? Why not me, Fuller? Why do you think I know you are lying? When the jokes were over, they brought a man in to interrogate. They strapped him down.

FULLER. You never did this.

GREGORIO. You do what they make you do. Or you die. And maybe your family dies — your mother, your father. *(A beat.)* The man they tortured wasn't important. He didn't know much. But he was all they had for training that day. For my family's sake, I tried to stay. I translated questions, answers — when he could answer. But finally I couldn't watch anymore. I ran out.

FULLER. Good.

GREGORIO. Not good. Some commanders, when they had a soldier like me, they sent them to another unit — somewhere unimportant, for the babies. But my commander didn't do that. He called me in. He said now that people were nervous about me, he had to do one of two things. Kill me, or take me on an 'operation'. To wipe out guerillas — far up in the mountains. I went.

FULLER. You had to.

GREGORIO. There's a small village, close to Honduras. Guerillas were often there. It was called El Mozote. A few hundred people lived there: men, women, old people, children. We killed them.

FULLER. What?

GREGORIO. We killed them. Our unit was ordered to kill them, and we killed them. Shot them, killed them with knives, clubbed them to death, strangled them. Beheaded some.

FULLER. You killed them? *You* did?

GREGORIO. My commander made me stand next to him. Made me watch everything. If I looked away, even for a moment, he told a soldier to come and rub some of the blood on my face. Finally my face was covered with their blood. So many children. I watched babies die — all of the worst things you can imagine happened before my eyes. For hours. While it was still going on, my commander said, "You were afraid I'd make you kill someone, but I didn't. You see? You are still innocent." *(A beat.)* At that moment, a soldier pulled a young boy out of a house. He was thirteen or fourteen. The soldier took a knife. He started to cut the boy with it, very slowly. The boy screamed. I took my pistol and shot the boy in the head. And the only thing I felt — the only thing — was relief. *(A beat.)* And then another soldier did it — pulled another boy out, younger, and started to cut him up. The screams.... And I killed that boy too. Then there was another, and another. Finally, I didn't wait for them to start cutting. Why bother? *(A beat.)* We did this for three days. Five other villages — smaller than El Mozote. Maybe we killed a thousand people this way. At night, we went back to our camp. The other men would sleep, but I laid awake, thinking of how we moved through the soft green mountains: silent, as if we were still an army. As if something could still hurt us. Finally, when the last peasants had run away, we left.

FULLER. I don't want to hear anymore.

GREGORIO. I didn't go home. I went to the ocean. I wrote a note to my family, saying I was going to drown myself. I left it in my clothes on the beach. And I disappeared.

FULLER. I don't want to hear this.

GREGORIO. But you have to. You are the only one who can hear this.

FULLER. Why? Why me?

GREGORIO. You think I could tell this to a good man?

FULLER. I'm — !

GREGORIO. What? What are you, Fuller? *(Fuller is silent.)* Some things you can only confess if you find the right man. For me, I never thought such a man existed. I thought I was traveling for nothing. But it wasn't so. I was coming to find you. *(Fuller picks up the atlas, then nervously sets it down again.)*

FULLER.   It's late. I should get some rest.
GREGORIO.   Good night.
FULLER.   Good night. *(Fuller leaves the room. Lights fade to black.)*

SCENE ELEVEN

AQUARIUM

Noon, the next day. A narrow spot illuminates a small fish tank in the middle of the room. Two feet long, a foot or so wide, the tank has colored gravel in the bottom, and several inches of water are in it. A small figure of a deep-sea diver — an aquarium toy — with an old length of tubing attached to it hangs in the water at the side of the tank.

Gregorio stands at the dresser. He is pulling clothes out of the drawers and putting them on top of the dresser.

Trace enters. He's been beaten. His face is cut and bruised. His T-shirt is torn.

GREGORIO.   What happened to you?
TRACE.   *(Moving painfully to the cot.)* What do you think? I found him. His name's Roy. *(Trace lies down heavily on the cot.)*
GREGORIO.   Are you ok?
TRACE.   Is Fuller here?
GREGORIO.   I haven't seen him since last night.
TRACE.   He'd laugh — wouldn't he — if he saw me now. "Told you so, Trace. Don't go near him. Dangerous man."
GREGORIO.   You need help?
TRACE.   Keep away from me! I've been beat up worse than this. Ten times worse. I'm fine.
GREGORIO.   You need a doctor.
TRACE.   I don't need a damn doctor! I need Roy to be more understanding — that's what I need. How come all your

fucking clothes are out?

GREGORIO. I have to go.

TRACE. Already? You just got here. Thought you were gonna turn this room into Gregorio-land. New nation, under God. Small, but nice.

GREGORIO. Hagen called. He said I need to move.

TRACE. How come?

GREGORIO. Hagen said someone called him — told him things.

TRACE. Things?

GREGORIO. It doesn't matter. He's taking me somewhere this afternoon.

TRACE. So you're leaving. Fuller's gonna miss you. *(Rising, still clearly hurting.)* I can hear him now. "Where's Greg? Where's my good boy?" *(Holding his side.)* Agh! Fuck.

GREGORIO. Lie down.

TRACE. *(Of the aquarium.)* What're you doing with that? Gonna steal it?

GREGORIO. I was looking at it. I used to have one.

TRACE. What for? Drinking water? Hey, you found my little guy. You found airhead. *(Trailing a finger in the water.)* I used to have fish in this.

GREGORIO. Good idea.

TRACE. Didn't care about 'em. I liked the water more than the fish. The way it looked. Used to shine flashlights through it at night. My favorite thing though was airhead. *(Holding the toy diver's air tube.)* I used to bury his feet way down in the gravel and really turn up the air pressure till the tank looked like it was boiling. The fish'd go nuts. And the guy, the diver — he was just stuck, you know? Stuck at the bottom of the sea, with all that air going through him. *(He blows hard into the tube. Air bubbles come out of the diver's helmet.)* I used to wonder who the little bastard was, you know? Me? Fuller? Sure as fuck wasn't Roy. Got a cigarette? *(Gregorio lights a cigarette, hands it to Trace.)* Where's Hagen taking you — Canada? Gonna keep trying new countries?

GREGORIO. Maybe.

TRACE. *(Sitting on the bed.)* What if you run out?

GREGORIO. I already have. *(Gregorio goes back to packing.)*
TRACE. I love to smoke. Fuller can't stand it. Once he quit, the whole world was supposed to. Everybody worries about it up here. Smoking. Stop fucking smoking! Add five years to your pitiful life. Die at ninety-five instead of ninety, sucking a tube in a hospital someplace. *(Laughs.)* I even get trade that's worried about it — about me. We'll be there, still breathing hard after a real hot sloppy one, you know? After a fuck it, let's-do-it-all-then-hit-the-free-clinic-for-the-penicillin kind of number? You know. And the guy won't be talking about clap or herpes or any of the shit that's coming out — the sex that gives you cancer in the legs, or whatever the fuck it is. He'll be looking at me smoke — *tobacco* — and he'll freak. About my lungs, for God's sake. I mean, our dicks are rotting off for all we know, and he's acting like instant Daddy — like I'm supposed to reach thirty. *(A beat.)* I like my work. I hate my life — my life is shit — but I really like my work. I was meant to take it all in. All the garbage, everybody's trash, all the shit they bring me. You can smell it on them — how much they hate being alive. They come to me; dump their life. Just dump it and go. I'm a trash heap. Rats and everything. Running all through me.
GREGORIO. Trace —
TRACE. Damn it, why'd Roy have to do that? You should've seen his house. It was even bigger'n I remembered. It had TVs in the wall, indoor pool. The way the light hit the ceiling in there — it was like a church made out of water.
GREGORIO. Is that where he beat you?
TRACE. They got any water where you came from?
GREGORIO. The ocean.
TRACE. Ocean — great. Place for all the blood to go.
GREGORIO. Go to sleep.
TRACE. And miss you leaving? No way. Promise me you'll get out of this Sanctuary shit though, man. Looks like a fucking dog show. I see your ass on TV, I just want to spit in your goddamn eye. Come up here, begging us to be nice to you — who the fuck do you think we are? *God, I tried to be so fucking nice!!* Tried to be everything he wanted! He's di-

vorced! Doesn't even have a wife! Why didn't he want me? Why the fuck didn't he want me? *(Gregorio opens the toy box. He pulls out a toy pistol.)* What are you doing?

GREGORIO. *(Handing it to Trace.)* Here. Kill yourself.

TRACE. What?

GREGORIO. I'm sick of your complaints: kill yourself.

TRACE. It's not a real gun.

GREGORIO. It's not a real life.

TRACE. Fuck you.

GREGORIO. Neither is mine. *(Taking another pistol from the toy box.)* Maybe I'll kill myself.

TRACE. You go first.

GREGORIO. No, you go first.

TRACE. Don't you have anything better — ?

GREGORIO. *(Pointing the gun at him.)* Go first, or I'll kill you!

TRACE. What the fuck's wrong with you!?

GREGORIO. Do it!! Do it!! Blow your brains out!

TRACE. Fuck you!

GREGORIO. *(Splashing water from the tank at him.)* Do it! *Do it!!* Don't be a coward!

TRACE. Stop that!! Shit — !

GREGORIO. Kill yourself or drown!! NOW!!

TRACE. *(Jumping up, shoving him away from the tank and splashing him instead.)* I'll show you who's drowning — !!

GREGORIO. *(Pointing the toy pistol at Trace.)* Stop!! I warn you!!

TRACE. *(Splashing him.)* DROWN, MOTHERFUCKER!!

GREGORIO. *(Pointing his toy pistol at the little diver, which he's taken from the tank.)* I'll kill him! Stop, or I'll kill him!

TRACE. *(Splashing.)* DROWN!

GREGORIO. *(Dropping gun and diver, trading splashes with Trace.)* YOU DROWN!

TRACE. YOU DROWN!!

GREGORIO. *YOU DROWN!!!* *(Trace suddenly breaks for the toy box and pulls out a toy machine gun. He points it at Gregorio. He shoots it — it makes a gunfire noise — as Gregorio dives across the bed and reaches in the toy box himself. He pulls out another toy gun*

203

— which also makes some kind of shooting sound — and fires it at Trace from behind the bed. Trace kicks over the cot and hides behind it. Both men fire for another moment, then Trace makes a dash for the toy box and pulls out a toy grenade. He pulls an imaginary pin and tosses it at Gregorio, who continues to fire.)

TRACE.   *EXPLOSION!!!!! (Gregorio pitches onto the bed, screaming and 'dying.')*

GREGORIO.   *Aggggghhhhhhh — !!*

TRACE.   Die! Die, damn it — die!!! *(Both men are by now laughing. The energy from the fight slowly dissipates.)*

GREGORIO.   See what I told you? It's not a real life.

TRACE.   I don't know — I think I'm really dead.

GREGORIO.   *(Gregorio rises, starts very slowly to pick things up, put them back.)* You know when I first knew life was not real? I was in the mountains, down there. Hiding.

TRACE.   Hiding? From what?

GREGORIO.   I stole things to live. Once I even stole a gun.

TRACE.   Oh yeah? From who?

GREGORIO.   A dead man. I was near a town. I heard gunshots. Someone was shooting people. That's not so unusual there. It was nothing big — a few men. Someone made them kneel by a ditch and shot them. Then they went away, and the families came out for the bodies. I waited till night and crawled down to the ditch. I wanted to sit there, I don't know why. The blood was almost dry on the ground. I could hear people crying in their houses. There was no light on, in the whole town. Then I felt something with my foot — a pistol. One of the men must've thrown it in the ditch so it wouldn't be found. *(A beat.)* It was loaded. I wanted to kill someone — wanted to kill myself. Wanted to kill the people in the town, because they were only people. There was only one bullet in the gun. I fired in the air. Straight overhead, in the dark. Then I listened. Not one door opened. A shot at night, and no one dared to look. I walked down the middle of the street, past all the houses, with the gun in my hand. When I got to the end of town, I dropped the gun in the road, and gave myself a new name. Gregorio. I am Gregorio Hernandez. Whoever I was before had died, and then he pretended to

204

die, and then he killed himself in the night with a single shot. And no one came to look. *(A beat.)*

TRACE. *(Rising dizzily, of the picking up.)* Let me help.

GREGORIO. You don't have to.

TRACE. It's ok. Just let me ... let me — *(Trace takes a woozy step or two, then suddenly collapses unconscious.)*

GREGORIO. Trace? Trace — ?! *(Gregorio hurries to him as the lights quickly fade to black.)*

SCENE TWELVE

BAG

Twenty minutes later. Trace lies on the bed, asleep. There's a washcloth on his forehead. Fuller sits near Trace. The room has been tidied up. There's now an old athletic bag sitting on top of the clothes on the dresser. Fuller stares at Trace for a moment, then looks over at the bag. Fuller rises and goes over to the bag. He looks at it carefully. Trace awakes.

TRACE. What are you doing?

FULLER. Nothing. Go back to sleep.

TRACE. *(Feeling his bruised face.)* God. How long have I been sleeping?

FULLER. Not long. Go on and rest. I'm right here.

TRACE. Where's Gregorio?

FULLER. Getting ready to leave. Go to sleep.

TRACE. *(Feeling his face again.)* Agh — !

FULLER. *(Adjusting the washcloth on Trace's forehead.)* I'll get you a doctor, as soon as he's gone.

TRACE. No fucking doctor. I'm fine. *(As Fuller presses too hard.)* Ow!

FULLER. Sorry. It's a good thing I came home when I did. Why won't you tell me what happened?

TRACE. I don't want to talk about it.

FULLER. Son, I'm just trying to —

TRACE. *Son?*

FULLER. What if you're hurt? He said you blacked out. You could be hurt in ways you don't — *(Fuller tries to lift Trace's shirt to look for any other injuries.)*

TRACE. *Get away!! (Trace pushes Fuller away.)* What do you care if I'm hurt? "Trace got hurt" — *there's* news. Look, I'll lie here till I feel a little better. Then I'll go. Ok?

FULLER. This is your room. You have the right to get well in it. Wish you'd tell me what happened. I don't even know who hurt you. It could be Gregorio for all I —

TRACE. It wasn't him. Christ.

FULLER. Then who was it?

TRACE.· Who the fuck do you think?! I found Roy. It was Roy, ok? Satisfied? *(A beat.)*

FULLER. How'd you find him?

TRACE. Got lucky. His name starts with D.

FULLER. And he's the one who — ?

TRACE. What's it matter? As long as someone beats me up — you know? As long as the job gets done. You were right about the piece of shit. Congratulations.

FULLER. Trace —

TRACE. "Trace," "Trace" — *shit!!* I'd rather be back with Roy. I'm getting out of here.

FULLER. *(Stopping him.)* No! Damn it, this is *your room.* *(Gregorio enters. He carries a couple of shirts. He and Fuller exchange a look, then Gregorio puts the shirts into the bag and starts to pack the clothes.)*

TRACE. So is Hagen here yet?

GREGORIO. Not yet.

TRACE. Where's he driving you? Europe?

GREGORIO. It's secret. What you don't know can't hurt. Right, Fuller?

FULLER. Don't use that bag.

GREGORIO. This? Why not?

TRACE. It's my bag. I don't care.

FULLER. It's got Trace's name on it. What if you get caught?

TRACE. So what? If they've got him, they won't want you.

FULLER. He's not using the bag.

TRACE. What's he gonna use?

GREGORIO. It's all right. *(Hauling his things out of the bag.)* I won't touch it. *(Gregorio tosses the empty bag onto the rug.)* Fuller doesn't want me to touch your things. I understand. *(Gregorio picks up a pillow from the cot and strips off the case. He begins putting his things in it.)*

TRACE. *I* don't understand. What the hell'd you do, anyway?

FULLER. It's not important.

TRACE. Hell, it isn't — what'd you do?!

GREGORIO. I was in the army. I killed people.

TRACE. Who'd you kill?

FULLER. Trace —

TRACE. *Who'd you kill?!* *(Gregorio looks away.)*

FULLER. Civilians. Innocent people.

TRACE. That true?

GREGORIO. Yes. I was ordered to.

TRACE. *(To Fuller.)* You told Hagen?

FULLER. Of course.

TRACE. Why?

FULLER. What do you mean, why? He killed people.

TRACE. Not here. *(To Gregorio.)* You didn't kill anybody here, did you?

FULLER. It doesn't matter. In El Salvador —

TRACE. *That's the fucking other world!!* That's not here! You brought this guy in your house. He was your fucking guest, for chrissake!

FULLER. He's a criminal.

TRACE. And you're not? *(To Gregorio.)* I'm going with you.

GREGORIO. What?

TRACE. Let me go with.

FULLER. Trace, you can't —

TRACE. Shut up! You don't think I'm staying around here, do you?

FULLER. Hagen'll never take you anywhere.

TRACE. Yes, he will. Look at me: honorary refugee. Hell,

207

I don't look *good* enough to be a refugee. *(To Gregorio.)* I know I could've been more hospitable and all, but —

FULLER.   You're not going anywhere.

TRACE.   *(Ignoring Fuller.)* I can be a whole different guy. Really. Shit, I don't have to be Trace anymore. You don't have to be Gregorio. They're not our real names. We can have new ones.

FULLER.   Trace, stay here. I'm not going anywhere. I decided. I'll be right here, I promise.

TRACE.   *Will you shut up!?* You had your choice — you didn't have to call Hagen.

FULLER.   God doesn't make choices easier. He makes them harder.

TRACE.   Oh. He does, eh? So does that mean when you fucked me it was bad? And now that you're fucking him it's good? Is that what that means? *(Fuller is silent.)* Fuck you. I'm leaving. *(To Gregorio.)* Let's go.

GREGORIO.   You can't come.

TRACE.   What do you mean I can't come?

GREGORIO.   You're not like me. You can't go where I go.

TRACE.   What do you mean? Hell, I'm your roommate, man.

GREGORIO.   No.

FULLER.   Trace —

TRACE.   I mean it! I can help you. I know guys. Not just here. Guys that go all over. Doesn't matter what town you're in — they're gonna know somebody. Hagen doesn't have all the answers. I can make calls.

FULLER.   Trace, he doesn't want you.

TRACE.   *(Picking up the bag, grabbing the pillowcase with the clothes in it from Gregorio.)* Here, take my bag —

FULLER.   He's not taking —

TRACE.   *(Stuffing the pillowcase into the bag.)* IT'S MY FUCKING BAG — YOU HEAR?! MINE! (To Gregorio.)* I can help you, man. We don't even need Hagen.

FULLER.   You have to wait for Hagen — ! *(Something in Fuller's tone makes them look at him.)*

GREGORIO.   Why wouldn't I wait for him?

208

FULLER. No reason. I mean, he'll be here any minute.

GREGORIO. Any minute? You know exactly?

FULLER. Not exactly, but —

TRACE. What's going on here?

GREGORIO. He's coming alone, right?

FULLER. Of course. Why wouldn't he be?

GREGORIO. You tell me. What did you and Hagen talk about?

FULLER. About moving you — what do you think?

TRACE. Someone else is coming. I can feel it.

GREGORIO. Is that true? Fuller, is that true?

FULLER. It's just Hagen!

TRACE. He's lying. He's fucking lying.

GREGORIO. Who's coming, Fuller? Who's coming here now?

FULLER. Just stay calm, ok? It's Hagen.

GREGORIO. *Who's he bringing with him!?*

FULLER. Nobody! I'm going upstairs. (*As Fuller starts for the stairs, Trace swings the bag hard in Fuller's face. Fuller slips and falls onto the bed, sliding down to the floor. Trace hits him hard with the bag two or three times.*)

TRACE. *You stay here!! You fucking stay here, you hear me!!? You — fucking — STAY!!* (*A tense beat.*) You gonna tell us the truth?

FULLER. I did.

TRACE. *Shit — !* (*Trace looks around the room, sees the scissors on the floor by the dresser, picks them up. Trace grabs Fuller by the shirt and holds the scissors inches from Fuller's face.*)

GREGORIO. Trace — !

TRACE. We're gonna have an honest moment here, Dad. You tell me who's coming with Hagen — *now.* If you don't, I'm gonna cut out your eye.

FULLER. No!

TRACE. You understand?! *YOU UNDERSTAND?!! Now who the fuck's coming!!?*

FULLER. Immigration.

TRACE. You piece of — !! (*Gregorio grabs Trace before he can harm Fuller. He swings Trace away, disarming him.*)

209

GREGORIO. Stop it!! *(To Fuller.)* So. Hagen too? *(Fuller's silent. To Trace.)* Come on.
TRACE. Where?
GREGORIO. *Now!*
TRACE. Ok — ok!
FULLER. No — Trace! Don't go with him! Don't — *(Gregorio and Trace hurry out. Fuller follows as far as the door.)* Trace! *Trace* — !! *(Fuller stares after them. Lights slowly shift.)*

SCENE THIRTEEN

FULLER

FULLER. *(Moving slowly around the room, running his hand over furniture — as at the beginning of the play.)* They took my car and abandoned it downtown. An hour after that, the police picked them up. Trace they let go. Gregorio.... The INS returned him to El Salvador two months after he was arrested. A year later, his body was found on the beach. There was a bullet in the back of his head.

It's been ten years since Gregorio was here. The fighting has stopped, for now. They finally got permission to excavate the mass graves of the victims at El Mozote. They're finding hundreds — mostly children.

Trace never came back. I finally got up the courage to tell Reverend Hagen the truth about who I was, what I'd been. He said we had to find Trace, so we looked all over town, the Russell Hotel, everywhere. But he was gone.

I went to other cities — drove around for days sometimes. No one had ever seen him. He'd be almost thirty now. Every week I look for him. *(Lights start to fade. Fuller sits on the bed and stares at the window. Lights fade to black.)*

THE END

PATIENT A

To Jeanne,
for every step of the way

We are all special cases. We all want to appeal
against something! Everyone insists on his innocence,
at all costs, even if it means accusing the rest of the
human race and heaven.
—Camus, *La Chute*

Assuredly we bring not innocence into the world,
we bring impurity much rather: that which purifies us
is trial, and trial is by what is contrary.
—Milton, *Areopagitica*

Patient A was first produced at Signature Theatre Company (James Houghton, Artistic Director; Thomas C. Proehl, Managing Director), in New York City, on April 23, 1993. It was directed by Jeanne Blake; the costume design was by Teresa Snider-Stein; the lighting design was by Jeffrey S. Koger; and the production stage manager was Kurt Engstrom. The cast was as follows:

KIMBERLY . . . . Robin Morse
LEE . . . . Jon DeVries
MATTHEW . . . . Richard Bekins

CHARACTERS

(in alphabetical order)

KIM, in her early 20s
LEE, in his 40s
MATTHEW, about 30

Lights up to reveal Matthew, sitting upstage. He very slowly pages through an invisible magazine. Kim enters. She looks around as though this is the first time she's ever been here. She notices Matthew, who gives her a small, friendly wave and goes back to his magazine. Kim sits downstage on a platform. Lee enters. He makes a gesture for Kim to lie down on the platform, parallel to the audience line. She does so, and closes her eyes. Lee looks down at her.

LEE.   *(Reciting in a natural tone.)*
"The wanton troopers riding by
Have shot my fawn, and it will die.
Ungentle men! They cannot thrive
To kill thee. Thou ne'er didst alive
Them any harm: alas, nor could
Thy death yet do them any good.
I'm sure I never wished them ill;
Nor do I for all this; nor will."

(To audience.)
I heard somewhere, years ago, stumbling forward or backward — I can't remember which — in my career, that if you have an actor lie feet-first to the audience, then it's a tragedy. But if you have her lie head-first —
KIM.   Should I do that?
LEE.   No, no. If you have her lie head-first, then it's a comedy. *(Staring at her a moment.)* Or it's the other way around. I can't remember. It was a director talking. Anyway, the position itself preconditions us.
KIM.   But you've got me lying sideways. *(Sitting up.)* That's

215

not anything, right? I mean, not tragedy or comedy.

LEE. Well —

KIM. Why? I'm not neutral.

LEE. I know — I know you're not. But I am. *(She gives him a look, then indicates Matthew.)*

KIM. Who's he?

LEE. Him? Oh, that's ... I thought he might be helpful later.

KIM. I trust you, you know.

LEE. I know. *(A beat.)*

KIM. What was that poem, anyway?

LEE. What?

KIM. The poem you were saying.

LEE. Oh — actually, that's one of my favorite poems.

KIM. It is?

LEE. It's not very current. Andrew Marvell. The "Coy Mistress" guy? *(She's unsure.)* Doesn't matter.

KIM. Was that the whole poem?

LEE. No, no. Only the beginning. It's actually a hundred and twenty-two lines long. Short lines. It's called, "The Nymph Complaining For The Death Of Her Fawn." Mid-1600s. It's in the voice of the nymph — or young girl. It's really about the loss of innocence. The convention however is that it's about the death of ... of a pet.

KIM. A pet?

LEE. A pet fawn. *(A beat.)*

KIM. I'm a little stumped by this.

LEE. I'm sorry. It's kind of personal for me. I'm trying to find a ... a resonance. Something that's evocative for me. Of you. Of your story.

KIM. I had a lot of pets.

LEE. It's not that literal.

KIM. Birds, a dog — no small deer.

LEE. It's more figurative than that.

KIM. Why do you have to be figurative? Why don't you just tell my story?

MATTHEW. He's a playwright.

KIM.   *(Looking at Matthew, then to Lee.)* Ok, who are the troopers?

LEE.   The troop — ? Oh, um ... "The wanton troopers riding by" — yes. That's actually a reference to the Scottish Covenanting Army which invaded England in 1640 —   •

KIM.   Stop.

LEE.   Yes?

KIM.   What have they got to do with me?

LEE.   Nothing ... directly. But they were raiders, lived off the land and ... killed a fawn. Or men like them did. It's all fiction anyway. The poem just needs the fawn to be killed by people who don't really ... take responsibility.

KIM.   Oh! Ok. Go on.

LEE.   Really?

" ... But, O my fears!
It cannot die so. Heaven's King
Keeps register of everything:
And nothing may we use in vain.
E'en beasts must be with justice slain,
Else men are made their deodands."

MATTHEW.   Deodands? *(They stare at Matthew.)*

LEE.   Legal term. Means forfeits. Not important.

KIM.   This is very personal for you, isn't it?

LEE.   Yes, I guess it is.

KIM.   'Cause it makes no sense to me at all. I was trained to be an actuary. You know? Working out mortality rates —

LEE.   This was a mortality.

KIM.   A *fawn?*

LEE.   You were a mortality.

KIM.   I'm going to do this my own way for a while. Ok? Just to get started. *(He nods. She makes a small gesture. He sits. She speaks to the audience.)* For those of you who don't know who I am yet — and it's already several minutes into the play and I'm sure that's some kind of playwriting mistake — my name is ... was ... Kimberly Ann Mary Bergalis. I came from a family of Lithuanian-American Catholics, for the most part. I'm using the past tense, by the way, out of respect for myself. The rest of my family's doing fine.

LEE. Past tense is a very workable choice.

KIM. *(To audience, giving him a look.)* I was born in eastern Pennsylvania, and grew up in a little town called Tamaqua. Lee actually came there for my funeral.

LEE. I was struck by — May I interrupt?

KIM. Is it poetry?

LEE. No.

KIM. Ok.

LEE. *(To audience.)* I was struck by the countryside. There are ridges everywhere you look. They loom over you. Towns in dark, narrow valleys. Buildings, roads, mines — all of it with this eternally leftover look. Even the fast-food places feel like they were built a hundred years ago.

MATTHEW. He thought —

LEE. Who would want to be buried here?

KIM. But he hadn't seen the cemetary. On top of the ridge, up among the trees. As far as you look, other trees, other ridges. And the sky — you're practically in the sky. It's a Lithuanian cemetary. Names like —

MATTHEW. Karalunas, Andrukitis, Shucavage, Pilashusky. And of course, Zebleckas —

KIM. My grandmother. *(Quickly, to Lee.)* Is this how he's going to be helpful?

LEE. Maybe.

KIM. *(To audience.)* Anyway, my grandmother was buried there, and I wanted to be buried next to her. And now I am, of course. I believe in an afterlife, and I'm with her now. In heaven.

LEE. Let's not get too much into that.

KIM. Why not?

LEE. It just makes me a little uncomfortable. Concepts like a literal heaven.

KIM. You don't believe in one?

LEE. I have no faith.

KIM. Really? So what's heaven for you? Things in the world?

LEE. Yes, I guess.

KIM. Like the poem?

LEE. Maybe.

KIM. So heaven for you comes in little bits and pieces?

LEE. Yes.

KIM. And ends. Finally.

LEE. Yes.

KIM. I see. *(To audience.)* When I was twelve, we moved to Ft. Pierce, Florida. I loved it. I was just beginning junior-high, and suddenly it was summer forever. I found a best friend almost right away — Geralynn. We were blood sisters. That got looked into later on. Sometimes when we didn't have anything else to do, we'd take a stupid little red plastic boat and go float in the Indian River.

LEE. *(To audience.)* Geralynn told me about this. The image stuck in my head.

MATTHEW. *(Without looking up.)* It did?

KIM. Geri and I would float in that boat in the sun for hours. Like we were the same organism. I don't know which gave me the most pleasure — the floating itself or being that close to another person. The river's not deep there, but I used to imagine that it went down forever, like the sea. That we were above a world that had no limit, just floating. *(A beat.)* My Dad was the financial director for the city of Ft. Pierce. His name is George.

LEE. *(To audience.)* A lot of daughters love and admire their fathers. Kim emulated hers. She sought his respect in everything.

MATTHEW. Sort of a perfect relationship?

LEE. A fortunate one.

KIM. My mother, Anna, in the first of a series of ironies the author wants me to observe — although I find them pretty unremarkable — was a nurse at a clinic that treated a lot of AIDS patients. *(A beat.)* After high-school I went to the University of Florida. I was a business major, and — *(Lee coughs quietly.)* Oh. He wants me to underscore this other irony. You know, that I was going to be an actuary, and that actuaries work a lot with statistics, and that eventually that's what I be-

219

came — a statistic, not an actuary. Ok?

LEE.   Thanks.

KIM.   I'm not sure these are technically even ironies.

MATTHEW.   Besides, didn't they do this on Channel 5?

LEE.   Humor me.

KIM.   The other irony — and believe me, this is the last one — is that when I was in high school I once tried to do a report on AIDS, but had to pick another subject, because there wasn't enough material on it in the library. Are ironies like poems for you or something?

LEE.   A little.

KIM.   So you actually get pleasure from them? 'Cause most people don't, you know. *(To audience.)* In the middle of my junior year, I needed some dental work. Two back molars had to come out. *(A beat.)* We'd just changed our dentist. Our new one was down in Jensen — Dr. Acer.*

LEE.   Dr. Acer.

KIM.   What?

LEE.   Oh, nothing. Dr. Acer, that's all. I've been thinking what to do with him.

MATTHEW.   What to do?

LEE.   All I can see is that terrible graduation shot of him that ran all over the country. *(To audience.)* Grainy, black-and-white.... The very quality of the shot — the remoteness it forced on you.... It made him look like a criminal.

MATTHEW.   A criminal?

LEE.   I'm not saying he was. There could've been accidents, oversights. Certainly no one ever proved that he willfully infected anyone. He even published a letter, the day before he died. It said he had HIV. It also said he'd been advised he could continue to practice, as long as he followed the guidelines of the Centers for Disease Control. If any of his patients was worried however, they should get tested. The last paragraph was quite touching.

MATTHEW.   *(Quoting it.)* "Please try to understand. I am a

---

* Pronounced, "Ack-er."

gentle man. To infect anyone would be contrary to everything I have stood for."

LEE.   As it turned out, he'd infected at least six of his patients with HIV. The questions these events raised were all ugly ones: had Dr. Acer deliberately transmitted the virus? Had he done it negligently? Or — even more disturbing — was he trying to follow the CDC's guidelines? No one knew the answers to these questions. And Dr. Acer was dead. All that was left was a blood sample and a tiny, black-and-white photo. *(A beat.)* This is all we have to judge by, so many of us. On one hand we see a young, composed, telegenic woman dying. On the other, this little grey, remote head. This dead man. This mysterious letter in a newspaper.

MATTHEW.   And you think that's fair?

LEE.   Some stories just push us in a particular direction. We have to face that, we have to give it its due in a sense — and yet struggle to withhold our final judgment.

MATTHEW.   And who are you to judge?

KIM.   Yes, who are you?

LEE.   Nobody.

KIM.   *(To audience.)* On December 17, 1987 I had two back molars removed by Dr. Acer. While it was an involved appointment, I don't remember much about it that was unusual. Of course, it was years before it seemed important enough to remember. I drove home on the narrow road up the coast, looking at the ocean and the trees. *(A beat.)* Less than four years later, I'd be dead.

LEE.

"Though they should wash their guilty hands
In this warm life-blood, which doth part
From thine, and wound me to the heart,
Yet could they not be clean: their stain
Is dyed in such a purple grain,
There is not such another in
The world, to offer for their sin."

MATTHEW.   That's a little extreme, isn't it?

LEE.   What? Oh — hyperbole is a central device of the poem. The fawn is seen as a perfect ideal of innocence. To harm it was a profound sin. I'm not saying that's Kim's story exactly.

MATTHEW.   Then what are you saying?

LEE.   That I miss ... innocence.

KIM.   *(To the audience.)* I started to feel sick in spring of 1989 — only about a year and a half after I had my molars removed. Part of the reason we didn't at first think of Dr. Acer was that it had been so recent. But I was definitely getting sick. I had a few sore throats that spring, and then I developed oral thrush. Little white patches in my mouth. The doctor was surprised. Normally they only see thrush in diabetics or people on a lot of antibiotics, infants, AIDS patients. They gave me some medication and it cleared up. A few weeks later though, the thrush came back. Meanwhile, we looked for diabetes. My grandfather was diabetic.

MATTHEW.   A basic medical principle: look for the likeliest first.

KIM.   I had a blood sugar test done. Everything was fine. Then I started fainting at work. I went to a hemotologist. They took blood, ran a lot of tests — no HIV test, though. I really didn't fit the profile.

MATTHEW.   Look for the likeliest first.

KIM.   The blood results weren't good. I began to have problems breathing. I went to a hemotologist/oncologist, who examined me for cancer.

MATTHEW.   Look for the likeliest —

KIM.   *I know.* I drove home to show my parents all the lab information. My Mom cried. She said my symptoms were so reminiscent of AIDS.

MATTHEW.   Did you have a test done —

LEE.   She asked —

KIM.   No, I said. There's no reason. *(A beat.)* I just got worse. I didn't have cancer. The doctors wondered if I was just hyperventilating. By December my parents had to come up and drive me home. Just before we left, a nurse called and said the new results had come in and that I had hepatitis. Hepatitis, I thought. That's lucky.

LEE.   When I grew up, it was the diseases that were dying.

Smallpox, polio, diphtheria — wonderful new drugs were killing off all the old killers. Billions of tiny white flags under the microscopes — that was the image. I think the public genuinely believed we could defeat any serious, infectious disease.

KIM.   Except for viruses.

LEE.   Except for viruses. They've been with us forever, presumably, though we didn't discover the first human virus until 1900.

MATTHEW.   Yellow fever. *(To Lee.)* Do I really have to do this?

LEE.   What do you mean?

MATTHEW.   This choral support. I mean, can't we just talk?

LEE.   We are talking.

MATTHEW.   No — to each other.

LEE.   This is important information.

MATTHEW.   But it's yours, not mine. I didn't even exist in the decade you're talking about. For that matter, do I exist now?

KIM.   What's it matter?

MATTHEW.   What's it *matter?*

KIM.   *(To Lee.)* Who is he?

LEE.   Can we just talk about viruses? We do not have all night.

MATTHEW.   I like her question. Who am I?

LEE.   *(To audience.)* Viruses infect every living thing. And while the vast majority don't kill their host —

MATTHEW.   Who am I?

LEE.   Which would be inefficient —

MATTHEW.   Do I have a name?

LEE.   Some do. *(To Matthew.)* Will you please shut up?! *(Matthew stares at him. Lee continues quietly to the audience.)* It doesn't always last. The great influenza pandemic of 1918 came, killed millions and left. Some viruses hover around us forever, like rabies. *(To Matthew.)* I'm sorry. *(A beat.)* I'm sorry. Please forgive me.

MATTHEW.   Who am I to forgive? *(A beat.)*

LEE.   *(To Kim.)* Meanwhile, you thought you had hepatitis.

KIM.   *(To audience.)* By the time my folks got me home, I could barely walk. I blacked out and crashed into the hall closet. The next day we got a call from the doctor's office. I didn't have hepatitis. It was a mistake in their labs.

MATTHEW. A basic medical principle: sometimes we make mistakes.

KIM. Our local doctor diagnosed me with bilateral pneumocystis pneumonia and had me hospitalized. Oh, yes — and for the first time I was tested for HIV. The test wasn't conclusive. So I had another one. That was inconclusive too. So I had one more. Five days after I turned twenty-two, the results came back positive.

LEE. What with the pneumocystis and the numbers, it was clear they were talking about AIDS.

KIM. The doctor gave me some time alone, before my folks came in. I began to cry. I looked out the window, and the clouds were moving against the sun, swirling. My life came into my mind. I thought about when I lived in Tamaqua, and the lake and ice skating, and then when I became, you know, a woman. I thought of everything, and that it was all over. No boyfriend, husband, kids, grandkids. My eyes were closed. Suddenly I felt as if someone was lying by my side. There was pressure against my whole side, a warmth — I felt it. I heard a voice that said it would all be ok. That everyone in the family would be able to handle it. And I opened my eyes and no one was in the room.

LEE. Kim was an adult of course, so the law said that only she could tell her parents.

KIM. My mother was the first to come in. She knew as soon as she looked at me. She came around and just lunged onto the bed and cried and hugged me and pushed my hair back, and ... comforted me. She talked about her own parents, who'd been killed years before in a car accident and how they'd be waiting in heaven for me, along with Grandma Zebleckas and even their dog that died, too. I think if she could have put everything that ever lived into heaven for me in that moment she would have.

MATTHEW. *(To Lee.)* Millions go through this.

LEE. And will.

KIM.   When we'd calmed down, my father came in. That was harder. I was his oldest. I remember he said —

MATTHEW.   *(Softly, as the father.)* "Oh, my God, no. No, please."

KIM.   And he shook, and he cried. I said "Put your head on my shoulder," and he did. And I ... petted his head, and said, "It's gonna be ok. We're gonna get through this." And Mom was rubbing his back, and he just kept crying and crying. He kept saying it had to be a mistake, that he didn't believe it, that it can't be. It just can't be. And I said, "Dad, it is."

LEE.   *(To audience.)* Kim's mother went to work the next day, trying to keep her mind off it. But the day after was Saturday, and there was nothing to do but think. *(Lee looks expectantly at Matthew, who's lost in thought.)* She had nothing to do but think. *(Matthew looks up.)*

MATTHEW.   Oh. *(To audience.)* It was a cold, wet, foggy day, but she had to get out of the house. So she went for a walk on the beach. Almost purposely she headed for an isolated area where some women had been attacked. She decided to look for a large piece of driftwood — a big club, she thought — and to beat the hell out of anyone who tried to hurt her. There was only one person on the beach, a retired man surf-casting. A few yards behind him there was a broken branch in the sand. Anna picked it up and glanced at the man, who said —

LEE.   Lady, I'm just here fishing.

KIM.   I'm going for a walk. I found out my daughter's very sick.

LEE.   Oh.

MATTHEW.   Then she strode down the beach, looking for someone guilty. She didn't find anyone. Then she came back.

LEE.   Looks like you cooled down a little. Want to talk about it?

KIM.   Not now.

MATTHEW.   She dropped the piece of wood and kept walking. When she was almost out of earshot he yelled —

LEE.   Lady! Life is unfair!

MATTHEW.   She didn't turn. She just walked home.

LEE.   *(After a beat, to audience.)*
"It is a wondrous thing, how fleet
'Twas, on those little silver feet.
With what a pretty skipping grace,
It oft would challenge me the race:
And when't had left me far away,
'Twould stay, and run again, and stay."

(To audience.) "It," by the way, refers to the fawn — or innocence — or I suppose, for me anyway, just life.

"For it was nimbler much than hinds;
And trod, as on the four winds."

(To audience.) I didn't meet Kim till the last months of her
life. She was in the hospital, she'd just had a transfusion. I'm
really pretty useless in hospitals. *(A beat.)* A few years ago a
friend of mine died. Congenital heart defect. She'd had sur-
gery when she was young, and that gave her maybe twenty
more years — but suddenly one day the sutures or plugs
blew, and.... So for the first time in my life, I went to an in-
tensive care ward, to see Serene, which was her name. It was
so *hot* in there. All this equipment, all these beds and noise
... I tried to smile, talk normally. She couldn't talk at all —
she had these tubes and things going into her throat. I'd
never seen the life in a person so ... pressed down into her.
My reaction was absolutely physical. I started to faint. Just
from being near this terrible force that was working in her. I
stumbled out into the waiting room, collapsed in the nearest
chair. I felt as though I'd been sealed in my own crypt.
KIM.   I saw that all the time. People who visited me,
journalists, friends. Some couldn't take it.
LEE.   When I first met you, I couldn't touch you.
KIM.   I know. I was used to that, too.
LEE.   I knew it was safe. I know it's safe.
KIM.   Just makes you human.
LEE.   It makes me common. I can take my place in the
clear majority. *(A beat.)*

KIM.   Maybe if I just went on with my story.

LEE.   We could try that.

KIM.   *(To audience.)* My case was reported to the state agency and also to the Centers For Disease Control in Atlanta. They couldn't figure out how I'd been infected. I didn't have any of the usual risk factors. I hadn't had any transfusions. I wasn't a drug user or hemophiliac. They ended up asking about some pretty unusual things.

MATTHEW.   What about this blood sister you're supposed to have had? This Geralynn — ?

KIM.   Yes?

MATTHEW.   When was that?

KIM.   Eighth or ninth grade.

MATTHEW.   And how did you, um — ?

KIM.   We took a pin and just, you know, pricked our fingers, rubbed our fingers together — and we came up with some contract that we were sisters forever and put the fingerprint by the names. We used a little safety pin. There was just a tiny dot.

MATTHEW.   How many people have you had intercourse with?

KIM.   None.

MATTHEW.   I'm talking about sex, now. Sexual —

KIM.   None. *(To audience.)* They had a very hard time believing that I'd never had intercourse. They came back and asked the questions again. And they made them more personal.

MATTHEW.   Have you ever used any birth control devices or pills?

KIM.   No.

MATTHEW.   Did any of your boyfriends ever use birth control devices?

KIM.   Once, in my junior year in college. But nothing came of it.

MATTHEW.   And what were the circumstances of his using it?

KIM.   He had ... placed the condom, and we were, you know, talking about it, and we were going to. And my roommate at the time had moved out two weeks earlier. Anyway, there was a slamming, and he thought she had come in, and my bedroom door was open. And he jumped up, and I said "No — it's not my roommate, it's someone across the hall." And he apologized and.... So nothing ever came of it. We both just went to sleep.

MATTHEW.   So you never — ?

KIM.   No.

MATTHEW.   Have you ever participated in oral sex?

KIM.   *(To audience.)* Some people at this age are really not prepared to discuss all this, you know? It makes them feel just ... very ... humiliated.

MATTHEW.   Have you?

KIM.   No. I haven't.

MATTHEW.   Has anyone ever performed oral sex on you?

KIM.   Yes.

MATTHEW.   And the circumstances — ?

KIM.   A different boyfriend, also my junior year. We'd been at a party. We went back to my place about two or three in the morning. He was kissing me, and he started removing his clothes, and we were lying on the bed, and he ... he performed, you know, on me. And he tried to have intercourse, and I said no. He didn't have a condom, or any.... And then later he tried again, and you know ... I said no. And, and then, you know, he got dressed and —

MATTHEW.   When you say that he tried to have sex, was he on top of you trying to insert himself?

KIM.   He ... he placed a hand in my vagina and I panicked because I wasn't sure of, you know, what was going on. Then I realized it was his hand, and — he was aggressive, but like I said, nothing happened.

MATTHEW.   When you say he performed on you, did he put his mouth on your vaginal area?

KIM.   *(To audience.)* If anyone wants my definition of eternity, this would be it. I had to answer these kinds of questions repeatedly for the people from the CDC. They came to our house several times and asked me things like this on the living room couch. Later, when I filed my suit, I had to answer the same questions over again in a room filled with eight or nine middle-aged men. Don't ever tell me I don't know what invasion of privacy is like.

MATTHEW.   Did you suffer any wounds or bleeding or soreness from this encounter?

KIM.   You mean *this* encounter, or the encounter with my boyfriend? *(To audience.)* Of course, the real embarrassment isn't even in the physical details they drag out of you. It's what becomes so obvious finally: that no matter how passionate I'd been about anyone in my life so far, it wasn't really passionate enough to ... try again after the door slammed. And then — for me, the door slammed for good.

LEE.
"I have a garden of my own
But so with roses overgrown,
And lilies, that you would it guess
To be a little wilderness."

KIM.   Are you going to read that whole poem?

LEE.   Just favorite parts. Honest. We're already on line 76.

"And all the springtime of the year
It — "

(To her.) The fawn, that is.

KIM.   I know.

LEE.
"It only loved to be there.
Among the beds of lilies, I
Have sought it oft, where it should lie;
Yet could not, till itself would rise,
Find it, although before mine eyes.
For, in the flaxen lilies' shade,
It like a bank of lilies laid.
Upon the roses it would feed,
Until its lips e'en seemed to bleed:
And then to me 'twould boldly trip,
And print thoses roses on my lip — "

KIM.   This is a long section.

LEE.   I'm almost done.

"But all its chief delight was still
On roses thus itself to fill:
And its pure virgin limbs to fold
In whitest sheets of lilies cold.
Had it lived long, it would have been
Lilies without, roses within."

KIM.   Well, that's pretty.

LEE.   I'm sorry you had to talk about those first experiences. There's a kind of loneliness that comes with first times. A longing. At least there was for me. You want it to go so easily, to glide, to be as effortless as that moment you first saw each other. You want your first time to be graceful as a smile. It's more like hand-to-hand combat. You struggle over every inch. This is all right, but that.... Up to here, but not.... You try to become completely lost in each other, and instead, you begin to understand what an elegant and effective prison the human body is.

KIM.   When did you lose your virginity?

LEE.   At twenty. (*Matthew laughs involuntarily.*) It could've been worse. Horatio Alger was nearly thirty when he lost his. The next day he wrote in his journal, "I was a fool to have waited so long."

KIM.   (*To audience.*) My family got tested for HIV. My blood sister got tested. My old boyfriends got tested. None of them was positive. Questions got down to using my roommates' razors — roommates got tested, all negative. If I'd been able to say, "Yes, I had a transfusion once, or once I slept with a bisexual man who I think used drugs," the CDC would've said —

MATTHEW.   Fine, thank you.

KIM.   And that would've been it. That's all they do in the vast majority of cases: find a risk factor, and assume that's what it was. But I was a puzzle. I used to wonder if maybe I hadn't stepped on something on the beach. A syringe, or —

MATTHEW.   And never noticed?

KIM.   You don't know what to think. You've got this disease.

The best experts in the country can't tell you how. Meanwhile you're hiding it from as many people as possible, you're going through a kind of terror you've never known, you feel *guilty*. You feel as though you somehow betrayed your family, because you see their pain. And you yourself — somehow you betrayed yourself. You failed to take care of yourself. But how? How?

MATTHEW. *(Sitting U., smiling pleasantly.)* Hi.

KIM. Hi. *(They're strangers. Matthew pages through his "magazine.")* It took almost six months to get into a treatment program in Miami. I was in it with three men I didn't know. There was an actor, and a turnpike employee and a man who worked with autistic and retarded children. They were all gay.

MATTHEW. *(Friendly.)* Pretty quiet in here today.

KIM. Yeah.

MATTHEW. My name's Matthew. *(He looks at Lee.)*

KIM. Hi, I'm Kim.

MATTHEW. You on the program?

KIM. Yes.

MATTHEW. Me too. Just getting the basic package?

KIM. Guess so.

MATTHEW. I have black, hairy tongue.

KIM. Pardon?

MATTHEW. From all the medications. Black, hairy tongue — it's a reaction.

KIM. Oh.

MATTHEW. The taste buds. They swell and turn dark. Don't worry, I won't show you. Just don't get scared if you develop it, that's all. It's a side effect.

KIM. Oh. Thanks. *(He smiles at her; she smiles back. Matthew goes back to "reading." To audience.)* We were getting AZT and CD-4. I was already getting pentamidine. I got a prescription for Bactrim, to keep the pneumonia at bay. But at least I was on a program, and we all had hope at the time. I didn't develop black, hairy tongue, but suddenly everything tasted terrible. Plus there was a lot of nausea. They said I'd have to work through it and keep eating. I lost six pounds in one week. Gained one back, thank goodness.

MATTHEW. That's good.

KIM. Thanks. I shouldn't be complaining. I was chubby in college.

MATTHEW. Really?

KIM. I ended up losing it. But I was — I looked like a porker. Well, I thought I looked like a porker; my friends thought I looked normal, but that I just weighed a little too much. And I probably could've lost ten pounds.

MATTHEW. Who couldn't? Back then, anyway. My lover was overweight, a little bit. By the time he died, he was so thin, I couldn't believe I'd ever been with him. "That's not the body I made love to," I thought. "Who is this person?"

KIM. How's your weight?

MATTHEW. Oh — um ... better.

KIM. *(To audience.)* It was my mother who first thought of Dr. Acer. There'd been rumors about him. Some people thought he had AIDS. So we mentioned it to the CDC. What about the dentist? They said there's no chance I got it that way.

LEE. We're not investigating transmission from the dentist —

KIM. They said —

LEE. It's a dead end.

KIM. I was never told they were investigating the dentist. But of course, that's exactly what they were doing.

LEE. *(To audience.)* The Centers For Disease Control are required to be extremely secretive about the HIV cases they handle. I personally see the virtue of that. One of the few stigmas in this country more powerful than that which is attached to homosexuality, is the one attached to terminal illness. More powerful still is the stigma attached to contagious terminal illness. In Florida, they burned a family out of their home. In Poland, they stoned buildings that housed children with AIDS. In Egypt, a woman with AIDS had to have her baby delivered by her mother, since no doctors or nurses would do it. So about all the CDC can tell you is that they either do or don't know how you got infected, and ... thank you very much.

KIM. Seven months after I was diagnosed, Jane Pauley had

a message for me on the evening news. She said the CDC had released a report that a young woman in Florida my age had in all likelihood been infected with HIV by her dentist. No one had called to tell me this would be on.

LEE. They couldn't.

KIM. This was the first moment I realized they'd been lying to me all along — staring me in the eye, knowing I had a disease that was going to kill me, and refusing to tell me the truth.

LEE. They did tell you the truth. This was how they told you.

KIM. Then may the rest of the world be as frank with them.

MATTHEW. *(To audience.)* There's an inflation that's not just economic. The price goes up on truth as well. Someone tells the truth that he's gay, and he's beaten to death. Someone admits he's HIV-positive, and his health insurance is cancelled.

LEE. *(To audience.)* A decade into this epidemic, the price of truth is at an all-time high. I don't know much about market forces; I was debilitated long ago by a liberal arts education. But it seems to me that the price was driven up when the AIDS epidemic ran directly into the real epidemic. The one we don't even see as a disease.

KIM. After the CDC announcement, my sister Allison said —

MATTHEW. It's going to come out; they're going to find you.

KIM. She said there'd be reporters all over the place. That what I really needed was a lawyer. Something — some kind of protection. But I didn't want anybody to know. They could've burned *my* house down. Finally I decided to do it. What if there were other people this had happened to? Was I really the only one in a country of 250 million? Were those the odds?

MATTHEW. For every three million seeds created by the red alder, only one will grow into a new tree. *(Kim looks at Matthew, who looks at Lee.)* Why did I say that?

LEE. Sorry. I looked up a lot of statistics — sort of in general.

233

MATTHEW.   And I'm just supposed to toss them in?

LEE.   They're counterpoint. You know ... to vary the presentation.

KIM.   I thought it was going fine.

LEE.   It was. I'm just drawn to statistics, that's all.

MATTHEW.   What? You mean emotionally?

LEE.   In a way. For example: *(To audience.)* A person would have to fly 30,000 times before they were due to crash in a plane.

MATTHEW.   What's emotional about that?

LEE.   Well ... the fear, I guess —

MATTHEW.   So if I say far more people die at railroad crossings every year than in plane crashes, you have a specific, definable emotional response?

LEE.   Yes.

MATTHEW.   And you feel something — fear or pity or ... when I say that?

LEE.   Yes.

MATTHEW.   And if I say I have AIDS, and I'm dying? *(A beat.)* Do you feel something then? That you can ... hold onto? *(A beat.)* I'm just curious.

LEE.   Of course ... of course. No, it's fine, just.... Let's go on for right now. *(A beat.)*

KIM.   *(To audience.)* We went to a lawyer. It was a big office down in West Palm Beach. Bob Montgomery — my lawyer — thought we should seek damages, that there might be quite a bit, in fact. But there'd be a price — and he didn't mean his fee.

LEE.   I mean your privacy.

KIM.   We filed suit against Dr. Acer's insurance company and called a press conference. I met all of America pretty much at once. Everyone wanted to see the young woman who'd done the impossible: contracted HIV just sitting in a dentist's chair.

MATTHEW.   The only one in the world. For a few months, you were the ultimate statistic.

KIM.   *(To audience.)* The only one in the world. *That* got a few people interested. After awhile, it got hard for me to go

234

places without being recognized. *(She looks around to Matthew, who smiles.)*

MATTHEW.   Hi.

KIM.   Matthew — hi.

MATTHEW.   I saw you on TV.

KIM.   Oh, right.

MATTHEW.   You looked very good.

KIM.   Thanks.

MATTHEW.   How's your treatment going?

KIM.   My T-cells are at 43.

MATTHEW.   Oh?

KIM.   They don't think the CD-4's working. I'm going off it.

MATTHEW.   I'm sorry.

KIM.   They wanted to switch me over to a ddI/AZT combination —

MATTHEW.   *(Nodding.)* Uh-hunh.

KIM.   But you have to weigh 110 pounds, and I don't qualify. I'm down to 102.

MATTHEW.   I'm sorry.

KIM.   I may not qualify for anything down here in Miami anymore.

MATTHEW.   What'll you do?

KIM.   Switch back to the clinic at West Palm Beach. It's much closer to home.

MATTHEW.   We'll miss you.

KIM.   Thanks. *(After a beat, to Matthew.)* Yesterday, I called my friend with AIDS. Her husband has AIDS too, and their little boy's trying to deal with the fact that both his parents are sick.

MATTHEW.   How's she doing?

KIM.   Not very well. She has herpes sores at least two inches long all over the inside of her mouth. It makes it hard for her to eat. She had absolutely no white blood cells. It got down to zero. They had to give her a transfusion. *(A beat.)* I don't know why I'm thinking about her.

MATTHEW.   I was going to walk over to Dunkin' Donuts. Want to come? *(She smiles.)*

LEE.   *(To audience.)* The mass media went uniformly crazy

over Kim's story. They'd just had Alison Gertz on the cover of
People two months before —
MATTHEW.   You know — HIV from just one date? White
girl? Upper East Side?
LEE.   And they'd done Ryan White and the Ray family and
well, they were more than ready for Kim.
KIM.   I was ready for them, too. I had a few things to say.
I was glad when all these people we'd only seen on TV
knocked on our door and asked us to choose between them.
MATTHEW.   Kim? You can't do both Donohue and Oprah.
KIM.   Why not, Mom?
MATTHEW.   *(To Lee.)* Why am I always her mother?
LEE.   Please.
MATTHEW.   Donohue's demanding an exclusive.
KIM.   I'd rather do Oprah.
LEE.   There's always Geraldo.
KIM.   Dad — please.
LEE.   How was your interview with Paula Zahn?
KIM.   Better than the one with Deborah Norville.
MATTHEW.   Oh, by the way — Larry King doesn't want to
interview you unless you're willing to fly up. Plus he doesn't
want your lawyer with you.
KIM.   Everybody wants me to fly to them. I can't make that
many trips. Maybe if I was eating well.
MATTHEW.   It's your decision.
KIM.   Let's hold out — ok?
LEE.   Kim? The *National Enquirer* called again. They doubled
their offer to $10,000.
KIM.   Not interested.
LEE.   They say they'll do the story whether they have you or
not.
KIM.   I'm not interested.
LEE.   They say they'll print a story about the dentist being
gay.
KIM.   What's that got to do with it? I don't see how these
people can live with themselves after they print this crap.
MATTHEW.   Kim? Oprah says if you want to do her show,
you have to come next week. She's going on vacation.

236

KIM. Ok. When's that film crew from the Netherlands?

LEE. Kim? *People* magazine said they'll fly your sister down from Gainesville on a private charter so she can be here for your interview.

KIM. *(To audience.)* It went on like this for a few months. Lasted a long time, I guess, as these things go. *Inside Edition* even sponsored a trip for me and my best friend Geralynn. I got to do some things I'd never done, and they got to have great ratings one night. We skiied in Utah, rode in a helicopter in the Grand Canyon and in a hot-air balloon in Palm Springs. That was the best. Geri and I just floating over these endless groves of palm trees in the desert. Floating again. For a few minutes, it seemed like a different planet. I started to imagine who might live down there. Maybe it was people who were not greedy, not vicious, not afraid. Maybe they felt pain when others suffered, joy when others succeeded. Impossible people, walking gracefully beneath the palms, approaching every new experience thoughtfully, generously — grateful just to be walking there at all. Then suddenly the balloon made a little jump, and I looked up and thought, "Here I am suspended above my dreams by nothing more than heat." It felt like riding in the hand of God — that gentle, that terrifying. And somehow I knew, that wherever that hand took me, frightened as I was, it would never let me go.

MATTHEW. I was going to go on a hot-air balloon. My friends arranged it for me. It was very windy that fall. We couldn't get a calm day. By the time the weather was good again, I couldn't walk.

LEE. Couldn't they have carried you?

MATTHEW. Wouldn't have mattered much by then. I'd gone just about blind.

KIM. In the middle of all the media attention, there was a pretty intense debate, of course. A lot of people didn't believe I was infected by Dr. Acer — no matter what the CDC said. But as more of Dr. Acer's patients turned up positive, it got harder to deny.

LEE. *(As a lawyer at a deposition.)* Doctor, where are you employed?

MATTHEW.   (As research scientist.) Los Alamos National Laboratory.

LEE.   And you were asked by the CDC to analyze the HIV nucleotide sequences as well as the amino acid sequences derived from the blood of this patient — referred to as Patient A — and the sequences derived from the blood of the dentist?

MATTHEW.   That's right.

KIM.   (To audience.) I was called Patient A a lot, since at first my name was off-limits. Then two of Dr. Acer's other patients tested positive, and we had Patients B and C. It felt insulting. As though they'd decided never to speak my name again.

MATTHEW.   At least they studied your case. Most of us never get designated anything. Just the research equivalent of a mass grave.

LEE.   Doctor, what did you find when you compared the sequences?

MATTHEW.   Well for example, there are eight amino acids constituting the HIV signature. As it happens, there are some rare substitutions in the sequence signature of the dentist, and these substitutions are also found in Patients A, B, and C. However, they are not found in any of the Florida control group. So far, in fact, we haven't found this signature anywhere in our data base — except among this dentist and these three patients. It's a unique signature.

LEE.   And what is the probability of that?

MATTHEW.   The probability?

LEE.   Yes, please.

MATTHEW.   (As himself.) Are you sure about this study?

LEE.   Believe me, this is the short form.

MATTHEW.   (As the scientist.) Well, the probability would be 6.3 times the log base E, times to the minus seventh power.

LEE.   And in English that would be — ?

MATTHEW.   One in a million. Now as for the nucleotides —

KIM.   (To audience.) I think the insurance company really thought about going to court until the other two patients were discovered. After that, the company agreed to a million-dollar settlement. They knew, as any judge reading the data would know, we got HIV the way we said.

LEE. *(A helpful, but odd person.)* Hello? I'm calling for Kimberly Bergalis. I too am a devout Catholic, though I live far away. I read in a national magazine about a clinic where a woman was cured of AIDS by exercise, natural diet and meditation. She only has scars now on her cells.

KIM. A lot of people wanted to cure me — especially after we won the settlement.

MATTHEW. *(A persisitent person.)* Hello, I've had a healing ability since 1987. I can cure the AIDS virus. AIDS is very similar to cancer, and if cancer can be stopped, so can AIDS. Remember, the newspapers don't print everything.

LEE. *(Another person.)* Hello, I'm sending a pamphlet about Urine Therapy.

MATTHEW. *(Overlapping, the persistent person.)* Hello, I'm calling for the third time. As a metaphysician, I have a healing ability. If you really want to save Kim's life, contact me at my New York office.

KIM. I'm sure it was with the best intentions.

MATTHEW. Those kinds of people called you?

KIM. All the time.

MATTHEW. Figures. I had to call them.

KIM. *(To audience.)* Others, from all over the country, sent books: "When Bad Things Happen To Good People," "God Calling." And they wrote really beautiful letters. A man fasted for 35 days in order to cure me. I was getting too sick to read much. It was easier to just lie there and watch the birds.

LEE. Kim's house takes getting used to. The living room's filled with five or six large birds with dangerous-looking beaks. They're not in cages — just around. And of course, they shriek a lot. *(Matthew shrieks like a parrot. He makes muted parrot sounds through the next two speeches only.)*

KIM. The birds show off for strangers. Didn't you like them?

LEE. No, no — I liked them fine. Birds have always fascinated me. It's just that the level of *life* in your house. All these creatures breathing and eating. Staring. I can barely take care of a cat. I'm always worried about what it's thinking. It

239

amazes me that people can draw all this life to them, that it somehow makes them more focussed, not less. The only birds I live with are in books.

MATTHEW. What books?

LEE. My favorite one's called *Extinct Birds*. The illustrations are quite —

MATTHEW. Pardon me — are we still on the point?

LEE. In a way. I think so. *(To audience.) Extinct Birds.* Um ... sometimes for relaxation I'll look through it. Not relaxation, really. It's more of an emotional experience. *(With a quick look at Matthew.)* It has what you'd expect: exquisite birds — all disappeared forever now. I knew all the stars: the Dodo, Passenger Pigeon, Great Auk. But sometimes I'll run across the most vivid picture of a bird I never knew existed — the Pink-Headed Duck, the Laughing Owl, the Paradise Parrot —

KIM. We had parrots.

LEE. Not this one. My favorite discovery was the Huia. That's "Hwee-Ah." New Zealand bird. Gone since ... 1907? For years naturalists thought that the male and female were two different species. They had completely different types of beaks, which has never been found in any other bird.

MATTHEW. I give this no hope at all of tying in.

LEE. The male broke up rotting wood with his short, thick beak, and the female would follow along extracting grubs with her longer, more delicate bill.

MATTHEW. And?

LEE. And therefore, when the bird was erased from existence, not only was it gone, but also its unique ... collaboration. That particular form of sharing is also dead.

MATTHEW. And all this gets us back to...?

LEE. I mean, we all discover that we're born into a world in which things have fallen away from us already. Irretrievably. Instances of life that — Forms of beauty. Things we never possessed, but somehow ... still feel we have the right to.

MATTHEW. You have the right to a bird from New Zealand?

LEE. No, to its uniqueness. *(To Kim.)* By the way, there is an irony.

KIM.   Oh — lucky.

LEE.   The Huia, a bird so beautiful it was hunted to extinction for its plumage, was named for its own distress call. *(A beat.)*

MATTHEW.   That's it?

LEE.   You see the connection, don't you?

MATTHEW.   You want to know what I see? I'll tell you. I see a person who's deeply emotional.

LEE.   You do?

MATTHEW.   Yes. And the farther he gets from something that's human, the deeper emotion he feels. As it descends the Chain of Being from human, to animal, to dead animal, to the idea of a dead animal —

LEE.   This isn't —

MATTHEW.   I wish I was the last specimen of some bird of paradise. Some final display of worth that even you could understand. Something even you could miss — in your soul — when I was gone. *(A beat.)* Anyhow, that's what I see. Thanks for asking.

KIM.   *(To audience.)* This was a relatively good time for me and my family. We were suddenly famous, we'd won this big settlement, and I was still having a lot of good days physically. Over the past year I'd been up to Pennsylvania to see relatives, old friends. Once I met a young man on the plane. He was, well, good-looking. And I still looked ok, and ... I could tell he was attracted to me. He didn't know who I was. I admit I sort of gave in to the fantasy for a little while — you know, of kind of flirting in a real sweet way. Not telling him. *(She looks at Matthew, smiles.)* Hi.

MATTHEW.   *(Turning to Lee.)* Oh, no. No, no. No way.

LEE.   *(To Kim.)* Sorry.

KIM.   It's ok. It was just a couple hours anyway. Then the plane landed. *(A beat.)* Not long after that, our priest started to call. Father Chris. We'd known him forever.

LEE.   Kim —

KIM.   He said —

LEE.   There's someone I'd like you to see. He's about your age.

241

KIM.   About my age and dying of cancer. But I went to see him. He wasn't doing that great. They gave him morphine shots while I was there. When I left, I cried and cried. I went three or four times that week. The next week, the boy died. Anyway, Father Chris made his point — at least what I took to be his point. I thought, "I have AIDS. But I can walk and see and feel and touch. I can run and bend." And of course there was another point that took me longer to understand. Father Chris was reminding me that in all likelihood, and sooner rather than later, I would be like this boy. When you're 22, it's hard to know what that is, unless you go and look at it.

LEE.   *(To audience, as her priest.)* No one wants to see the priest coming. People see me on my way, dressed in black — they know what it's about. Mortality is my job. Plenty reject what I do, and that's their right. But for those who believe —

MATTHEW.   I'm lapsed.

LEE.   For those who believe — eventually they don't see death coming, dressed all in black. They see life.

KIM.   *(To audience.)* Anyway, I was grateful. I had a church that supported me, I had my family, the community, I had money — I knew how many people with AIDS didn't have any of that. My Mom worked in a clinic. I knew what those people went through.

MATTHEW.   Then why did you inflict more pain on them? *(Kim looks at Matthew, then at Lee.)*

KIM.   Is that why he's here?

LEE.   Sort of. One reason.

KIM.   Thanks a lot.

LEE.   I have to be responsible.

KIM.   *(To audience.)* I called a few people bastards before I died, and frankly I don't regret it. I resented what that dentist did, but more than that I resented the authorities who told him he had a right to keep practicing and keep his secret. After all, when you die for a public health policy, I think you have the right to question it pretty strenuously. And this principle doesn't just apply to me. AIDS activists, who themselves die every day for any number of public health policies, aren't the least bit shy about making their views known. And like myself, they take advantage of whatever public forum is offered.

MATTHEW.   But you had a broader forum. And you were speaking for so many fewer people.

KIM.   *(To Lee.)* Is he going to be this way from now on?

LEE.   It's the chance you take. You put a character on-stage —

KIM.   *(Irritably.)* Oh, *right!* *(To Matthew.)* This may seem like a very selfish point of view, but I considered my life to be more important than a debatable public health policy. Four more people will probably die because of what Dr. Acer was allowed to do. Exactly how many lives should a public health policy be worth?

MATTHEW.   You want an honest answer?

KIM.   Yes!

LEE.   *(To audience, as he intervenes between the two.)* Actually, the answer is quite variable depending on who's in the White House, how much money's to be made and what kind of field-day Congress and/or the media are having. But public health policies have in the past gone for a price of — easily — hundreds of thousands of lives. That's why to many it seems so ... paltry to talk about the six lives in this case. After all, it's been a couple years. Other physicians have succumbed to AIDS, and so far none of their patients was shown to be infected.

MATTHEW.   Which is the whole point.

LEE.   Is it? I mean, we're doing studies and we think we're right when we say we don't see any further cases. But people with a risk factor are just charged off to that risk factor. Some of them, for all we know — and I'm certainly not talking about many — might have been infected by a health care worker instead. And we just never noticed.

MATTHEW.   Do you really believe that?

LEE.   I don't know. But do you really believe that no health care worker will ever infect a patient with HIV again?

MATTHEW.   Not if they follow universal precautions.

LEE.   If. People die for if. She died for if. I don't know

243

what to think about a phrase like "universal precautions." I mean, haven't we all seen enough episodes of *Emergency?* The blood goes flying — before people can get gloves on. Doctors try to stick hypos into men who've been shot in the gut, flopping around like fish. People get stuck. How confident do I feel when I hear a phrase like "universal precautions?" They're not universal. They're only as universal as we can make them. And is that good enough?

MATTHEW.   Absolutely.

KIM.   Never.

MATTHEW.   Public health policy has to be made for 250 million people. Not six, or a hundred or ten thousand — 250 million. The only solution to this epidemic lies in the work of the medical community. We can't turn them into a persecuted class.

LEE.   So someone dies? Or may die?

MATTHEW.   Someone dies every day, of something! You spend all this time and effort over the lives of a few people —

KIM.   Whether it's a few —

MATTHEW.   A *few! (To Kim.)* You knew some people who died of AIDS-related causes? I knew hundreds. I spent years watching my acquaintances, my friends, my lovers — the one true family of my world, *my world* — die one by one. And no one in the rest of this country gave a damn. They were happy in fact — either that homosexuals were dying *per se,* or that the disease seemed thankfully to be confined to a single, disenfranchised group. Then I got to watch as the rest of America discovered HIV case by heterosexual case — from Ryan White, to Alison Gertz, to you, to Magic Johnson to Arthur Ashe. I got to watch tributes to the courage of these brave, suffering human beings. Outpourings of affection from people they would never meet, whose thoughts were with them every day, whose eyes filled with tears that these lives could be cut short, that these lives — which were so precious that no amount of publicity was too much — had been mutilated by a virus that was clearly meant for someone else. Then I got to die. In oblivion. Because no matter how many thousands of us die, we will never be visible to you.

LEE. *(To audience.)* It's hard to write about a mass of people. Far easier to focus on an individual. I like to think — I hope it's true — that it's hard for me to dismiss any life. But I suppose I do. And not just out of fear or misunderstanding. *(A beat.)* My brother died when he was twenty. Many years ago. One-car accident. It was an old car, no seat belts. The kind of seat belts that would have saved his life were still years away, though the technology had been there for decades. We as a society were sacrificing maybe 10,000 people a year this way. It really wasn't a big enough number to make us change our public policy. He's been dead for over 25 years. And each year, on April 16th, though I don't plan to, I notice that it's his birthday again. Someone dies every day, of something. *(A beat.)*

"Oh, help! Oh, help! I see it faint:
And die as calmly as a saint.
See how it weeps. The tears do come
Sad, slowly dropping like a gum.
So weeps the wounded balsam: so
The holy frankincense doth flow.
The brotherless Heliades — "

(To Kim.) The Heliades were the sisters of —

KIM. It's all right.

LEE. They were turned into poplar trees. And their tears into amber.

"The brotherless Heliades
Melt in such amber tears as these."

KIM. Not that long after my trip out west, floating in the balloon, I took a turn for the worse. Hospital, transfusion — that's when Lee met me. My lawyer had given him a really nice picture they'd taken of me the fall before, and I was glad, because I was beginning to look a lot worse. When I left the hospital this time, I started keeping my diary on tape, 'cause I was too weak to write. I'd lie on the couch all day, making tapes. You can hear our parrots on parts of them. Sometimes, I'd talk to my sisters. Allison held up really well, but Sondra cried a lot. She was only eleven. I was kind of another mom to her, and I knew it wasn't good for her to lose somebody right then. Anyway, she'd start crying and just couldn't stop sometimes, and I'd have to think of things to cheer her up. Like once I said, "Listen — every time there's a graduation, or if you give a big speech, I want you to save a seat for me. If you get married, I want there to be a seat. And you know what? I guarantee you, you'll feel a presence. You're going to be happy, and you're going to smile, and you're going to say, 'Kim's here.' Ok? Now, I want that seat. You've got to promise me. If you have a child, I want a seat when you have that child. It might make me sick, but I want to see that first child born. Ok, now I'm getting too mooshy and enough has been said, but is everybody ok? Does everyone feel a little better?" 'Course, by that time we were *all* crying. *(A beat.)* Not long after that, speaking became harder. I was weak and my voice had turned into this monotonic whine wrapped around what was becoming a kind of constant pain. By the end of May, I couldn't speak at all. I was at home, and I had a nurse, but we weren't doing much medically. Just treating symptoms. I was on the couch all summer, silent.

MATTHEW. You weren't so silent in September. *(Indicating the audience.)* May I? *(She nods.)* Kimberly, as America loved to call her, was by her own definition, an "innocent" person with AIDS. And she was right, of course, since who isn't? But she was more than just innocent in the public mind. She was a virgin who'd been outraged — everybody's daughter, the dream of the republic. And while she'd never have a chance to have a go at the Virgin birth, she was at least guaranteed the Virgin death.

KIM. Are you saying I wasn't a virgin? Because the insurance companies made me take two full physicals. They drew pictures of my hymen.

MATTHEW. No, I'm not denying you were a virgin. Or as close as we get to it anymore.

KIM. Thank you.

MATTHEW.   It really doesn't matter what you were. The only thing that mattered was what politicians could make of you.

LEE.   *(To audience.)* Which was, as one commentator put it, "the Willie Horton of AIDS."

MATTHEW.   Exactly. And mandatory testing laws were drafted. Disclosure laws. You proved a great opportunity for a number of powerful people who hate homosexuals: Pat Buchanan, William Dannemeyer, Jesse Helms — it was a very admirable crew.

KIM.   They agreed with my position.

MATTHEW.   And that didn't scare you?

LEE.   It scared me. Still does.

KIM.   I wasn't fighting homosexuals. I wasn't fighting people who had AIDS, or doctors or ... I just don't think any doctor should go into my body if he has HIV and hasn't told me. I didn't care what sort of politicians agreed with that, or why they agreed.

MATTHEW.   Sort of a one-issue person?

KIM.   Yes, I sort of was.

MATTHEW.   *(To audience.)* Anyhow, this wonderful law they'd drafted — called the Kimberly Bergalis Patient and Health Providers' Protection Act — was going to be voted on in the fall, so in September they had hearings. Kimberly was invited to be a witness.

KIM.   My voice came back — it didn't sound any better, but it came back — in August. I wasn't able to walk much by the time of the hearings. We took the train up.

MATTHEW.   Her parents accompanied her. By now, the ugly political reality was this: the new law being debated was a dead letter. It was more than a year since Dr. Acer's case had been uncovered, and surveys had found no other health care worker in the country having infected a patient with HIV. Public furor was beginning to ebb. The Bergalises may well have guessed this, but came anyway because it would at least provide a public forum — something that was getting harder for them to find. Kim's comments to the committee were brief and didn't offer anything new in the debate —

KIM. *(Cutting him off with her comments to the committee.)* "I'd like to say that AIDS is a terrible disease that we must take seriously. I did nothing wrong, yet I'm being made to suffer like this. My life has been taken away. Please enact legislation so that no other patient or health care provider will have to go through the hell that I have. Thank you." *(To Matthew.)* For the record.

MATTHEW. *(To audience.)* Her father also spoke, and seemed to suggest that if these congressmen didn't pass this law they were probably all damned to hell. Which, considering what they did for a living, may have been a foregone conclusion. In any case, the Kimberly Bergalis Act was supported only by the committee's right-wing Republicans, and never even came up for a vote. Kimberly's speech —

KIM. Was the last public act of my life.

LEE. After testifying, the family went to the White House. A tour had earlier been arranged. There had been some mixed signals as to whether President Bush and his wife — who were home at the time — would be greeting them personally. The Bergalises didn't know who they'd be meeting from the Administration. The answer was, in its way, sublime.

KIM. Nobody.

MATTHEW. The President's personal quarters are on the second floor. He doesn't have to come down. Oh, he would be down later — there was a dinner that evening for the King of Morocco.

KIM. We saw the place-settings.

MATTHEW. In the end, they were shown around by a reluctant Secret Service agent.

LEE. Kim's mother told me she had an almost irresistible urge to shout up the stairs.

MATTHEW. *(As Kim's mother.)* George?! Babs?! We're here! Come on down! *(A beat.)* George?!

LEE. George?!

MATTHEW. Millie?!

KIM. My family wheeled me out of the White House, and we all went home to Florida.

MATTHEW. We hope you've enjoyed your tour of the

248

American political process.

KIM.   After the trip to Washington, as far as most of America was concerned, I was pretty much used up. Too sick for talk shows, Congress wasn't going to pass my law, the President had missed his photo opportunity. Time to go back to the couch and count the parrots and ... pass away.

MATTHEW.   Pass away. A phrase obviously not invented for AIDS.

KIM.   I lived two and a half more months. It's easier to die in public life than in real life.

MATTHEW.   I wouldn't know. You're right about real life, though. What was my list? Pneumonia, blindness, dementia finally — for which I was grateful, since it allowed me to forget about the enormous debt, and the fact that almost everyone I knew had gone out of my life before I did.

KIM.   You were alone?

MATTHEW.   Oh, no. There were medical personnel.

KIM.   I wanted to die at home. Not every family can bear that. I mean, you've been so disfigured. You wonder who they're looking at when they talk to you — if maybe afterwards they don't go into the bedroom and look at your old high-school picture.

MATTHEW.   I hated my high-school picture.

KIM.   Me too. *(Quietly.)* I don't want to talk about when I died.

LEE.   *(To audience.)* Anna and George told me that Kim had good nights and bad nights. Of course the good nights now resembled the bad nights of a few months before. Kim hadn't yet experienced the final effects of the disease. Incontinency, incoherence. The intense pain. But these were coming, they knew. One day in December, Kim suddenly thanked her nurse for having taken such good care of her. That night, getting her ready for bed, Anna and George said to their daughter — and this is something I can only imagine since I've never fathered children of my own —

KIM.   You can let go, Kim.

MATTHEW.   It's ok.

KIM.   You don't have to worry about us.

MATTHEW.   You don't have to go through the pain.

KIM.   You can just let go.

LEE.   That night Anna decided to sleep on the floor of Kim's room, next to her bed. Sometime later the dog came in, and laid down on the floor beside her. One of the things I admire about the Bergalises is how unassumingly they accept the work of living. And dying. All those months they kept Kim part of their family, part of their household. Each day she was on that couch in the middle of the living room. They didn't want to be apart from her. Each night they bathed her and put her to bed. It was clear she was going to die soon. The only question was, in how much pain? That night, very late, in the dark, Anna woke to a kind of scratching sound, a rattling. It was the dog. He was shuddering in his sleep and his claws were rattling against the door. Then Anna noticed Kim's breathing had stopped. Anna felt her. There was no pulse. Her body was still warm. Anna stood there for a moment, holding Kim's hand and the oddest emotion welled up in her, and she said to Kim —

MATTHEW.   I'm so happy for you.

LEE.   And she stood there in the ineffable excitement of the dark, feeling something beautiful had happened. Like a child on Christmas eve, suddenly certain that the house had been visited, and the long dreamed-of gift had at last been given.

KIM.   Mom waited for a while, then went and woke my Dad and told him. They sat there for a long time, in the stillness that's already come to so many parents, and will come to so many more.

MATTHEW.   Someone held my hand when I died. I think it was the day nurse. She had a peculiar smell.

LEE.

"Now my sweet fawn is vanished to
Whither the swans and turtles go:
In fair Elysium to endure,
With milk-white lambs, and ermines pure.
Oh, do not run too fast: for I
Will but bespeak thy grave, and die."

(To audience.) The Nymph — the young girl, the speaker of

the poem — is planning her own death, because she can't survive in a world that has murdered innocence.

MATTHEW.   Sounds like a quitter.

LEE.   I suppose. *(To audience.)* But I sympathize with her. You know, one recent estimate I saw suggests that at present rates, as many as a billion human beings — nearly one out of every six people in the world — could be HIV-infected as of the first couple decades in the next century.

MATTHEW.   Don't do any more statistics.

LEE.   Why not?

MATTHEW.   I want you to describe something.

LEE.   What?

MATTHEW.   My funeral.

LEE.   *(Uncomfortable.)* Your...?

MATTHEW.   When I died. Did they bury me? Cremate? What?

LEE.   What did you direct?

MATTHEW.   I kept putting it off. By the time I started planning, I was too sick to — Was I buried?

LEE.   It was cold. The ground was — A tough time to bury, anyway. You were cremated.

MATTHEW.   Ah.

LEE.   One relative. A cousin. Actually, she married into the family.

MATTHEW.   *(Nodding.)* Mm-hmm.

LEE.   She didn't know you very well, but ... she's a natural at tying up loose ends. She flew in quietly, accepted your ashes, knew she couldn't bring them home, so ... she thought about where to scatter them.

MATTHEW.   Which was?

LEE.   Where do you think?

MATTHEW.   The park?

LEE.   She waited for a warm day. She even asked where they plant the roses in the summer. And there, at noon, under a brilliant March sun —

MATTHEW.   Oh.

LEE.   There were a lot of ashes. The box was heavy. It felt like a gallon of milk. So it took a long time. And a lot of rosebeds.

MATTHEW.   And then she flew home?

LEE.   Without looking back.

MATTHEW.   Well ... I suppose that's all you need.

LEE.   I suppose. *(To audience.)* It'll take a lot of effort to achieve one billion infected people. But we may have what it takes. Sometimes what concerns me most is that a cure will be found — for HIV, for all the deadly viruses we've begun to encounter. I suppose we'll declare victory again, ignoring as always the larger disease: the cowardice, the viciousness with which we behaved. It's the epidemic that's been with us from the beginning. Palpable everywhere, instantly recognizable, but with no simple acronym.

KIM.   So you think that if we find the cure for AIDS tomorrow, we'll still have failed? *(A beat.)* How does the poem end?

LEE.   The poem? It's nothing much. Just sort of an extended image. The girl, still in tears, imagines her own gravesite. You know, complete with a statue, and —

KIM.   Let me hear.

LEE.   Really? *(She nods.)*

"First my unhappy statue shall
Be cut in marble; and withal,
Let it be weeping too — but there
The engraver sure his art may spare,
For I so truly thee bemoan,
That I shall weep though I be stone:
Until my tears, still dropping, wear
My breast, themselves engraving there."

You understand? The statue will weep and —

KIM.   *(Nodding.)* Keep going.

LEE.
"There at my feet shalt thou — "

KIM.   The fawn.

LEE.   Yes.

252

"There at my feet shalt thou be laid,
Of purest alabaster made:
For I would have thine image be
White as I can, though not as thee."

KIM.   That's the end?
LEE.   Yes.
KIM.   I'm not going to have a statue.
LEE.   I know.
KIM.   But I was innocent.
LEE.   The world is innocent. You know why?
KIM.   Why?
LEE.   Because the opposite of innocence is not guilt. It's knowledge.
KIM.   And we're in the dark?
LEE.   Completely.
KIM.   How do you know?
LEE.   Because I have no faith.
KIM.   No faith at all? *(Lee shakes his head no.)* Then we're different. *(Lights slowly narrow in on Kim during the next speech.)* Eight months before I died, I was in pretty bad shape for a while. And I wanted to be prepared if something happened, so I was making all these plans and I realized maybe I should have the final blessing — the Sacrament of the Sick — so I made a phone call to a priest. Not Father Chris; he was out of town. This was around nine in the evening. And this priest said he'd come over right away. I said, I don't need it right now, but eventually I'd like to have this done. And he said, "No, no, no — I'm coming right over," and he hung up. So suddenly I'm trying explain to my parents why there's a priest coming to our house at 9 o'clock at night. They think I'm telling them that I'm dying tonight. And it's just this big mess. Everybody's crying. "What are you saying to us?" And I say, "No, I'm not dying tonight. I just need to talk to him and have this little blessing." And they didn't believe me. "Why are you having this done, Kim? Do you know something you're not telling us? Did you get some kind of calling?" I said *no.* I started crying and said the main reason I wanted him here

253

was that I was afraid to go to sleep, because I was afraid I wouldn't wake up. And that's one of the main reasons I hadn't been sleeping lately. Anyway, the priest came over, and we sat down in my room and he said some prayers, and I told him about a vision I thought I had a week before. I was in the dark and saw this dim light that moved around and went farther and farther away. And it turned into a bunch of little children, and they were waving at me and laughing. And it sounded like they were saying, "Come play, come play." Actually, I wasn't sure if they were saying, "Come play" or "Goodbye," but it sounded more like, "Come play." And then they disappeared. And the priest said that sometimes it's not always a vision — sometimes it's just a hallucination because I have a fever of 103 or 104. He said maybe it scared me, that they were calling me, and made me think it was my time. He said, "When the Lord is ready, He'll be ready. Don't necessarily think it's over yet." And my Mom brought up a good point. She said, "Why are you so sure that it's not going to get any worse? That it's going to be a quiet death, and not some more terrible thing? You may have more things happen to you." And that's something I never thought about. I just thought how *I* can't take this pain anymore, and how *I* feel about this pain, and how *I* want to be out of my misery before it gets worse. But God might not take me now. So that made me think. Well, anyway, the priest was really nice, and he gave me the Sacrament of the Sick, which I discovered I'd been getting all along at church, at weekly Mass. It's the exact same thing. And he gave me First Holy Communion, and then he left and I just felt so good suddenly. I started thinking again about the cemetary where I was going to be buried, and all the names —

MATTHEW.   (*Quietly, in the background, as she continues.*) Zebleckas —

KIM.   And how I'm going to lie right next to my grandmother on top of that mountain —

LEE.   Pilashusky —

KIM.   And how I'm going to lift up and just fly away into the heavens —

MATTHEW.   Shucavage —
KIM.   And how God's going to come down and take my hand —
LEE.   Andrukitis —
KIM.   And how my body's just going to be this thing I used while I was on this Earth.
MATTHEW.   Karalunas —
KIM.   Anyway, then this peace came over me, and I was able to sleep.
LEE.   Bergalis. *(Lights fade to black.)*

THE END